Sovereign Shame

Sovereign Shame

A Study of *King Lear*

WILLIAM F. ZAK

Lewisburg
Bucknell University Press
London and Toronto: Associated University Presses

Associated University Presses
440 Forsgate Drive
Cranbury, NJ 08512

Associated University Presses
25 Sicilian Avenue
London WC1A 2QH, England

Associated University Presses
2133 Royal Windsor Drive
Unit 1
Mississauga, Ontario, Canada L5J 1K5

Library of Congress Cataloging in Publication Data

Zak, William F., 1945–
  Sovereign shame.

  Bibliography: p.
  Includes index.
  1. Shakespeare, William, 1564–1616. King Lear.
I. Title.
PR2819.Z28   1983   822.3′3   82-74489
ISBN 0-8387-5056-7

Printed in the United States of America

To the memory of my mother, Catherine

"Sorrow would be a rarity most beloved,
If all could so become it."

But what e'er I be,
Nor I, nor any man that but man is,
With nothing shall be pleas'd, till he be eas'd
With being nothing.

Richard II

Contents

Preface

This book originated from an intuition that the old king and father we encounter initially in *King Lear* is a man in hiding. In the first scene, when Lear hints at a "darker purpose" associated with the bribes he is about to proffer as gifts to his children, on a symbolic plane he unwittingly directs our attention to some still obscure truth about himself that we must uncover if we hope to understand the man and the extraordinary actions that follow. Indeed, were Lear not more than the sum of what is revealed about him from his overt actions and intentions, especially in the early scenes, his plight would never earn our sympathy or take on the seriousness necessary for tragic effect. Lear appears to play a peremptory, self-important, willfully impatient part in a ludicrous series of comeuppances following his foolish banishment of Cordelia and Kent; even more significant perhaps, at no point in the play's evolution does he ever face a conspiracy of circumstances that forbid turning toward Cordelia for forgiveness and relief.

But though Lear's access to Cordelia—or even to the loving community of Kent and the Fool, for that matter—may always be clear of external obstacles, I do not believe it is ever free of the most deeply rooted and crippling of internal inhibitions: a hidden, unacknowledged shame at himself, a shame so profound and tyrannical that it drives him in the first place to the absurdity of the love auction and thereafter into the ever noisier and more extreme forms of "distraction" from himself that lead to madness and Cordelia's death. Like some severe fault in a great stone which cannot sustain the stresses that test and finally fracture its apparent integrity, this dreadful weakness—Lear's occluded anxiety about personal worth, about deserving love—lies buried within his ever-adamant will and person. Much of this study is an attempt to explain and justify the validity of this claim about Lear by revealing how persistently the play's language and dramaturgy revolve around and hint at this unspoken and seemingly unspeakable secret. Although Lear himself may be but dimly aware of this secret, it nonetheless dignifies his nearly hapless, admittedly self-induced misfortunes and elevates his story to tragic proportions.

However, the book is not a case study in psychoanalytic method. The language and emblematic mirroring of characters in the action, not formal psychoanalytic theory, led me to formulate these reflections upon the state of Lear's soul. There have been, of course, numerous psychoanalytic readings of *Lear,* perhaps the most important of which may be the recent and brilliant interpretation Stanley Cavell develops in *Must We Mean What We Say?* But if I am correct in believing that Edgar, Edmund, Gloucester, and even Albany all suffer privately a version of the malady afflicting Lear, identifying the shame in *Lear,* as Cavell and the Freudians do, with hidden incestuous desire is questionable. I will argue that the problem of shame the play invites us to reflect upon is a far more complex and fascinating dilemma of human experience than Freudian formulae or therapeutic pathology generally urge us to believe, a fact also observed by Carl Schneider in *Shame, Exposure and Privacy,* an incisive critique of most psychoanalytic analyses of shame.

Schneider's seminal study, a self-described experiment in philosophical anthropology, establishes a theoretical framework for a discussion of shame that is congenial to my sense of the problem Shakespeare dramatizes in *King Lear.* Schneider argues that psychologists have for the most part disvalued shame, treating it simply as a psychic inhibition to be overcome, or, at best, as an isolating problem to be controlled, rather than as a significant, if ambivalent dimension of all human experience. For him and the philosophical tradition he codifies, however, shame is a human drama in which we may decline to participate only at a frightening cost in self-mutilation and severance from human community. It is not shame that isolates us from others, but our unwillingness to acknowledge and properly cultivate it in ourselves: it is our flight from shame that isolates us. Schneider's argument reinforces my sense, derived from the literary tradition of pastoralism, that Shakespeare sees the essence of the tragedy in *King*

Lear as a flight from shame that keeps man from a redeeming participation in human community.

In considering the observations of philosophers from Aristotle to Scheler and Sartre, Schneider distinguishes two varieties of the shame experience, each of which has a positive human import we should try not to banish. It is an easy matter to concede the central human benefit in what he labels "discretion-shame" (the "sense of shame" opposed to "acting shamelessly," which is thus associated with the interdicts and restraints of conscience); yet Schneider argues convincingly that even "disgrace-shame," a far more ambivalent experience of our failure to live up to our highest ideals of ourselves, inevitably involves a positive component as well. Shame of either sort is more than a simple feeling and always implies a disposition toward acts, contemplated or committed; thus it reflects an order of law and is consequently an inseparable partner of our very awareness of value. As the Russian philosopher Vladimir Soloviev declares, shame is the "true spiritual root of all human good and the distinctive characteristic of man as a moral being."

Though perhaps too exclusively ethical in its orientation, the suggestiveness of Schneider's distinction with regard to the situation in *Lear* can be clearly discerned. If we may be granted a momentary shift in the inflection of Albany's words to Goneril, we might say that Shakespeare presents all the principal characters in *King Lear* as "self-cover'd thing[s], for shame." But the shame that drives Cordelia, Kent, and the Fool into love's disguises is primarily a matter of discretion, not disgrace—though they acknowledge that dimension of their lives, too, as we shall see. Theirs is the "discretion that discerns [Lear's] state, /Better than" Lear himself ever does; and neither his disgrace nor theirs ever urges them to flight, either from themselves or from each other. In Lear, Edmund, Edgar, and Gloucester, however, the matter is disastrously reversed. Banishing discretion, they remain "self-cover'd things, for shame," to hide, even from themselves, in a desperate and isolating flight from the sense of their own disgrace. But we will not fully appreciate the complexity of Shakespeare's presentation of the problem if we only address the action. It seems to me that the dimensions of "dis-grace" Shakespeare dramatizes, especially in Lear, are as much ontological and psychological as they are moral. I will argue that if, from the abdication onward, Lear flees the sense of disgrace in his acts there, he is also fleeing a yet deeper and more significant sense of personal worthlessness that makes it difficult for him to stop to consider, let alone admit, his specific sins in the opening scene.

If, then, Cordelia, Kent, and the Fool live in the "proper sense of shame" that Schneider claims "goes hand in hand with our acknowledgment of radical sociality," one of the great ironies in the play is that, try as they might, they are unable to convince the others to accept the peace they share. This book will explore the paradoxical logic of this irony. The first chapter focuses on the curious absence of a significant tragic dilemma in the play: nothing external to Lear's own thinking and feeling, as I have already suggested, forbids or even inhibits him from acknowledging his folly and turning to Cordelia. The second chapter reinforces this sense of anomaly in Lear's behavior by demonstrating that Cordelia, Kent, and the Fool share a pastoral ideal and together constitute a loving community from which Lear persistently flees and that, as a consequence, he repeatedly jeopardizes. The third and fourth chapters, in arguing that Lear is too ashamed of his shame to face himself or his daughter, try to account for Lear's failure to make this "conversion," the turn to Cordelia and the others, which would have transformed the bleakest of Shakespeare's tragedies into the first of the late romances.

It gives me great pleasure to acknowledge the many people who have helped make this book a reality. The critics who have most spurred my thinking about the play are cited repeatedly in the notes, so I would like to offer special gratitude here to a number of people whose inspiration and aid have greatly eased my labors throughout this book's composition. Years ago as an undergraduate at Boston College, my vision of what the life of a scholar and teacher might accomplish was first fired by the brilliant teaching of Richard Hughes. The stirring memory of his classes remains to this day mingled in me with the standard of excellence he set in everything he put his mind to. George Kernodle, James Devereux, and Marianne Novy were all kind enough to read the manuscript in earlier drafts and offer valuable suggestions for its revision. James Welsh repeatedly took the time to encourage me in my work and actively helped me to place the manuscript with a prospective publisher, no small accomplishment these days. Both of the chairmen I have worked under while writing the book, Francis Fleming and Thomas Erskine, sustained me with their affectionate support for me and the project; and Margaret Onley typed much of the book—large parts of it repeatedly—with the care and efficiency one learns, unfortunately, only too easily to take for granted from her. My colleagues and dear friends, Tony Whall, Jerome Miller, and Francis Kane, have jested me out of the depressions and weariness that inevitably attend the writing and revisions of a study of this kind; and in perhaps a greater proof of their kindliness, they have borne, without a hint of mockery directed toward me, the insistent renewals of what must eventually have seemed to them my manic and tiresome enthusiasms for this and that gargoyle in the cathedral. They read and reread the various manuscripts, scrupulously edited and reedited them with me, offered suggestions and even the defense of my honor whenever I (stung by some criticism) hinted at the need for such fidelities. In short, a man could not ask for better coauthors and friends. Finally, my wife Kit deserves a special word of thanks. Despite the fact that this book has meant more sacrifice for her than for anyone else involved in its creation, she has nonetheless still found the time somehow, among her many other accomplishments, to charm nearly all of my days.

[1]

A Tragedy of Fools

> This would have seem'd a period
> To such as love not sorrow, but another,
> To amplify too much, would make much more,
> And top extremity.
>
> Edgar, *King Lear*

> Thus we play the fools with the time.
>
> *2 Henry IV*

Introduction

One of the most striking of the many troubling features in the final scene of *King Lear* is how the play circles upon itself in its concluding moments. Lear's "Pray you undo this button" (5.3.310) recalls not only his attempt to disrobe before Poor Tom in act 3 but also the initial divestiture that precipitated Lear's torment. In the end Lear again begs from Cordelia the exact thing he entreated from her at the beginning—words that would reassure him of their continuing love and intimacy. We end as we began with Lear futilely begging Cordelia for some word that would save him. In one sense, then, little that is essential has changed in the course of the play despite the tormented advances Lear has apparently made in exploring his and the world's miseries. His suffering and the attempts he and we have made to discover some sense in it ultimately come to mean nothing more than that Lear has returned, now raving and utterly lost, to the point at which he began. A generation ago critics of the play often argued that act 4's reconciliation between Lear and Cordelia transformed, or at least mitigated, the bleakness of the close and that Lear dies happily, either hallucinating that Cordelia lives or else ex-

17

periencing a true vision of transcendent reunion. The best
critics of the past twenty years, however, have taken a much
starker view of the play and its conclusion.[1] Although willing to
grant the beauty and importance of the reconciliation scene in
human and moral terms, very few have seen its relevance to the
world order (or lack of it) that the last scene appears to imply.
Judah Stampfer, for example, calls the finale "the tragedy of
penance" in which a penitential Lear is brutally struck down in
an "imbecile universe," a world without "charity, resiliency, or
harmony."[2] Nicholas Brooke argues that the humane values
embodied in the play are important but "can have no reference
beyond themselves, no ultimate sanction." For him

> the process of these last two Acts has continually set ideas of
> poetical justice, the avenging gods, against the perceptions of
> experience; and has not only made it impossible to retain *any*
> concept of an ordered universe, but also has promoted the
> reflection that any system of order results in very strange
> notions of justice. And in the end the subtlest and most
> tempting order of all is undone—the order of repentance,
> forgiveness, redemption and regeneration is reversed in un-
> regenerate Lear's tottering broken-hearted into madness and
> death.[3]

Helen Gardner sums up the prevailing view in this way: "No
consolation is offered us, for there is none which this world, the
world of the play, can offer."[4]

Regarding the notion that Lear dies believing Cordelia lives,
S. L. Goldberg speaks for recent criticism against the older
view:

> It would be no answer to the real question [of the play's
> meaning], for instance, even if, as Bradley argued, Shake-
> speare has Lear die believing Cordelia is alive. (Nor of course
> did Bradley suppose it was.) We know Cordelia is not alive;
> and to take Lear's delusion (though it may be only a hope) as
> the basis for some final optimism in the play, as some critics
> do, is really to take the delusion as a kind of personal declara-
> tion on Shakespeare's part—an assertion of *his* hope or be-
> lief—but one so visibly at odds with the impersonal dramatic
> facts as to be both gratuitous and sentimental.

The "impersonal dramatic facts" culminate in Lear's anguished
question: "Why should a dog, a horse, a rat have life,/And thou
no breath at all?" (5.3.307–8). That this question

comes so irresistibly not only to his mind but to ours as well, and yet is left echoing in a void of ambiguous silence, seems the only truth the play continually and finally discovers—the very facts of subjective human experience testifying to the lack of any "clearest gods," of any certain objective meaning or Justice that our inner life directly answers to, or even, with spiritual insight and effort, it might answer to. Seen from this angle, the action is a series of destructive "ironies," abrupt reversals, breaks, sharp disjunctions, each one of which sub-tly engages our assent, but which together form what Frank Kermode would call a gathering "apocalypse," a process wherein reality declares itself in the very revenge it takes upon every belief, upon every expectation, or assertion of meaning or value with which men try to contain it.[5]

But if we acknowledge that the often brilliant work of recent critics has provided us with readings of *Lear* whose acute awareness of the play's complex ironies must be reckoned with, we need not, therefore, conclude that the only interpretation of the collective force of such irony is that Lear and the others inhabit an imbecile universe or, at best, that, as Goldberg de-clares, the play is "continually self-qualifying" or that it "does not offer us anything like a single, straightforward, clear-cut attitude to life, or a guaranteed moral vantage point."[6]

If Lear's universe were truly absurd, without intelligent or intelligible design, one would expect it to visit its ludicrous con-tradictions and reversals upon one or all of its characters with-out a discernible pattern of selectivity, that is, randomly. But this is not the case in *Lear*. In one way or another every charac-ter in *Lear* suffers, and suffers greatly; but the peculiar note of grisly yet nearly farcical humiliation succeeding a character's declaration of expectation or desire is reserved for a spe-cific group of "good" characters, namely Lear, Edgar, Glouces-ter, and Albany. That ironic note is not heard in Shakespeare's treatment of the "villains" of the piece or, more impor-tant, in his depiction of Cordelia and the Fool. Though the latter are betrayed and terribly victimized, they never become the ridiculous victims of the repeated trapdoor ironies that fol-low hard upon the speeches and actions of the other good characters, especially in the later scenes of the play. These facts should begin to make us question whether the real issue of the tragedy has anything to do with disorder in the heavens and to ask instead some simpler but unanswered questions about why a certain group of apparently good men should be singled out for such Shakespearean irony. As I hope this essay will show, Cordelia and the Fool are exempted from such irony precisely because they represent what Professor Goldberg has despaired of discovering in the play, a "guaranteed moral vantage point," not, of course, because they or their virtues can be assured of continued existence in the *Lear* world or anywhere else, but, rather, because there is nothing in the nature or condition of things generally that forbids their continued existence—except man's own wasteful prodigality.

What follows, then, is an attempt to argue that *Lear* cannot be accurately construed as an early anticipation of the theater of the absurd. The play is tragic not because its characters inhabit an imbecile universe but because well-intentioned men, with opportunities to do so, do not act to make the play the romance it could and should have been. When we see Lear again begging a word from Cordelia at the close, we do acknowledge the cruel irony that has brought this "poor perdu," after so much suffering, back to the exposed point at which he began. But that irony is not the result of some last, ghastly prank of a heaven gone mad; instead, it is a cruelty Lear unwittingly inflicts upon himself because he has been unable to acknowledge the implicit corruption in his initial attempt to beg a saving word from Cordelia. So profoundly, in fact, does Lear continually mistake his own condition that when Cordelia speaks of her fear for his life, she also speaks the truth about his death: his "ungovern'd rage" does "dissolve the life/That wants the means to lead it" (4.4.19–20).

Lear's Final Distraction: Ixion on His Wheel

In his now classic discussion of the "comedy of the grotesque" in *King Lear,* G. Wilson Knight took a major step forward toward identifying the anomalous tragic design in this most tormented of plays. He brilliantly defined and illustrated the persistent strain of ridiculous, absurdly incongruous, often cruel humor running throughout the situations, incidents, and dialogue of the play, elements that significantly distinguish its dramatic development from that of any other of the major tragedies. Though Knight did not explore the problematic relationship between this strain of grotesque comedy and the traditional and elevated conventions of tragedy, he nonetheless

identified and formulated an insight into the play's dialectic
that had not been and still needs to be explored if we wish to
comprehend *Lear*'s unique tragic design.

At a later point we will have to try to suggest how this current
of grotesque comedy in *Lear* can simultaneously allow for the
emergence of the sublime tone ordinarily aroused in tragic
drama and how this play's absurd and at times fantastic incongruities can be reconciled with tragedy's demand for inevitability. We will have to determine the relationship between the
cruel, sometimes bathetic ridicule in *King Lear* and tragedy's
exalted, if terrible, dignity and pity. How are we to explain the
apparent contradiction, for example, between Lear's nearly
childish pranks and tantrums and conventional tragic stature?
These relationships are much more difficult to resolve satisfac-
torily than has traditionally been thought, at least in part because the pervasiveness of the grotesque comedy, although
amply illustrated by Knight and others, has nevertheless been
underestimated and its specific nature and effect ill defined. In
the last scene of the play, for example, from Lear's return to
the stage until the curtain, the terrible pathos of the action
should not prevent our recognition that elements of the ridiculous continue to remain a prominent part of the action. Nor
should we, with Knight and the absurdist critics who have
found his insights so congenial, attempt to define the nature of
the comedy there or anywhere in the play as a "cosmic mockery," the "unknowing ridicule of destiny," a "mankind deliber-
ately and comically tormented by 'the gods.'"[7] Such a view
would appear to have gazed unflinchingly into the abyss the
play has uncovered, but actually, if unintentionally, it only
confirms what Edmund sarcastically names an "admirable evasion" in us "to lay" our "goatish disposition[s] on the charge of a
star" (1.2.126–28). Professor Knight's subtle shift from the de-
monstrable fact that man is repeatedly depicted as absurd and
almost grotesquely comical in *King Lear* to the less than inevitable conclusion that he is by implication something of a pathetic
cosmic victim suggests, as we shall see, a more flattering and a
more pathetic image of man than the play can or does sustain.
To identify the element of the grotesque in that way overesti-
mates the responsibility the divine bears for man's inveterate
foolishness and its consequences; and, conversely, it implies a
more conventional tragic dignity in the characters than careful
analysis of their behavior will support. We cannot simply con-

jure away the grotesque and bathetic way that the action com-
plicates this final scene, a scene that incongruously and
repeatedly distracts us from sympathetic concentration on
Lear's grief.

As Knight had apologetically observed of an earlier incident
in the play, at the finale, too, it may indeed seem a "sacrilegious
cruelty" to consider how the scene's ironies ridicule Lear. But
we have little choice because such ridicule is as real as it is
painful. If Lear bearing Cordelia in his arms emblematically
suggests a "secular *Pieta,*" as Helen Gardner has proposed,[8] he
is not subsequently permitted to retain such dignity unqualified
by absurd mockery—much of it unknowingly self-initiated and
self-declared.

In the bitter eloquence of inconsolable grief Lear does unquestionably stand well above the company he keeps in these
last moments, an awesome and sympathetic figure. For four
acts and with growing amazement we have watched Lear
undergo increasingly complete dispossession, and we have seen
him resist his torments with an unflinching fierceness of heart.
We have watched as the gathering force of his titanic suffering
gradually splintered his sanity; yet even madness could not
break his spirit. Although staggered by the final blow, in the
end his spirit remains unyielding in its resistance to the outrage
and injustice of Cordelia's death. He cannot comprehend how
those he speaks to can have "tongues and eyes" (5.3.259) and
not be using them to assault the heavens and bring them down
for this atrocity. We may not have begun the play with great
respect or sympathy for the old king; but even as we observed
him grow helplessly distracted we also realized that we could
begrudge him neither his bravery in challenging his suffering
nor the heroism of his persistent, unrelenting hope to discover
the import of his miseries regardless of how sinister their latent
significance. To the end he remains undaunted and incorrupt-
ible in this respect even if, as Professor Knight laments, he has
only regained his tenuous hold on sanity for a final hideous
torment.

It is certainly very curious, then, why Shakespeare does not
allow Lear's terrible pathos an uninterrupted stage. Instead he
loads the last lines with a series of ironic and even absurd incon-
sequences whose nearly laughable incongruities constantly
threaten to break the spell of our attention to Lear's grief. Later
in this chapter I will discuss Albany and Edgar's parts in this
alternately bitter and bathetic comedy. But they play merely

minor, supporting roles in this regard; the leading threat to the
dignity of Lear's anguish is Lear himself. Take, first of all, his
initial greeting to Kent:

KENT: [*Kneeling.*] O my good master!
LEAR: Prithee away.
EDGAR: 'Tis noble Kent, your friend.
LEAR: A plague upon you, murderers, traitors all!
         I might have sav'd her.

(5.3.268–71)

Though moments later Lear will tentatively recognize the man
before him as Kent, at this moment he is apparently too be-
sieged by his grief to notice him. Because of his anguish we do,
of course, forgive Lear's peremptory dismissal of the man
kneeling before him and his outraged indictment of both Kent
and the others as "murderers, traitors all!" But it is not
insignificant that Lear's actions do need our forgiveness—he is
certainly in the wrong on both counts here. In fact, it can
hardly be considered an accident that Shakespeare stages this
first meeting between an undisguised Kent and Lear since the
opening scene to mirror its central features in miniature: Lear
again mistaking Kent's gesture of friendship for an act of
treason;[9] his exploding suddenly into violent execration that
seemingly masks from himself his own anxieties by projecting
upon others a responsibility and shame he himself bears but
cannot acknowledge; and the pronouncing of a second, if
somewhat less formal banishment, "Prithee away."[10]
    Lear's behavior here, by uncomfortably reminding us of the
old king's disavowal of his social responsibilities and bonds in
the first scene of the play, tends to undercut or at least temper
our sympathy for him as a distraught father. Why would
Shakespeare, even momentarily, call us away from our attention to the immediacy and intensity of Lear's grief to confront
the irony in his recapitulation of one of his initial errors? We
need not question whether Lear is "still cursing, still understanding nothing" in this scene, as George Orwell would have
us believe,[11] in order to conclude that Shakespeare may indeed
be hinting that there remains a blindness, a moral occlusion in
Lear's sense of himself and his actions that his reconciliation
with Cordelia at the conclusion of act 4 has neither shriven nor
redeemed. It may be more than we have a right to ask that Lear
acknowledge anything but his intolerable grief. But thereafter

Lear will be lucid enough to recognize Kent by name; a proper recognition of Kent would have brought the old king some "fellowship of bearing" in his anguish and preserved the dignity of his grief from the self-ridicule he enacts instead. It would also have demanded, however, a more critical and difficult confrontation with himself than Lear has habitually been able to make in the play.

Full recognition of Kent would have involved his recalling and then acting upon three facts that remain blocked in Lear's consciousness. First, he would have had to recollect the circumstances of act 1, scene 1, and his actions there and, subsequently, expressed self-recrimination and personal contrition for his central role in Cordelia's fate instead of the inappropriate vaunt, "I might have sav'd her." Second, recognizing Kent would have involved an admission on Lear's part that Cordelia was not the only person he had sinned against and from whom he should beg forgiveness. But instead of an apology to Kent the distraught king can only manage what for us, in these circumstances, is grotesquely ironic praise for his good servant, Caius—"He'll strike, and quickly too" (5.3.286)—praise for the one weakness of Kent's fidelity, the weakness that, moreover, incongruously equates Kent in our minds with Cordelia's hangman and Lear's own vengeful retaliation, neither of which is remotely appropriate to the essential nature and extent of Kent's self-sacrifice for the king throughout. An even more ludicrous, if similarly unwitting insult to Kent follows directly in Lear's confusion about Caius's death. When Lear tells Kent that Caius is "dead and rotten" (286) it is likely that in his despair he presumes that anyone who has been in faithful service to him has suffered Cordelia's fate. Battered by one blow after another, he must assume that the heavens never rain but always pour grief upon him. But what are we to make of the irony of these words, unexpectedly spoken to the very man they speak of, a man who, if no longer in the best of health because of his service to Lear, is still very much with him? As much of a distraction as such an incongruous speech may be in the midst of what should be simple grief for Cordelia and her father, it is, nonetheless, what the absurdity of Lear's words leave us with.

Nor is the incongruity merely the accidental irony that arises when our expectations are reversed or surprised in the course of external events; this incongruity directs us toward the analysis of character. We have to question how intimately and personally concerned Lear is about Caius-Kent if he can readily and with relative indifference presume upon the fact of his death. His words here would seem to indicate an attitude toward his "good servant" not that irreconcilable with the good-natured but personally uncommitted way in which he retained him:

> Follow me, thou shalt serve me. If I like thee
> no worse after dinner, I will not part from thee yet.
> (1.4. 40–41)

His mistaken claim about Caius may also lead us back to reassess the profound pathos of a similar pronouncement—"She's dead as earth" (5.3.262)—made just previously over Cordelia's limp body. The speech loses none of its power to move, of course; but we may wonder how completely Lear's grief for Cordelia centers on Cordelia herself and how much it is shadowed by an unconscious self-regard perhaps tinged with the paranoia we saw in Lear's sense of isolation among his rescuers in act 4, scene 6: "No seconds? All myself?" (194).[12] Only the force of something akin to paranoia, though now manifested in a man virtually exhausted, can explain why here, too, also among friendly rescuers, Lear so inappropriately urges a "plague upon you, murderers, traitors all!" (5.3.270).[13]

The fury of the curse with which Lear guards his exclusive right to grieve for Cordelia seems to give credence to the suspicion that Lear's lament for Cordelia is unconsciously self-regarding. If Lear had truly been able to acknowledge Kent fully, the third fact he would have recognized was that his "grief hath mates, and bearing fellowship" (3.6.107). He would have had to acknowledge that Kent loved Cordelia in that he unselfishly defended her when Lear was banishing her, and that Kent has thus earned a right to share the stage in their mutual grief for her. By including Kent in his indiscriminate curse, Lear is allowed to sustain his childlike illusion of the exceptional quality of both his love and his grief for Cordelia but at too high a cost to himself and to those who love him—his final, conclusive abdication from the sustaining community of man, the fellowship of bearing represented emblematically in the play by the untiring concern and community of suffering among Kent, the Fool, and Cordelia.[14]

Though he has no idea that he has been doing so, Lear has repeatedly taken this community for granted, unheedingly sinned against and presumed upon it, only now to abdicate a final time.

> And my poor fool is hang'd! No, no, no life!
> Why should a dog, a horse, a rat, have life,
> And thou no breath at all? Thou'lt come no more,
> Pray you unto this button.
>
> (5.3.306–10)

Whether we read "no, no, no life" as a wailing lament or more bitterly as Lear's cursing sentence of all life to death, the finality of his despair comes through clearly enough. It may puzzle us, however, why Shakespeare, in a moment when Lear is clearly preoccupied utterly by his grief, should suddenly force us to recall the long absent Fool.[15] Even granting that we regain a coherent response to the immediate situation after we realize that "fool" is probably used metaphorically here to suggest Cordelia's innocence and is thus a term of endearment, we also must admit that Shakespeare has startled recollection and provoked our curiosity without satisfying us. We have been made to feel at least momentarily like Albany recalling his prisoners—"Great thing of us forgot" (5.3.237); and we want to know what has happened to the Fool. What arouses in us a sudden concern for the Fool finds no corresponding awakening of care, however, or even jog to memory in the preoccupied king. This is understandable; but it is also terribly ironic in that Lear's obsessive, utterly exclusive preoccupation with his loss of Cordelia suggests a final occlusion and avoidance, one last, unknowing repetition of his sundering of the communal bond "t' intrinse t' unloose" (2.2.75) that began the play. It is not at all that we begrudge Lear his grief for Cordelia at this moment, but only that others also deserve a portion of his concern and grief; for we recall that, throughout, three have suffered and cared for Lear unremittingly. But the two who remain alive also remain beyond Lear's "distracted" recognition—one again banished and the other forgotten as the king in his willfully self-imposed exile mistakenly imagines himself with "no seconds, all myself" and welcomes death. Lear's absolute devotion to the memory of Cordelia's unique value need not have assumed the shape of the despairing desire to die with her. Rather, it could have been transformed into the effort to live like her: to ac-

knowledge Kent as she had done ("O thou good Kent, how
shall I live and work/To match thy goodness? My life will be too
short" [4.7.1–2]) and to seek the Fool as she had sought hers—

> A [century] send forth;
> Search every acre in the high-grown field,
> And bring him to our eye.
>
> (4.4.6–8)

The troubling and pathetic details in Lear's failure to recognize Kent properly or recall his Fool complicate our response to
the play's final moments in at least two ways. Even though Lear
is desperately fixated on the betrayal of his last and only hope,
Shakespeare does not place his sense of loss in a consistently
flattering or wholly sympathetic light; nor does Lear become
for us, as we shall see more fully in a moment, the completely
pathetic victim of a mocking heaven that snatches Cordelia
from him, because even now we find him blindly rejecting potentially healing alternatives to his terrible despair. Lear is at
least as much his own worst enemy as are the heavens—a fact
quite consistent with Lear's character and the events of earlier
portions of the play and one suggestive, more generally speaking, of a curious lack of inevitability in the play's tragic design.
In order to illustrate this idiosyncrasy, let us return to one of
Lear's remarks quoted earlier—"I might have sav'd her"—to
explain how, as I claimed there, it is but a foolish and distracted
boast. It is ironic, in one sense at least, because we feel Lear has
so utterly misconstrued his own situation. We feel rather that
Cordelia might have saved him because, as Regan's dramatic
irony rightly suggested to Lear early on,

> You should be rul'd and led
> By some discretion that discerns your state
> Better than you yourself.
>
> (2.4.148–50)

For us, this has the symbolic force of an oracle Lear never
understands. Regan unknowingly declares what we have now
repeatedly been noting in the final scene—that some blockage
in Lear's consciousness always prevents him from seeing his
own situation and action clearly enough for him to become his
own best counselor. The symbolic "discretion" that could and
should lead Lear is his daughter Cordelia, a reading that is

reinforced by the fact that in the Renaissance the word *discretion* referred both to the freedom to decide to act according to one's own judgment and with circumspection and to the ability to hold one's own counsel, to be silent when speech would be inconvenient or, (more relevantly here) inappropriate. As we have just noted, even dead, Cordelia could have provided such "rule" to Lear had he been able to yield to her example of prudent care for the life of those she loved by lovingly acknowledging Kent and seeking for his Fool to bring him aid.

But the real ludicrousness of Lear's boast only emerges because what Lear claims here—when he should more truly recognize in himself Cordelia's executioner than her thwarted savior[16]—is unfortunately only too true. He could, in fact, very easily have saved her. All he needed to do to save Cordelia, and himself for that matter, was to muster the courage to face his other two daughters when Cordelia requested that they do so after the battle had been lost: "Shall we not see these daughters and these sisters?" (5.3.7).[17] For no sooner have the pair been led from the stage and Edmund ordered their deaths, following Lear's "come, let's away to prison" speech, than Albany enters with his immediate and insistent demands for the liberation of his two captives. Albany would not have been deflected from his purpose only to get lost in the complications of his troubled personal relationships with Goneril and Edmund had Lear and Cordelia been on stage to greet his entrance.[18]

But Lear does not ask or protest; and this apparently trivial avoidance on Lear's part instead leads to lethal consequences. If that moment is not unarguably climactic, it is certainly characteristic, even typical, of the seemingly inexplicable element of the ludicrous we must face when we consider the question or problem of the inevitability of the tragedy in *King Lear*. We might take *Hamlet* as a contrast in this regard. Hamlet, like most great tragic figures, acts out his fate within the grip of a genuinely unavoidable and therefore terrible dilemma. The incidental ironies, absurdities, and deflations we confront in the character and action in *Hamlet* do not fundamentally undermine the seriousness of our sympathetic involvement with the cornered protagonist, unable to ignore a beloved and virtuous father's call for justice and yet unable to exact murderous revenge. What can he do, we ask helplessly; what could anyone do? Such questions, asked of *King Lear,* however, risk self-parody. What can Lear do? Why, at any time he can quite simply turn to Cordelia instead of repeatedly turning away from her and what her living, fully human openness means. At any point in the dramatic action—even, as we have already suggested, at the very end—such a "conversion" would metaphorically and perhaps even literally save the old king. The obscure reasons why such a choice remains blocked in Lear's consciousness and the difficulty of the spiritual struggle that such a conversion demands require more discussion, but in the play's action Lear's release from his agon depends on terms as simple as those he himself had set in his offer to Burgundy: "Take her, or leave her" (1.1.204). "Election," in Lear's spiritual fate, as in Burgundy's material one, does (Burgundy's disavowal notwithstanding) "make . . . up in such conditions" (206) and no others. But because Lear, in his deepest personal relations as in his resignation of kingship, can never be absolute either for love or retirement but always insists on "reservation[s]" (2.7.255) for himself, he never—not even in the reconciliation scene—transcends Burgundy for France and acknowledges that the choice that transforms tragedy to romance is as simple and as complicated as "taking" Cordelia, turning toward grace as France did: "Thee and thy virtues here I seize upon" (1.1.252).

Though the depths of Lear's unease can in no sense be plumbed by his acknowledgment that he has done Cordelia a terrible wrong, Lear could have begun there. In every version of the Lear story available to Shakespeare, all of whose plots it should be kept in mind are cast not in the tragic mode but in the pattern of familial reconciliation and restoration common to Shakespeare's late romances, a consistent feature is that at some point in the middle of Lear's trials he correctly identifies his sin in abusing and exiling Cordelia, repents his folly, and makes a pilgrimage to France to seek forgiveness from her. In Shakespeare, Lear never initiates any similar expiational journey; instead, an unacknowledged but no less "burning shame," as Kent specifically remarked of Lear's final refusal to face her, repeatedly and persistently "detains him from Cordelia" (4.3.46–47).

This self-detention and the subconscious mask hiding it from himself are both clearly revealed in a self-accusing remark Lear makes just after Goneril, in demanding that he reduce his train, has given him the first clear indication of which way the "wind sits." Striking his head in rage he cries out—

> O Lear, Lear, Lear!
> Beat at this gate, that let thy folly in
> And thy dear judgment out!

(1.4.270–72)

We are moved, of course, by the extremity of Lear's frustration, his self-accusation, and his self-laceration, both literal and metaphorical; but we are not completely overcome by them. Lear's anger is not yet the result of any profound enlightenment; nor is it unshadowed by the possibility of theatrical posturing meant to shame, rebuke, and perhaps even manipulate Goneril into a change of heart. Clearly, Lear's choice of metaphors suggests he is living in the paradoxical comfort of self-accusation, the delusion that his "folly" is a foreign invader that has driven out indigenous "dear judgment" and is not itself native to the walled fortress of.his defensive self. The metaphor aids Lear—whether consciously or not—in presenting himself before Goneril as the father more sinned against than sinning, a role that rebukes Goneril even if it does not awaken her slumbering conscience. But even if we ignore this delusion and grant the premise that folly has taken the stronghold, Lear's strategic response—in effect, cutting off his nose to spite his face—seems like an unacknowledged and ironic triumph for folly. What sort of wisdom stands impotently beating at folly's gates when dear judgment is known no longer to be within and can so easily be sought without? What but folly can be won there, even if one should vanquish folly? It is doubtful that at this point in his trials Lear identifies his "dear judgment" in any but perhaps a subliminal way with Cordelia; but when we recall the "discretion" that Regan aptly told Lear should "discern your state/Better than you yourself" (2.4.149–50), we do. Consequently, Lear's speech and behavior here become an emblem of his agony throughout—frenetic gestures of impotent revenge alternating with and compounded by acts of self-directed and self-defeating rage, each and together a brave and noisy mask to distract the utterly mortified king from the silent, unvoiced accusation whispered by his valorous soul's better part, his own "dear judgment," embodied from the start in prudent Cordelia whose "voice was ever soft,/Gentle, and low" (5.3.273–74). So completely does Lear succeed in this that even at the conclusion Cordelia's dead silence only spurs him to fly into a final, defensively thunderous distraction. Much like a runaway so ashamed of his shame he can only bear to compound his miseries, a "child-changed" and immensely touching Lear prefers a violent tear through a storm-ridden waste, "distracting" himself in both senses of that term, rather than facing the music of his folly by going home to himself and Cordelia. Though shelter is always at hand, he insists instead on braving the torturing elements to make a grotesque but ultimately successful effort to "punish home" (3.4.16).

Lear is never trapped in a predicament as Hamlet is; he confirms his own prison, confining himself to exhibition in the beginning and to the end.[19] Harsh as that judgment is, it nonetheless masks a pathos perhaps yet more extreme than that with which we respond to Lear's grief for Cordelia hanged. Lear's only sense of dilemma may be in one sense little more than an idle and melodramatic fabrication of his own mind; but he lives out this pretense of a predicament in complete seriousness of purpose, apparently without suspicion of himself or his true situation. From the outside, we may deplore or perhaps even grow impatient with Lear's failure to take the one step of introspection that would give him the distance to recognize how false his dilemma is; once inside with him, however, we begin to suspect that there are deeply moving reasons why the Lear who wanders dispossessed and displaced in the play does not realize that if he is lost he is lost in a labyrinth containing one gateway that will allow a safe return to his loved ones. It is unthinkable for Lear to suspect himself or his true situation because to do so would uncover the wound that the first scene of the play momentarily threatened to tear wide open; it would expose before himself and others the humiliating fact that the predicament he needs to believe in is but self-protective avoidance of the real issue—a shame at himself in his weakness and vulnerability that Lear has not been able to acknowledge, even to himself.[20]

As we shall argue in succeeding chapters, a hidden shame is the only satisfactory explanation for the touching absurdity of the love auction the old king stages in act 1, scene 1, a piece of theater so foolish that neither vanity nor political sophistication would have attempted it. In this regard, *Hamlet* once again provides a striking contrast. It can hardly be a mere coincidence of structural patterning that the ultimately decisive action in *Hamlet* awaits the last scene, whereas in *Lear* it precipitates the drama. Both Hamlet and Lear balk at their worlds; but also, and more important, they are alike in that they balk at themselves in their worlds. But Lear's horror at the evil he must confront is not, like Hamlet's, bred in troubled anticipation of his complicity in it; it is lived instead as a deep anxiety about retrospection—a fear of confronting the sins he has already committed against Cordelia and Kent[21] and, even more significant, a fear of unearthing the abject shame that led him to act at the outset in ways so unlike himself and his best hopes. Hamlet may be obsessed by flight toward inwardness; but Lear is obsessed throughout with its opposite—flight and hiding from inwardness and self-analysis. What D. G. James claimed of Hamlet is perhaps even more true of Lear: from the banishment to the curse upon friends as "murderers, traitors all" Lear consistently attempts to "excuse himself."[22] This should not, we must hasten to add, be confused with a meanness of spirit that would knowingly insist on rationalizing crime. It is a more complex phenomenon and one that begins to suggest the limits of the defining power of grotesque comedy in the play as well as the tragic depths that subsume it. Lear may act meanly enough, may often appear ludicrous or even puerile; he is never beyond the undignified iteration of ironic reversal. But his spirit is neither trivial nor mean. It is grand; and the anguish that moves him to unknowing rationalization and ever more confused distractions from himself and his true condition communicates directly with some dread recess in the being of each of us and touches us, as it touches Cordelia, almost too deeply for words.

Kent's inconspicuous but summational statement, "He but usurp'd his life" (5.3.318),[23] is perhaps the best indication in the play of what the complexity of our response should be to Lear's long challenge to his destiny. Kent does intimate that Lear has consistently acted wrongly in seizing and wielding by force powers he had no right to exercise over his own life and those of others. His great bravery, then, in facing the winds and persecutions of the skies was always in another sense simply the forced march of a cowardly evasion, the furious assertiveness of a pretender attempting to preserve his false position and dignity at any cost rather than admit the secret identity of the true king. The ironic result is that Lear persists in a foolish contention to "course his own shadow for a traitor" (3.4.57–58). If, instead, he could have stood very still and looked within, he would have discovered the treasonous "pretender" there. What gives these curious paradoxes about Lear tragic dimension is that if he is a criminal usurper, his chief victim is himself as rightful and beloved king. Unless we are to assume that Lear is merely the foolish object of our ridicule, a conclusion inconsistent with the dimensions of his suffering if with nothing else, there must be a good reason why Lear prefers to remain a tortured pretender rather than recognize his rightful identity as king. The answer can only be that he feels such a profound shame at himself that he finds it too painful to do anything but avert his gaze. His tragic nobility emerges out of his agonized and unspeakable suspicion that he is neither rightful king nor deserving of love. As Cordelia's character shows, greatness of spirit can be built on the risky foundation of such vulnerability; but in Lear vulnerability remains simply a horror to be fled so intently that if we take Kent's metaphor seriously we must conclude that even in death Lear remains an impostor.

Tragedy in Farce

If the absence of a real dilemma in Lear's world distinguishes him from a long line of heroes and heroines from Agamemnon and Antigone to Antony and Hamlet, it nonetheless links him intimately to Othello and provides us with another useful approach to the peculiar tragic perspective *King Lear* sustains. Once we look beyond the single-minded structural concentration of *Othello* and the extensive diffusion of dramatic interest in *King Lear,* a matter we will be returning to presently, we come upon a number of similar points in the two plays that, though perhaps obvious, are nonetheless revealing.

As tragic dramas go, both plays are unusually restricted in scope and focus to the realm of the familial and domestic. Though each exhibits significant tangential relations to the larger public world and some more historically minded critics might even argue that Lear's tragedy in fact derives from an essentially political error, still, for nearly all of the play Lear is fundamentally and nearly exclusively of concern to us in his role as father in "domestic and particular broils" (5.1.30), only indirectly as king;[24] Othello concerns us in his role as husband, not soldier, except insofar as his identity as military campaigner aids us in understanding his sense of himself as a husband. In this they are both, relatively speaking, unlike Macbeth, Antony,

Coriolanus, or even Hamlet; for our interest in the latter characters and their predicaments is thoroughly implicated in and complicated by the public roles that mingle uneasily with and intrude into their domestic and private lives.

Furthermore, if in *Lear* and *Othello* the arena has shrunk, so, in a sense, has the stature of the principals. If Lear's antics risk reducing him to the stature of old fool become babe again, a skeletal synopsis of the unmistakably comic plot convention that underlies Othello's torment promises little better to the Moor. An ugly older man, prominent if not rich, who somehow manages to marry a beautiful young girl soon finds himself possessed by sexual jealousy, fear of marital ignominy, and loss of face—it is hardly a promising prospectus for a tragic plot.[25] In fact, it is hard to imagine a tragic hero in a more inherently foolish position or a character whose weakness is more conventionally ripe for ridicule. Even Lear starts out with better odds. Also, as with Lear, Shakespeare forbids Othello a true dilemma, as if he were trying to challenge his creative capacities to transform an unlikely vehicle into a significant tragic action. If Lear need only choose Cordelia, Othello need only choose Desdemona to break the seemingly magnetic force binding him to Iago and sustaining the tragedy's tenuous sense of inevitability. One could conjecture that Othello does, loosely speaking, have something of a dilemma in determining whether Iago or Desdemona is truthful; but reflection reveals that Othello does not in any significant way realize that he has a choice as to whom he should believe. Had he truly realized that he had a dilemma and simply had enough trust in Desdemona and, even more significant, in himself to doubt his own suspicion and consequently make the most elementary efforts to adjudicate the question before those concerned, the gossamer fabric of Iago's deceit would have collapsed.

The reason Othello does not do something of this sort may suggest a final similarity between the two protagonists, a similarity less than overt because Lear's wounded self is even more subtly defended and hidden than Othello's from the risky, uncertain ministrations of the open air. As we shall see, though Lear pretends otherwise, he lives, even more than the Moor, in shame before the painfully probing eyes of others and in fear that any exposure of his vulnerability to such scrutiny will only produce worse harm. In the most guarded reserve of their souls, both Lear and Othello suffer alone a noble agony that

only serves to smooth the way to self-torment and the wanton
destruction of the women they most love. In both, the aching
wound that they cannot acknowledge explicitly even to themselves is an anxiety about personal worth, a profound insecurity
about their deserving love. It is this alone that suddenly transforms the seemingly self-possessed public leader of the early
portions of *Othello* into Iago's helpless dupe and the respected,
still vigorous, if aged king into a ranting, petulant child.

If the similarities we have been referring to seem to predict a
more obvious and extensive likeness between the two tragedies
than actually exists between them, the reason is largely Shakespeare's manipulation of tone and chosen scope in each. *Othello*
could have become a play more permeated by elements of grotesque comedy than *Lear;* but, in fact, it does not. Shakespeare
carefully mitigates Othello's folly and otherwise guides our response to him in ways that protect him from the open ridicule
that Lear's own behavior and Shakespeare's management of
distance and tone invite in *King Lear.*

In *Othello,* the early going, especially act 1, establishes Othello
as a moral leader of heroically enviable proportions and stature, if not social position, more like Christ before his captors
and judges—dignified, self-possessed, and psychologically triumphant—than a likely candidate for jealous folly and a mad
crime of passion. The sudden collapse of his character before
Iago's insinuations in act 3 shocks us out of the relatively
unqualified moral admiration and affection we feel for him. In
Lear, of course, the collapse is just as shocking and inexplicable,
but it daringly opens the play. Consequently, our wonder is as
much or more the result of such a thing happening over a trifle
as that Lear has done it; for in the first scene we do not gain
enough knowledge of nor respect for Lear to be morally disappointed in *him,* though the banishment itself upsets us greatly.
The first scene is a blow from which our developing relationship to Lear never recovers. However harshly we must judge
Goneril and Regan's culpability in trying to wash their hands of
responsibility for their father's care and feeding, the Lear who
will not "stay a jot for dinner" (1.4.8), rewards retainers for
tripping up insolent house servants,[26] and flies into violent
rages whenever he discovers his dignity in the least slighted by
his daughters could never remotely recall Othello's triumphant
dignity. In addition, in the early action the Fool's irreverent
ridicule punctuates Lear's "scenes" and invites us, even forces

us by its repeated insistence, to keep the distance of a hard-headed critical intelligence between Lear and whatever sympathy we may begin to feel for him.

Othello may have no true dilemma, but trusted Iago's unaccountable malevolence and unrelenting torture do tend to emphasize for us a sense of external malice in the conditions of Othello's existence from which we fear he is not likely to find a way to extricate himself. This tenacious predation tempers our judgment of Othello's folly and criminality with an equally emphatic awareness of his diabolical victimization.

Lear's problems, by contrast, seem self-initiated and largely self-perpetuated. No rabidly persistent torturer significantly qualifies our sense of his folly. Goneril and Regan's behavior withstands little comparison to the enormity of Iago's malevolence. For one thing, Iago has no legitimate grounds for his resentment of and antagonism toward Othello whereas Lear's daughters do. Though their subsequent reactions to Lear's "unruly waywardness" (1.1.298) are, of course, morally unjustified,[27] their accusations do not misrepresent the fact that Lear's behavior has been and remains rowdy, willfully demanding, and disruptive. Moreover, their immediately fearful suspicions of Lear's "unconstant starts" (1.1.300) exhibit the prescience of a legalistically oriented if less than generously motivated self-defense. If, to their amazement and dread (since they doubt that they hold a similarly preferred place in the old king's doting heart), faithful Kent and beloved Cordelia could be banished, they reasonably infer that Lear could just as rashly and unexpectedly "offend" (306) them and once again seize the power he presumably gave away. Lear does not belie their fears when at Goneril's first check he threatens to "resume the shape which thou dost think/I have cast off for ever" (1.4.309–10). In addition, despite the fact that they have some basis for their antagonism and Iago none, they react far more diffidently than he in their malice, to the degree that one recent critic has been able to develop a lengthy, carefully supported, though not finally convincing argument that little in the first two acts prepares us properly to believe in the daughters' later villainy.[28] In any case, morally scandalous and emotionally chilling as the closing of Gloucester's gates may be at the end of act 2, it does nonetheless seem defensible to claim that whereas Iago was only satisfied when he had gratuitously planted and twisted the knife in the Moor's heart, Goneril and Regan's malice appears

more fearfully defensive, as if, even allowing for an element of
self-justification and pretense in their own explanation of the
need for their harshness, they were content, literally and metaphorically, to "disarm" the threat Lear represents to their security. All they desire is to render him powerless to turn on and
reverse his graciousness to them as one might defang and de-
claw a dangerously unpredictable cat that had given indications
it could turn from fawning devotion to viciousness.[29] If Regan's
claim can be at all trusted—"I'll receive him gladly,/But not one
follower" (2.4.292–93)—were Lear, left to his own devices in
the storm, once able to swallow the humiliation administered by
these daughters made mothers, he could at least return to dry
comfort if not to respect, reverence, or love. More important,
nothing the daughters do prevents him, once out of doors,
from seeking Cordelia and her forgiveness. He is not the
target, as Othello is, of an active, relentless desire to do irrepar-
able personal harm. With ironic reluctance we must agree with
Goneril to a degree that we never consider agreeing with Iago:
"'Tis his own blame hath put himself from rest,/And must
needs taste his folly," (2.4.290–91), even though we also know
that a good portion of Lear's folly is his foolish gamble on the
character of Goneril herself.

If the contrast between the villainy of Iago and Lear's daughters mitigates our sense of the ridiculous in Othello's fall and,
conversely, intensifies our sense of Lear's folly, Shakespeare's
manner in the final acts of each play further compounds this
effect. After Othello's capitulation or conversion to Iago's view
of things in act 3, so intensely and unrelentingly are we forced
to concentrate upon Othello's experience that although we
evaluate and judge Othello we are never really tempted to
ridicule him even at his most ludicrous and absurd moments.
In *King Lear*, however, we see little of Lear himself in the last
two acts; what is more, his behavior when he is on stage har-
monizes with the broadening, persistent presentation of ludicrous incidents and reversals that make up the roller coaster
movement of the last two acts. During the diffusion of dramatic
interest in the fourth and fifth acts, in which the Gloucester
subplot, including Edgar's revenge upon Edmund, an offstage
war, and the love relations among the daughters, Edmund, and
Albany all play themselves out, Lear appears on stage only four
times. Though each of these appearances represents an intimately personal and significant moment in Lear's torment, in

the poetic tapestry woven in the final acts they become somewhat obscured and reduced in scale by the sheer volume of
busy movement and the number of dramatic events and
character revelations flanking them. More important, all four
of Lear's scenes themselves subordinate their expected
thematic preeminence by repeatedly embodying a dimension
of the larger pattern of sequential and incongruous ironies of a
grimly humorous cast that "open like a series of trap doors"
upon the dramatis personae throughout acts 4 and 5.[30] This
pattern, in its apparently gratuitous bedevilment of men, even
in their best intentions and pathetic weakness, has occasioned
the current wave of interpretations of the play as reflective of
metaphysical absurdity.

I have already spoken at length of the ironic aspects of Lear's
last scene and speeches and the profound irony in his earlier
evasive refusal to see Goneril and Regan as Cordelia requested,
only to "confine" himself to "exhibition" yet again and commit
himself, in the wisdom of second childhood, to the often remarked "trap door" irony of his claim for the invulnerability of
fettered prisoners: "The good-years shall devour them, flesh
and fell,/Ere they shall make us weep" (5.3.24–25). No less is
true of Lear's mad encounter with Gloucester near the end of
act 4, in which among other grotesque ironies and incongruities
Lear counsels adultery because "Gloucester's bastard son/Was
kinder to his father than my daughters/Got 'tween the lawful
sheets" (4.6.114–17). He condemns all women with misogyn-
istic disgust even as Cordelia, we know, is actively seeking to
bring him aid and relief. Then, in presumptuous despair (given
Edgar's later victory over Edmund) he argues that whenever we
"[plate sin] with gold . . . the strong lance of justice hurtless
breaks," (165–66), and goes on to preach a sermon on patience
to Gloucester that, within ten lines, degenerates into a violent
revenge fantasy ("Then kill, kill, kill, kill, kill, kill" [187]) only to
give way, at the entrance of Cordelia's men, to mistaking his
rescuers for captors. In these sequentially ironic juxtapositions
and reversals, Lear takes his less than completely commanding
place beside the others in the dramatis personae in a poetic
universe repeatedly leveled by nearly farcical irony.[31]

The hint of the farcical in the last two acts of *Lear* and its
thematic consequences will soon lead us to a claim about the
essence of Shakespeare's tragic vision in the play. But for the
moment let us glance at the behavior of Edgar and Albany,[32]

the characters most responsible for moving the action to its
close in act 5, in order to exemplify the commanding presence
and operation of the elements of the ludicrous in the play's
resolution, repeated elements that cleverly serve to distract
us—like some features of Lear's final speeches themselves—
from unequivocally sympathetic concentration on the old king's
final ravings.

Given the brisk dramatic pace of the ingenious, often underestimated fifth act of *King Lear*,[33] it is ironic that unnecessary
delay should be the situational pattern of farce welding its
structural unity. If Lear's evasion of self and reluctance to acknowledge his shame always "detain him from Cordelia," even
in his apparent concentration upon her in his final speeches,
then the rest of the cast in act 5, especially the prime movers,
Edgar and Albany, also do their unconscious and ludicrous best
to avoid the central issue—the rescue of Lear and Cordelia.
Themselves obsessively "distracted" by their own personal
preoccupations from fully and responsively acknowledging the
situation they know their personal trials are but a part of, they,
like Lear, make their embattled insistences, usurping our attention and detaining us from Cordelia and the king. Though they
occupy the center of the stage, both Albany and Edgar remain
somewhat beside the point, just a bit absurd, as Shakespeare
insinuates by stationing us in the way that he does in act 5; it is
as if, having once been engrossed in a friend's story at a party,
we find him or her interrupted by two others insistent in their
turn on telling what to them are compelling but to us are com-
paratively tiresome tales.

We watch with an understanding of inevitable human weakness as the well-intentioned Albany inconspicuously slides into
allowing the fatal delay in the return of the captives whom he,
as commander in chief, had demanded of Edmund as the first
priority. In the process, he surrenders his generous power to
rescue the king and Cordelia to his personal hurt and subconscious rage to settle his marital scores against Goneril and Edmund (5.3.40–89).[34] Although powerful personal feelings of
betrayal overwhelm his sense of the immediacy of the need for
a generous rescue of the king and Cordelia, our sympathy for
him does not completely shield him later from our sense of his
foolishness as he suddenly blurts out his lapse of memory—
"Great thing of us forgot!" (237). After having distractedly
called Kent's attention to the dead sisters before Edmund has

had a chance to reply to his question about Lear and Cordelia's whereabouts, Albany confusedly rushes an even more confused Edgar offstage without a token of reprieve. Then he summons the gods to defend Cordelia, seemingly without acknowledging that he himself should and could have saved her, only to see his prayer answered immediately by Lear bearing Cordelia dead in his arms.[35] Nor does he cut much of a figure as he lamely tries to establish an official tone and juridical atmosphere in the midst of the unspeakable waste of life all about him and the deflating interruptions of Lear's nearly mad raving. It seems as if he cannot quite decide what else to do; and so he does what he presumes he is expected to do—assume a role of virtuous command. The pretense neither suits him nor the situation, however;[36] consequently, he acts the fool, absurdly declaiming, for example, given the circumstances, that "all friends shall taste/ The wages of their virtue, and all foes/The cup of their deservings" (303–5), only to hear the gallery send up its answering mockery—"And my poor fool is hang'd" (306).

If we look carefully at the language and intent of these final speeches, in fact, much of what Albany officially proclaims is as inappropriate to the situation as Lear's "official" yet grotesque greeting of Kent here—"[You] are welcome hither" (290). Having declared that Lear has gone out of his wits, Albany decides that the best "comfort" he can apply to Lear's "great decay" is to abdicate and make the deeply disturbed old man king again, as if it would be a comfort to the broken Lear—not to speak of the small consolation it would offer his beleaguered people—to heap again upon his shattered mind and heart the weight of kingship's responsibilities. No sooner does Lear foil this act of good will by dying than Albany tries to abdicate again, this time in deference to Edgar and, perhaps, Kent as well. Though Albany is undoubtedly well intentioned, it is a curiously ironic act of generosity that would proffer to the "friends of my soul" (320) as the "wages . . . their virtue" has "more than merited" (303) his abdication from the fellowship of "bearing," asking them instead to "rule in this realm, and the gor'd state sustain" (321) by themselves.

In fact, in what is very likely the most significant irony in his attempts to reestablish order at the conclusion, Albany's manner of expressing his "intent" (297) to abdicate because others, he blindly presumes, would better "sustain" the weight of state cares clearly invites us to recall the "darker purpose" and chaotic consequences of Lear's "fast intent" (1.1.38) at the outset to "shake all cares and business from our age" and "unburthen'd crawl toward death" (39, 41), "conferring" (as if they were honors) the weight of state cares upon "younger strengths" (40), backs that are not spared by Lear's decision to add the dead weight of himself and his 100 knights "by you to be sustain'd" (134). The effect of déjà vu in Albany's abdication results not only from the similarity of language and metaphor in these two speeches but also from our implicit recognition that both kings are, in fact, pretenders, even perhaps to themselves, each in the indulgence of his self-conceived helplessness feeding the illusion that this self-protective "reservation" for himself is instead a generous act or at least a disinterested token of respect.

The crowning irony in this chronicle of men's repeated capitulations to the pretenders in themselves, usurping their lives in their futile tyrannies, does not come to rest, however, in Albany's apparent repetition of Lear's initial folly in abdication. It continues, as we shall see, in the presumption of Edgar's remarks at the close in succeeding to Lear and Albany's pretense of power. Edgar and Albany's recapitulation of Lear's errors confirms that though the curtain may fall, there is no end to the succession of fools. We never learn: neither from the mistakes of others, nor from our own, however catastrophic the consequences. We do not learn; we only forget or, at best, remember too late the "great things" we have forgotten. This is the one inevitability that the tragic vision in *King Lear* keeps before us. Lear's fate does not die with him. It lives on, begins all over again in the incomprehension and presumption of Edgar's assumption of power. But let an explanation of Edgar's importance at the close wait until we rehearse his role in the proceedings leading up to the finale, especially in act 5.

That Edgar's actions should form part of the context of avoidance and unnecessary delay in act 5 should come as no shock to anyone who has taken even a cursory glance at Edgar's career from the beginning.[37] Initially, of course, he avoided his father when a confrontation with Gloucester's suspicions, though admittedly a heroic risk, would have both confirmed a loving son's trust in his father and exposed Edmund's plot against him. Then, disguised as Poor Tom, at the end of act 3, scene 6, when he appears to have no compelling reason to avoid helping the king, Edgar lingers behind to hide himself rather than help Kent and the Fool carry Lear to Dover. The irony of this avoidance is more than compounded by the consolation Edgar, lurking alone, derives from the sight of Lear borne off by Kent and the Fool: "How light and portable my pain seems now,/When that which makes me bend makes the King bow" (3.6.108–9). Edgar appropriately concludes how "light and portable" his burden is compared to the king's, and he wins our sympathy in his expression of sympathy for Lear. But if we also compare his burden to Kent and the Fool's burden of active love, Edgar's philosophical consolation shades into mere rhetoric. Unlike Cordelia who knows love's burdensomeness, Edgar here unwittingly declares that his love is little more "ponderous" than his "tongue" (1.1.78). He may "bend" under his experience of grief but not humbly enough to help carry Lear's litter. His well-meaning affection for the king does not urge him to suffer or risk himself for him. Edgar's self-absorbed attempt to cheer himself up by weighing his woes against the greater misery of the king suggests that he does not really know the meaning of the satisfactions of the companionate suffering he speaks of. For Edgar, "bearing['s] fellowship" implies no genuinely communal fellowship but only the self-centered satisfaction of knowing someone is under burdens heavier than one's own. Though his words speak of it, he does not know the miraculous birth of muted but mutual joy from the ashes of suffering love, when "grief hath mates and bearing fellowship" (3.6.107).[38]

Lying hidden and alone in surrender to the snail's instinct for self-preservation ("lurk, lurk" [115]), or, at best, in the lingering dream of self-justifying vindication of innocence, Edgar's affection for the king lies open to the charge France leveled at Burgundy: "Love's not love/When it is mingled with regards that stands/Aloof from th' entire point" (1.1.238–40). The same accusation might just as rightfully be made regarding Edgar's astonishing delay in revealing his identity to his father and his decision, instead, however well intentioned, to remain disguised and drag Gloucester about the countryside in order to deceive him into a superstitious faith that his "life's a miracle" (4.6.55).[39] He could much more simply confirm in Gloucester a genuine faith by performing a miracle himself (namely, by revealing himself), something that is and ever remains in his power to do.[40] For our first glimpse of the blind Gloucester in act 4 revealed his undespairing hope in and a prayer for this simple but miraculous healing: "dear son Edgar . . . Might I but live to see thee in my touch,/I'ld say I had eyes again" (4.1.21, 23–24). But in Edgar's conscious decision making, as in Lear's, what appears to us an obvious remedial course of action remains occluded; and Edgar, though earnestly seeking to do good, merely usurps himself as he persists in playing out a series of needlessly artificial roles rather than simply presenting himself to his father. Throughout the play Edgar acts from high-minded motives, either in the uncompromising hope of reestablishing the good or of punishing evildoers; but, even so, there remains a telltale element in his character that qualifies our estimate of his virtues and good intentions. In matters of love, and otherwise, too, Edgar consistently "stands/Aloof from th' entire point," fastidiously reserved and theatrically "distant" even from the people he cares for greatly.[41] Whether costumed in the self-pitying rhetoric of poor, naked Tom or in the hero's armor as chivalric knight restoring his unjustly sullied honor, Edgar is always somewhat "brazed" to full personal involvement with and responsiveness to others.[42] From the beginning, when he readily falls the dupe of his brother's practice, he is never quite "all there" in any situation he undergoes. Act 5 certainly offers no exceptions to his distracted, preoccupied manner.

At the beginning of Act 5, for example, Edgar does two very curious things in quick succession. First, after secretly presenting Albany with Goneril's damning letter to Edmund urging, as he had earlier soliloquized, a "plot upon her virtuous husband's life" (4.6.272), Edgar unaccountably refuses to wait there until Albany has had a chance to read it:

ALBANY: Stay till I have read the letter.
EDGAR: I was forbid it.
         When time shall serve, let but the herald cry
         And I'll appear again.[43]

                                                    (5.1.47–49)

Had he stayed, Edmund, who appears alone immediately thereafter, could have been harmlessly placed under arrest or, at worst, driven to a desperate attack on both his accusers with little likelihood of success. In any case, the completely unnecessary waste of life in the ensuing battle between France and England and the risk of danger to those Edgar cares for—Gloucester, Lear, Cordelia, Kent, and Albany himself—might have been averted. Why does Edgar presume that he can only settle with Edmund after the battle has been fought and won, even at the risk of the man's life he has purportedly brought his letter to save (cf. 5.1.44–46)? Why the unnecessary delay? One can, of course, deny the meaningfulness of the questions as would those who tell us that Shakespeare is preeminently interested in "drama," in furthering his plots, not in character consistency and probable motivation. But even an apprentice playwright would know enough to avoid calling attention to an absurdly motivated act in the way Shakespeare does here in the quoted exchange between Albany and Edgar. The only possible explanation, though not completely satisfactory (since there is never an adequate explanation when "great things" of us are "forgot"), is that Edgar is preoccupied, is simply not thinking of these things or, at best, not thinking clearly about these things. He is apparently so distracted with imagining the orchestration of his own heroic vindication that he has no time for the trifling checks of common sense. He cannot come to a genuinely heroic rescue "in time" because he is living in his dream of the future, in the never-never land "when time shall serve" *him* in his glory.

We next discover Edgar a scene later stationing a wearied Gloucester under the shade of a tree and promising "comfort" should he ever be able to return to him again. The presumption is immediately ridiculed, however, as he returns to the stage, frantically shouting for Gloucester to endure yet more wandering, and then again in the comical picture of him preaching a bizarre brand of stoicism nearly on the dead run.[44] We realize, of course, that more motion, more flight, more evasion will not cure what ails Gloucester's body or his soul; the only genuine "comfort" Edgar could provide—rest and community—he does not think to offer him. Edgar's famous aphorism—"Ripeness is all"—too often treated out of its context, is utterly inapposite and beside the point in that context. The language of enduring the "going hence" even as the "coming hither" (5.2.10) that Edgar appropriates from a wisdom of patience in suffering smacks of puffery in the mouth of a man preaching forbearance in suffering only as a means to escape greater suffering, a man for whom "going hence" is reduced from an acceptance of death to a self-protective search for a safer place to hide. The "ripeness" Edgar speaks of, whatever else it demands of our spiritual self-discipline, clearly demands by force of the metaphor a yielding trust in our fruitful subjection to the service of the time being, something we have just seen Edgar refuse Albany and see again here in this harrying treatment of his father. Such yielding is certainly not something he lives since nothing can ripen when continually uprooted or in perpetually evasive motion.

Except for the speech that darkens the lights at the close, Edgar's final significant act is his ironically "pat" role in his challenge of and victory over Edmund in which he again comes on "like the catastrophe of the old comedy" (1.2.134), much in the sense Edmund meant the phrase in the context of his own theatrical plot in act 1. For Edgar's role is at once comedic and "pat" because we know that in his eyes the scene actually plays, like Edmund's earlier one, exactly the way he had rehearsed it. Edgar has for some time now lived by directing and orchestrating events and situations with an eye toward this denouement in which poetic justice will prevail, and now reality actually seems to serve his wishful thinking. It is a perfectly familiar sort of dream. Edmund has dealt him an apparently wanton wrong, and he is merely intent on justice and the vindication of his own innocence. But in making his challenge he fails to suspect that what he is doing here may not be as exclusively good as he imagines it. So intent is Edgar on his own righteousness that he does not imagine that even in acting to assert the right there is a real danger of doing wrong. His means secure him from the stumbling dread and anxiety of living blind as he lives out, instead, the visionary artifice of a self-vindicating dream.

What seems "pat" to Edgar seems too pat for us; and his entrance and actions in act 5 when he overthrows Edmund are not so much apt or opportune as they are theatrically cued. We know that reality has not truly served in spontaneous obeisance to him; rather, he has subtly manipulated it to serve his own fantasies. Consequently, we see him stumble even when he sees his way clear to victory; we hear him falter because his periods are so smooth, never halting or even embarrassed by their own tactlessness. His speeches, most of all, betray him. Their stiff, studied rhetoric, the absence of the supple responsiveness to the ever-contingent demands of personal interaction that makes all generous speech anxious, combines with the stylized nature of the chivalric challenge itself, already an antiquated, merely theatrical ritual in Shakespeare's day, to make the scene a kind of set piece staged with solemn deliberateness while the fates of Lear and Cordelia hang in dreadful peril at every moment.[45]

In an emblematic tableau that is obviously too pat, Gloucester's bastard son bred in the "lusty stealth of nature" and the
"legitimate" Edgar combat as mighty opposites for the "largest
bounty" of their father's lands.[46] Here again, and just as misguidedly as in act 1, scene 1, two children obey a ritualistic
summons and "nature doth with merit challenge" (1.1.53).
However, an emblem that would identify Edgar simply with the
virtue of law justly triumphing over brute acquisitiveness or
unbridled opportunism would not merely oversimplify the situation here, it would radically misconstrue its meaning. Clearly
Edmund's claims of "nature," however abused in his insistence,
do have "merit" unanswered of Edgar as they had been of
Gloucester. Any absolute assertions about the savagery of his
nature must come to terms with the highly civilized way he acts
throughout this scene—his generosity of spirit, his civility, his
grace and honesty in defeat, his willingness to forgive a triumphant adversary, and his desire and ultimate decision to do
good despite the acknowledgment that he has done great evil.
Certainly his manner is far more winning than victorious Edgar's whose legalistic case for "merit" presents no evidence of
the mercies of the heart toward Edmund, even in defeat, or
toward Gloucester for that matter—no "nature" in the sense of
spontaneous familial affection that Lear meant when he used
the word in ordering the challenge among his daughters in
act 1, scene 1. In fact, in arguing the "merit" of the legitimacy
he defends so righteously, Edgar does not even seem to recognize the corrupt presumption in his avowal of a legitimacy
founded on the exclusion of "nature's" fraternal kinship and
essential equality in blood. Otherwise he could never have re-
sponded with such inappropriate and obscene cleverness to
Edmund's simple offer:

EDMUND: If thou'rt noble,
          I do forgive thee.
EDGAR: Let's exchange charity.
          I am no less in blood than thou art, Edmund;
          If more, the more th' hast wrong'd me.
          My name is Edgar, and thy father's son.
          The gods are just, and of our pleasant vices
          Make instruments to plague us:
          The dark and vicious place where thee he got
          Cost him his eyes.

                                        (5.3.166–74)

The ambiguity in Edmund's use of the word *noble* probably reveals the pathetic insecurity of one who, rudely born, so desperately desires social acceptance and respect that even at his slaying he would offer forgiveness to his adversary could Edgar show himself a "man of quality or degree" (5.3.110).[47] Even so, any offer of forgiveness in such circumstances argues a degree of civilized graciousness and merit not evident in Edgar whose clever idea of an "exchange" of "charity" (167) is to identify Edmund as a venereal "plague." The rhetorical effectiveness in this complicated trope demands that Edgar identify his dear father's blindness as a just *quid pro quo*, the "dark and vicious" disease of venereal blindness rhetorically and judicially coupled to and balanced by the "dark and vicious" socket of Edmund's mother's diseased womb.[48]

Edgar's insult, however elegant and clever in rhetorical design and in the service of his defrauded righteousness, subtly declares the corrupted heart of a cavalier's nobility, when he jests in brazen worldliness about his own father's "pleasant vices" (171), tastelessly sacrificing human concern to an attempt at a well-turned phrase. In this, significantly, Edgar confirms that he is indeed his lubricious father's son, recalling as he does here Gloucester's sexual jesting at Edmund's bastard "blood." Edmund's plague is not venereal. It has grown and been fostered in reaction to the corruption of a civilization that makes him "stand in the plague of custom" (1.2.3), the corruption of the custom of legitimacy that refuses to acknowledge him son or brother to persist in naming him a filthy jest. The gods have had nothing to do with making Edmund the instrument of plague that he is, nor has anything in nature made his hard heart—certainly not his mother's libeled womb or even his father's engendering. The only truly "dark and vicious place" where Edmund was "got" (5.3.173) is the benighted heart of Gloucester, then of Edmund himself, and finally of Edgar, too, all of whom are unable to recognize or acknowledge in him anything but his bastardy.

Certainly the Edmund we meet in this scene is a grander figure than that. Unlike Gloucester or Edgar, and perhaps because of their exclusions, he magnanimously honors a claim of nature, not one of legal "degree," in facing his nameless challenger. Ever the opposite of the self-protective Edgar we have been following, Edmund "disdains" what "safe and nicely I might well delay/By rule of knighthood" (145–46). Then, having misguidedly, though with real dignity, absorbed Edgar's insult and accepted the verdict his brother pronounces upon him, he goes on to perform an act of repentance "despite of mine own nature" (245), spurred presumably by his reflection that for once at least "Edmund was belov'd" (240). The pathos with which we come to realize that Edmund knows so little about the experience of being loved that he could mistake the lust of Lear's daughters for it and that even the corruption of love for a man believing it to be love can inspire a truly gener- ous act only adds to the sympathy with which we experience Edmund's death. It certainly forces us to disagree with Albany whose response to Edmund's death is the myopic—"That's but a trifle here" (296). The manner of his death is, rather, of the neglected essence:

> Some good I mean to do,. . .
>   Quickly send
> (Be brief in it) to th' castle, for my writ
> Is on the life of Lear and on Cordelia.
>
> (5.3.244–47)

To do good, truly act generously, and be brief in it—it is a counsel both Albany and Edgar might well have paid more heed to in their "trifling" delays in making their efforts to save Lear and Cordelia.

It is even understandable that Edgar, flushed with victory, cannot resist telling, with repeated rhetorical flourishes, what seems to him but a "brief tale" (182) of his trials and exploits.[49] But we find it difficult to concentrate on what he is saying or hear him out, preoccupied as we are by the unconcluded tale of Lear and Cordelia. If Edgar must persist in telling tales, we wish that they might be yet briefer and more to the point. Let us take his unconsciously comic supplement to the tale of his exploits and his father's death as an illustration of his tendency to "amplify too much" (207). So affected, presumably, has Al- bany been by the account of Gloucester's death that he begs Edgar to speak no more sorrows:

> If there be more, more woeful, hold it in,
> For I am almost ready to dissolve,
> Hearing of this.
>
> (5.3.203–5)

One cannot be certain of the depth of Albany's sincerity here, but what is almost certain is that Edgar, perhaps generalizing from his own tendency to rhetorical exaggeration, treats Albany's request as a mere pretense, as a challenge to his rhetorical powers to move an audience. Glowing from his first tale's success, he hurries, heedless of Albany's request, to try to outdo himself in a manner that compromises the depth of his grief for his father since he trifles with his death.

> This [Gloucester's death] would have seem'd a period
> To such as love not sorrow, but another,
> To amplify too much, would make much more,
> And top extremity.
>
> (5.3.205–8)

Edgar has sinned against his grief for his father's agony and death if he can speak of Gloucester's eyes as "bleeding rings/ Their precious stones new lost" (190–91), in the way he had moments earlier or if he can speak of him with such self-conscious rhetoric and enthusiasm that his death is but one among other moving stories—and not even the climactic one. Even in the rhetorical framework in which Edgar's language invites us to think of these tales, his supplement is a breach of decorum. Rather than leave well enough alone, he "amplifies too much," with bathetic results. At least the placement of Gloucester's death provided a certain climactic power, finality, and resolution. It was an appropriate "period" to a tale. His supplement, its rhetoric flatly declarative and clichéd and its drama oafish ("Whilst I/Was big in clamor," "with his strong arms/He fastened on my neck and bellowed out," "threw [him] on my father/Told the most piteous tale of Lear and him" [208–9, 212–13, 214–15]), also ends with anticlimactic inconclusiveness when Edgar, answering his own demands, "left" his story's unnamed hero "tranc'd" (219), his fate hanging in a suspense worthy of a matinee movie serial.

It is a revealing irony, as we shall soon see, that this "top extremity" speech we have been examining within a context of nearly comic character revelation can, out of context, so easily be read as an aptly symbolic description of the tragic effect of this play of trapdoor reversals, answering all attempts at consolation and purposeful resolution in acts 4 and 5. Certainly the pattern of avoidance of love's "entire point" that we have been

examining in the behavior of Edgar and Albany, does, in mirroring Lear's persistent folly, "amplify too much" and "top extremity" for those who do not love sorrow. Similarly, except for
Cordelia's ideal and peaceful synthesis of the claims of nature
and law, inclination and duty, in the eager fidelity to her
"bond" we will be examining in chapter 2 we see the tragic
pattern of "nature's" challenge with "merit" and vice versa mul-
tiply so amply that eventually we may begin to suspect that it
will never cease. Goneril and Regan militantly answer Lear's
challenge to verbal joust, then continue their battle with each
other over the rights to Edmund's natural favors. Kent repeatedly wounds his merit by conceding to his hot-blooded
nature. Edmund, the natural son, declares all-out war on legitimate Edgar; Edgar, when he gets the chance in act 5, merely
returns the favor. Gloucester lives at war with himself for half
the play, deciding whether to yield to his nature or meritori-
ously stand up for the king and the other half, with Edgar's
help, debating the lawfulness of his inclination to suicidal surrender. In the first several acts of the play, he cannot say
enough about the merits of his natural son, believing the legitimate has betrayed him; but once he finds Edgar has been
"abused" (4.1.22) he never has another word or thought presumably for Edmund, even to wonder at the causes of his villainy. Albany, "the virtuous husband," literally challenges
Edmund, just as Edmund had already implicitly challenged his
legal rights to Goneril. Lear, in exile, begins and persists for
some time in a furious contention against "nature" as a man of
"merit," "more sinn'd against than sinning" (3.2.60).[50] He pro-
ceeds in acts 3 and 4 to even more complicated arguments
about the irreconcilable relations of nature to justice and law,
and he ends the play renewing his battle with nature in his last
speeches, this time challenging her with Cordelia's "merit." The
cumulative effect of the unyielding repetition of these sorrows
seems also to "top extremity." As Richard Fly has recently put
it, the play resists all efforts at closure.[51] It is, therefore, somewhat ironic that recent discussions of King Lear have tended to
emphasize the importance of the language of the last judgment
at the play's close; for there is no "promis'd end" (5.3.264)
awaiting us in this dramatic world.[52] There is no end to it at all.
The king is dead, long live the king. Edgar's final, summational
lines bitterly confirm the continuity of the unbroken succession
of Player Kings, the lords of misrule. The words that close the

play begin a new one very much like, one suspects, the one we have just witnessed.

In response to Albany's request to "rule in this realm, and the gor'd state sustain" (321), Edgar concludes:

> The weight of this sad time we must obey,
> Speak what we feel, not what we ought to say:
> The oldest hath borne most; we that are young
> Shall never see so much, nor live so long. (5.3.324–27)

Despite their pat couplet rhymes and assured antithetical balance, Edgar's remarks reveal that the persistent pattern of contention between nature and the laws of merit, between inclination and duty, remains unsettled, unresolved at the close despite the implicit, reconciling lesson of Cordelia's life and speech. We do not know, of course, whether Edgar is saying what he feels here or what he thinks "ought" to be said; if he is saying only what he believes he "ought to say," he is a hypocrite. On the other hand, if he is saying only what he truly feels, it is certainly not what he "ought to say," as we shall see. Troubled by a false note in Edgar's urging here, Professor Rosenberg expressed his doubt about Edgar's future by pointing to his role-playing past—"How much in other times has he spoken as he felt?"[53] One might add that on those rare occasions when he has spoken as he felt, as, for example, when he spoke to Edmund after his victory or perhaps here, he did not say what he ought to have said. In both cases, Edgar offers hopelessly simplistic solutions to questions the complexity of which he does not even understand. For someone like Edgar, unconsciously intent on himself primarily, speaking what he feels is simply a matter of indulging the self's desire for self-expression; speaking what he ought to say, an equally easy matter of protecting the self in a ritualistic rhetoric's studied conventions. Even the choice between one and the other is not difficult because neither torments or troubles him significantly; instead, each in its own way feeds his unconscious self-satisfaction. Only Cordelia and the Fool realize how terribly difficult and painful, even, in a sense, impossible it is to "speak what we feel" and conversely how dreadful it would be—in fact intolerable, given the love they feel for Lear and their sense that the "ought" must not be perverted—to retreat to the safety of a conventionally polite and ritualistic rhetoric. Only they, knowing how difficult either is, also know that there is no easy choice between speaking what we feel and what we ought to say. What we feel must be reconciled with what we ought to say; what we ought to say, with what we feel. In the midst of the embattled contentiousness surrounding them, only Cordelia and the Fool know the painful compromises of self and the anxious demands upon their capacities to respond to complexity made by the self's hallowed desire for a peacefully diplomatic reconciliation fair to both inclination and duty, to feeling's love and ought's rights. Only they—not the warring—know the dear cost of life to create this fragile peace.

Edgar does not yet understand—any more than Lear ever does—the unobtrusive sacrifices made in these secret peace deliberations and negotiations Cordelia constantly conducts within; for, in a conventionally pious deference to his elders, Edgar ingenuously claims that the "oldest hath borne most." Insofar as his remark may refer to Gloucester, we must question whether Edgar is speaking what he feels; insofar as it may refer to Lear, we know he is not speaking what he ought to say. Cordelia, the youngest, has "borne" the most from a Lear who sets his "rest/On her kind nursery" (1.1.123–24) from beginning to end. She has had to bear with him, not vice versa; for him, tragically, she always remains an indulgence spawned by his insecurity. In fact, Lear exhibits no genuine forbearance whatever in the play; for his protests about what he has suffered and his need for patience are themselves a self-justification rather than a self-sacrificial cross he bears. How indecorous is Edgar's, "we that are young/Shall never see so much, nor live so long" (5.3.326–27),[54] with Cordelia dead before us. Forgotten among the contentious dead, she has been inelegantly dismissed from the stage of the living, her singular graciousness unrecognized, her "virtues" still "unpublish'd" (4.4.16).

But it is not simply because he overlooks Cordelia's importance that Edgar fails to say what he ought to say here. Albany, we recall, had urged him to "sustain" the "gor'd state." In a revealing, yet seemingly unreflective continuation of Albany's metaphor, Edgar bows to the oldest who have already "borne" the most, but then modestly avers that he, too, "must obey" the "weight" of this "sad time" in his own small way. One would think Edgar might have learned at Gloucester's death the devastating effects that "top extremity" from dragging the gored about on one's back. His small way does not suggest the genuine humility and care of Cordelia's "better way" but, rather, merely promises a grotesque mimicry of his elders, especially Lear himself. If the state has indeed been "gor'd" then one ought with others in that community of wounded sufferers (one of whom is Edgar himself) to minister to its wounds, and like Cordelia and her physicians, provide peace and rest, not heave it on one's own shoulders in a show of superior strength only to do it and oneself yet greater damage as one stumbles further on. This faulty "assumption" of power on Edgar's wounded part points to the most ludicrous way in which what Edgar says here is not what he ought to say. Edgar has not only overlooked Cordelia's example and avoided the lesson implicit in Gloucester's death, but he has also forgotten his own highest wisdom in the play. For in his last words he does not "obey" the "sad time" except in the negative sense that, like the others, he presumes upon it rather than humbly standing in the service of the instants of sad time's being as they come. Edgar's last words presume upon his capacity to dictate the future and thus block the acknowledgment of his ongoing weakness and contingency. In them, he reveals himself as another pretender to kingship: "we that are young/Shall never see so much, nor live so long." He ought to remember that words, the tools of creative self-discovery, always prove ineffective shields when used as defense against vulnerability: "the worst is not/So long as we can say, 'This is the worst'" (4.1.27–28).

The diffusion of dramatic interest in acts 4 and 5 serves its purpose most effectively in delineating Shakespeare's tragic vision in *King Lear*. If Lear himself is the dramatic center of this vision he is not also its circumference; what he provides in depth, Gloucester, Edgar, Edmund, and Albany, as we have begun to see, reveal in breadth—a needlessly wasteful and almost absurd exhibition of themselves. But this nearly absurd dramatic universe should in no way be construed in metaphysical terms as some "cosmic mockery." Far from it. Chaos that "tops extremity" does so with a ludicrous edge because its amplitude builds so exclusively and wantonly from the human failure to recognize and prudently seize available grace. We cannot safely or meaningfully remove the "top extremity" speech from its context of comic character revelation to make of it a detached metaphorical summation of the trapdoor metaphysical economy presumed to constitute the play's vision. At every turn, even when Lear, with Cordelia dead, surrenders another opportunity by failing to recall his Fool, each and all of them could come to a heroic rescue "in time." They could redeem themselves at any and every moment, but they persist in their folly.

If tragedy's paradoxical melding of pity and terror can be meaningfully distinguished from the two forms of simple melodrama, that which excites terror at criminal villainy and that which arouses pity for innocence victimized, *King Lear* repeatedly suggests its tragic inevitability that men willfully and criminally continue to choose their own victimization, destructively challenging nature with merit when they could live graciously, like Cordelia, in a generous accord between them.[55] The element of the grotesque in the repeated ironies and deflations does not necessarily indict the gods for using man as a comic plaything in their wanton "sport," to borrow Gloucester's term.[56] To presume so is but an evasion of the fact that over and over again, man himself is the only idle trifler playing with human life here, making his "shame" a "pastime" (2.4.6).[57] The more men try to prove or uphold their value in this play the more they sin against it. The more they attempt to flee shame, consciously, as in Edmund's case, or unconsciously as in Lear's and Edgar's, the more they compound it and the evils they suffer.

Zeus's first words in *The Odyssey* aptly correct the absurdist orientation of much of the best current criticism of the play:

Oh for shame, how the mortals put the blame on us
gods, for they say evils come from us, but it is they rather,
who by their own recklessness win sorrow beyond what is
     given.

The tragic irony in *King Lear* is not that man is a weak and absurd misfit in the cosmic disorder of things. After all, Cordelia is weak and the Fool absurd enough; but both are quite at home in their universe, even under unnecessarily and unusually adverse conditions. Nor is either of them subjected to the trapdoor deflations mocking the others at every step and speech, especially in the last acts. Oddly enough, it is Regan who correctly states the situation of man in the play's world when, with mean incomprehension, she tells Lear: "being weak, seem so" (201).[58] The play does not focus on man's intrinsic weakness so much as on his presuming he need not be so, his tendency to repress the fact that he is at best a happy beggar who can and should take nothing for granted. Instead, he would play out the theatrical pretense of kingship. Absurdly and unrelentingly, despite the plainest facts, he insists he can subdue the present and secure the future to his imperial sway. In this he proves the true absurdity that forms the play's tragic essence. To revise Gloucester's half-truth (a revision needed, given how he behaves even after his blinding), even our defects can become a faulty means to secure us and thus prove an accommodation that obscures our true needs.

Though man is, by nature, a freakish creature who often deserves laughter—a featherless biped—he need not cripple his state further by hiding his defects or by brazening them out; he should, paradoxically, "cultivate" them and, thus, harmonize nature and merit. Cordelia and the Fool, though greatly pained by the miseries they see others experiencing, know, nonetheless, that it is neither appropriate nor wise to be so ashamed of what is shameful in us that we fail to face ourselves and, consequently, live out a pretense of virtue, never honestly meeting each other or establishing true community. Gloucester may nearly boast to Kent of having overcome his shame for the bastard he engendered, but we know that he has neither faced his shame nor grown humbled by it. He has, instead, merely grown insensitive to it, compounding it rather than learning from it, nurturing Edmund's bastardy rather than Edmund himself. Both Gloucester and Edmund wrongly insist that their shame is barren when, in fact, it is the only soil in which their virtues can be cultivated. Similarly, Cordelia knows that Lear's shame is not an intolerable offense against the person he imagines he might otherwise have become; it is the very precondition of that character's possible flourishing. It is solely because Lear, Gloucester, Edmund, and Edgar cannot imagine so cultivating themselves that so much unnecessary devastation results.

But however torturing and grotesque the effects of their unwitting failure to face themselves, Cordelia's presence in the play also teaches us that our final response to them should not be judgment since in their hearts they are clearly more frightened than vicious, more threatened and unsure of themselves than selfish. Like her, we only wish that they might share a "better way" to cultivate shame than the pretense of shamelessness. Although man can be a contemptible animal, he is not irredeemably so. If this featherless creature cannot fly (the play is filled with the "images of revolt and flying off" [2.4.90]—all ultimately unsuccessful), he need not in self-contempt "top extremity" by cutting off his legs to spite his deformed wings and "crawl toward death," moving in self-pitying and self-condemning abdication from communality. For such logistical maneuvers are themselves as much a part of the revolt against acknowledgment of who we are and can be, as much a flight from self as their seeming opposite. Rather than fly or crawl we can, instead, with natural dignity, genuine merit, and the muted joy of fellowship stand together even when we "stand condemn'd" (1.4.5), as Cordelia, Kent, and the Fool reveal in their solidarity.

Man need not merely usurp his life; he can responsively live it, standing in each "instant" come what may, not fleeing the present as he orchestrates imperial designs upon his brave future. Such living, of course, is no easy accomplishment. In a sense, it is not an accomplishment at all but at best an abiding attitude of humility. Only through the dreadful insecurity involved in our truest acts of bravery, the continued submission of ourselves to the ever-changing demands of the moment and the people in them, ourselves included, and our untiring acknowledgments and admissions of our "mere defects" and failures, can we, like Cordelia under the tutelage of her shame, learn humility's difficult lesson, be "eas'd/With being nothing," and through that grow into the fully human stature of what Shelley called "self-empire and the majesty of love." In her natural slowness (France remarks upon the "tardiness" in her "nature" [1.1.235] not to censure but to praise her) Cordelia knows that the strange "art of our necessities . . ./[that] can make vild things precious" (3.2.70–71) is no alchemical quackery that can transform the security of our "means" from lead to gold instantaneously and at our impatient will, as Lear thinks it is when he makes the statement; her slowness is, instead, a lifetime discipline, an art of living, that can gradually but miraculously transform the open and honest admission of our defects into emerging self-respect and the most shameful deformities of those we love into something precious. "Things base and vile, holding no quantity,/Love can transpose to form and dignity" (*Midsummer Night's Dream* 1.1.232–33). The reason such art is "strange" is not the inaccessibility of its mysteries but our refusal to become familiar with its practice. As Kent claims, Cordelia comes "seeking to give/Losses their remedies"

(2.2.169–70); but few of us are willing to follow the dreadful cure of her homeopathy.

Cordelia is unquestionably the key to the play's sustaining vision. Readings that focus on Lear's redemption too conveniently tend to forget her death or trifle with it by denying its importance, as if they agreed with the logic that denies the importance of Cordelia's own life and happiness in Lear's "come, let's away to prison" speech. So-called absurdist readings, on the other hand, presumably following Gloucester's equally questionable accusation of the meaningless heavens, tend to forget the overwhelming meaningfulness of Cordelia alive in the play. Neither position adequately accounts for the subtlety of Cordelia and the Fool's vision and heroism, and both thus avoid a full recognition of the play's complexities. Cordelia and the Fool unobtrusively manifest the ideal tact, prudence, and engagement with life the others lack. As we shall see in the following chapter, the living virtue they embrace when the others—especially Lear and Edgar—unknowingly flee, is depicted as a version of pastoral open to all. The music of their voices, a music lovingly beckoning us as it beckoned Lear and Edgar, is the harmony we must listen for in the silence if we hope to find our way to a "better place" than our shame.

[2]

The Pastoral Norm

Fleeing into the Storm: Lear and Edgar

In a provocative insight born of a comparison of the dramatic development and resolution of *King Lear* to *As You Like It,* Maynard Mack has established the structural indebtedness of *King Lear* to the "shape of pastoral romance."[1] He has revealed how the structural development of the tragedy alludes to the pattern of extrusion from court, sojourn in a natural setting, and restoration to serenity through ritual death and rebirth (this last at least apparent in *Lear*) that constitutes the action in *As You Like It.* But ultimately Professor Mack concludes that *King Lear* alludes to this pattern only to overturn it and become instead "the greatest anti-pastoral ever penned." Although this conclusion is unquestionably valid at the plot level in *Lear,* it is seriously misleading if not simply false in regard to the play's thematic vision. The first section of this chapter will examine several indications in the text that the play's meaning does not in any way undermine the pastoral ideal since the ultimate reality of evil in *Lear* is, as we shall see, not cosmic or even natural, but human. This human evil does not emerge from any ineradicable human maliciousness; it grows almost incidentally from a condition, primarily evident in Lear and Edgar, that is not itself intrinsically corrupt—a suspicion of and anxiety about lack of personal worth. Moreover, as we shall see in the second and third sections of the chapter, imagery and conventions peculiar to the pastoral mode extensively cluster about Cordelia, the Fool, and, at times at least, Kent. Together the three of them form an ideal community, a contentedly peaceful and gracious social order whose simple existence confirms the play's version of pastoral, a "better way" than the brazen and

58

contentious sophistications of the others at Lear's court. Their living example exposes many of the others' agonies as superfluous; their own graceful bearing, ignored by the others as superfluous, finally shows itself as the "true need" Lear and the others cry for but never recognize.

When Professor Mack, explaining the antipastoral case, emphasizes that in *King Lear* "nature proves to be indifferent or hostile, not friendly" to man,[2] he overlooks how much more inhospitable are aspects of the natural settings visited in exile from court in the late pastoral romances, or even in *As You Like It* where Duke Senior in Arden speaks of

> the icy fang
> And churlish chiding of the winter's wind,
> Which . . . bites and blows upon my body
> Even till I shrink with cold.
>
> (2.1.6–9)

King Lear's single storm presents us with nothing in nature to compare with the harshness of Belarius's long life in a rocky cave so stark that Imogen mistakes it for a lair. The storm covers no Sycorax or Caliban, only "cub-drawn bear" and "belly-pinched wolf" (3.1.12–13), which, if conventionally predatory, are here seen in a curiously pathetic, familial, and humanized light and harmlessly removed to their caves. Men are the only animals not tamed by this storm, a tempest that discovers that man is himself his own most tenacious predator.[3] Humanity alone, in the distress of this otherwise taming storm, "bemonster(s)" its natural "features" to "prey on itself" (4.2.63,49), heaping human injury upon human insult in the course of a potential natural catastrophe.

No one would deny that nature proves our weakness by its intermittent revelations of the terrible "extremity of the skies." But, as Duke Senior argues, we might as easily claim such extremity sublimely grace bearing as condemn it for being hostile or indifferent blue. The sky is not the hidden, tainted source of this play's poison. Men themselves create tragedy here by "amplify(ing) too much"; thus they "top" even nature's "extremity" (5.3.207–8). In an unconscious show of histrionics in *Lear*, able-bodied men consistently masquerade as beggars or else self-righteously play at being gods. As a result, the natural "feature" of the human voice, its "soft/Gentle, and low" speech (273–74), capable of open and humble recognition of and communication with ourselves and others, is "bemonstered" by howling curses and pettish whining. Between these theatrical extremes Lear, Edgar, and Gloucester—and Edmund and Albany, too, for that matter—oscillate toward self-destruction throughout. Lear himself unknowingly but accurately identifies the true poison when, mistakenly claiming Edgar as an emblem of unaccommodated mankind, he tells the masquerading beggar: "Thou wert better in a grave than to *answer* with thy uncover'd body this extremity of the skies" (3.4.101–2, italics mine). Lear's gesture of pity for Poor Tom symbolically represents a Shakespearean accusation of them both since Edgar's "roaring voice"—by his own admission a "presented nakedness" designed to "outface The winds and persecutions of the sky" in order to "enforce . . . charity" (2.3.14,11–12,20)—mirrors Lear's striving in his "little world of man to outscorn/The to-and-fro-conflicting wind and rain" (3.1.10–11) for the same purpose. The irony in Lear's remark to Edgar about "answering" the extremity of the skies is not simply that we know something that Lear does not—that Edgar is not "unaccommodated" but is, in fact, using his very nakedness as a disguise, making his defects his accommodation. The irony, as we shall see, is unfortunately more complex and self-incriminating than that.[4]

Let us examine, then, how Edgar and Lear "answer" this extremity of the skies both to determine the extent of their confusion about themselves and their conditions and to suggest the pastoral virtues they unwittingly abjure in the process. The disguise Edgar has taken makes a symbolic statement of the greatest importance in *King Lear*. As a masquerading bedlamite, Edgar's human voice in his ensuing "play" distorts its natural features to alternate exclusively between "lunatic bans" (curses) and a masquerading beggar's "prayers" (2.3.19), both designed to "enforce charity" from anyone he meets, even those more unfortunate than himself—the impoverished villagers and farmers who are not, like him, only recently down on their luck but find they must work the "low farms,/Poor pelting villages, sheep-cotes, and mills" (17–18) in perpetual penury. To "preserve" himself (6) in the hope of thwarting corruption in high places and again regaining his own social preeminence an Edgar intent only on his abused innocence will unscrupulously, even if unconsciously, impose upon the weak. Though Edgar finds the duplicity of actual bedlamites a "horrible object" (17), from what we can infer from his speech he sees his own mimicry of their behavior as at worst a necessary evil. The unwitting corruption in Edgar's stance gains dramatic immediacy when we consider that the "beggars" Edgar meets are not only faceless villagers, but king, fool, father, and brother, to all of whom he is intimately bound; it gains ironic complexity when we recall that Lear and Gloucester are themselves also, if even less consciously than Edgar, in an agonized and yet wholly pathetic masquerade as lunatic beggars, alternately praying and cursing in attempts to enforce charity from both god and man alike. Without conscientious objection to his own behavior, as if merely to preserve himself were more than ample warrant, Edgar wantonly "takes the basest and most poorest shape/That ever penury, in contempt of man,/Brought near to beast" (2.3.7–9). Surely Shakespeare wants this statement to mean much more to us than it does to Edgar. The most shameful form of penury is not, as Edgar believes, nature's seemingly contemptuous and arbitrary sentencing of some men to impoverished circumstances; more shameful is a poverty of spirit that would parody men in distress before their very eyes in order to preempt charity from them—men even more urgently in need of charity.[5] In his absorption in his own miseries Edgar is, of course, always unaware that his behavior is but a self-involved parody of those in greater need than he. But that fact should not completely exonerate him from moral culpability in the matter. The burden of the moral life consistently includes the felt need—accepted or rejected—to transcend our self-absorbed living and extend ourselves to others.

Though Edgar always acts with conscious generosity, he does so in unwitting contempt for the man in himself and in others he meets, because, rather than fully participating in their plights, he subtly imposes upon, trifles with, and needlessly bullies those even weaker than himself—Lear, Fool, Kent, Gloucester, and the fallen Edmund. One of Gloucester's servants has the dramatically ironic final word in Edgar's peculiar case: the bedlam's "roguish madness" does indeed "allow itself to any thing" (3.7.104–5). Though the servant commits the very crime he unknowingly indicts Edgar for, his words do, nonetheless, represent for us a true and serious accusation of Edgar's subtle wantonness in his disguised dealings with others. As in Lear's case, however, the unappealing surface of Edgar's behavior masks depths to which we are more sympathetic.

What makes Edgar's pattern of behavior more exasperating and pathetic than heinous and brings to his wantonness a degree of exculpation is the implict contempt in which he seems to hold himself. When in self-defense Edgar decides, "poor Tom/That's something yet: Edgar I nothing am" (2.3.20–21), we are forced to conclude that "the quality of nothing hath not such need to hide itself" (1.2.33–34) in this self-disguising parody of man's natural "shape," a dignified shape Cordelia, by contrast, finds possible even when in the most reduced circumstances and in the greatest danger before her father. But Edgar's shameless pretense is mitigated by the unacknowledged shame that encourages it. While we must put aside until later the question of how Cordelia has achieved the paradoxical miracle of a living harmony between acknowledgment of her shamefulness and lack of worth and her assured self-respect, clearly Edgar has tragically failed to achieve a similar miracle in his own life and person. Whereas Cordelia lives in disregard of herself and her self-defense, Edgar lives to protect himself at all costs even though and, in fact, precisely because he is apprehensive that the essence of his being, his intrinsic self, may be worthless and contemptible. Edgar would not rush to conclude "Edgar I nothing am" unless, unlike Cordelia, he could neither truly accept nor live out the reality of what he proclaims—his own insignificance and impotence. Hence, while Cordelia gains heroic stature by humbly accepting her own insignificance, he merely contemns himself, shucking his identity as Edgar as if it were no more than an empty mask. His central crime, like Lear's, is a sin against himself. In trying to flee his own fear of powerlessness, he only confirms his impotence.

Our suspicion that Shakespeare wants us to see Edgar as a "self-cover'd thing, for shame" (4.2.62) who "bemonsters" his "features" as he assumes his disguise will be confirmed if we look closely at the emblematic juxtaposition of this short scene (2.3) with those directly preceding and following it.[6] The previous scene concluded with Kent in the stocks. Kent, too, we recall, like Edgar, had been banished and had taken a disguise; but Kent disguised himself to "serve where thou dost stand condemn'd" (1.4.5)—with Lear. He had hidden himself to risk himself; Edgar "stands aloof" in hiding to "preserve" himself. Kent in the stocks suffers a malignant fortune "such as basest and [contemned'st] wretches/For pilf'rings and most common trespasses/Are punished with" (the language echoing Edgar at

2.3.7) and suffers yet worse later; but despite his awareness and acknowledgment that he is clearly in a "shameful lodging" (2.2.172), his contemptible fortunes do not lead him to disfiguring contempt for himself or to the more contemptible effort to outdo and "outface" fortune's persecutions by cursing or begging to enforce charity. Not only does he not curse or beg, but even when, unsolicited, Gloucester offers in charity to "entreat" for him, he declines the offer rather than risk having Gloucester incur Cornwall's wrath: "Pray do not, sir. . . . Some time I shall sleep out, the rest I'll whistle./A good man's fortune may grow out at heels" (155–57). We will be discussing at greater length the grand accomplishment in Kent's equanimity here, his more than stoical calm in the face of his confinement to the stocks; but for the moment suffice it to say that, unlike Edgar, he will no more try to take to his heels than will the "tarrying" Fool who sings his song to Kent in the scene following Edgar's speech.

> That sir which serves and seeks for gain,
>   And follows but for form,
> Will pack when it begins to rain,
>   And leave thee in the storm.
> But I will tarry, the Fool will stay,
>   And let the wise man fly.
> The knave turns fool that runs away,
>   The Fool no knave, perdie.
>
> (2.4.78–85)

The first four lines of the Fool's jingle are prophetic because they declare our recognition that the love and devotion the Fool bears the king are unreciprocated. Lear may cry about monstrous ingratitude vulturing his heart, but it is he who will "pack when it begins to rain/And leave" Fool "in the storm." But Lear is not the only one to whom the song makes implicit reference. In promising to stay a fool by declaring his unconditional fidelity to Lear, the Fool opts for what a self-disguising Edgar declines; and in his prophetic jingle, he indirectly reveals the pathetic egocentricity of Edgar's behavior and speech in act 3, scene 6, when he watches Kent and the Fool bear Lear toward Dover in the storm.

Perhaps we might turn now from a consideration of Edgar to examine the way Lear, too, repeatedly "answers . . . this extremity of the skies" and thus forbids pastoral reconciliation and restoration. We might well begin with a look at Lear's en-

counter with Kent before Gloucester's castle. Lear consciously
identifies with Kent sufficiently to see in his servant's humiliation a fearful premonition of his own; otherwise he would not
have argued so repetitiously with Kent about who placed him in
the stocks (2.4.12–27), nor, presumably fearful of embarrassment, forbidden anyone to enter with him to meet Regan and
Cornwall (59–60). In precisely the way Gloucester had warned
Cornwall the king would react (2.2.145–47), Lear naturally
enough sees himself in his messenger "slightly valued" when he
asks "what's he that hath so much thy place mistook/To set thee
here" (2.4.12–13) and then protests, " 'Tis worse than murther/
To do upon respect such violent outrage" (23–24). Certainly,
he is not ultimately worried about the "respect" due Kent-Caius
because once Kent has been freed his response is to sin against
Kent's self-respect and Kent's "respect" for him by dismissing
him: "O, are you free? Some other time for that" (132–33).
Lear's repeated banishment of the good serving man who is
always with him—both Kent himself and the Kent in himself—
is an inconspicuous but also ingenious Shakespearean emblem.
For the seemingly insignificant and distracted dismissal of a
servant as superfluous to the grand importance of the moment
turns with terrible economy into a foolish and tragic refusal of
every instant's saving grace. Could he join Kent now, as he is
perfectly free to do—theoretically at least—in the freedom of
Kent's devotion to another, he would metaphorically and perhaps literally be restored to Cordelia. But a Lear utterly preoccupied by the love or lack of it he elicits from his daughters now
that he is no more a king pitiably prefers "some other time" for
joining Kent, only to confine himself to exhibition yet again
before Goneril and Regan. So, as a result of anxieties about his
worth, a worth he does not know how to confirm, when Kent
leaves the stocks, Lear metaphorically enters them.

We know, then, that although it is true that Lear identifies to
an extent with Kent when he confronts this mirroring image in
the stocks, he does not realize the full import of their identity
and difference.

KENT: Hail to thee, noble master!
LEAR: Ha?
         Mak'st thou this shame thy pastime?
KENT: No, my lord.

(2.4.4–6)

Kent has, of course, played the riotous fool with Oswald at Gloucester's. We should not shun the facts, whatever we may think of Oswald. Cornwall argues justly in his reprimand when he claims Kent's own "disorders/Deserv'd much less advancement" (2.4.199–200); and Kent must have acknowledged as much in his heart to bear the indignity of being stocked so graciously. But admitting one's foolishness to oneself is simpler than acknowledging it before others. When Lear enters, Kent embarrassedly jests, makes light of his plight, to deflect attention from his shame, hailing the chief in a transparent pretense that there is nothing out of the ordinary here. In mocking himself, his hidden hope is to preempt the ridicule he feels he deserves and thus enforce charity by his helpless, if unspoken, begging. Lear's reprimand chastens him immediately, of course, but cruelly because of its offended tone and unconscious self-righteousness. Intent on his own anxieties, Lear cannot see Kent's embarrassment; he sees only that his own dignity may be being mocked or at least insulted—even when the service may be faithful and the praise honest—if it comes from a ridiculous, humiliated clown.

Lear is so instinctively threatened and offended by the humiliating sight of Kent stocked like the basest of wretches that he does not recognize in his accusation of Kent's ploy the mirroring identity between Kent's shame and his own: in dealing with his daughters at the outset he jested self-consciously about "crawling toward death" in the hidden hope of preventing the ridicule he feared might be awaiting his weak and useless old age if he could not enforce their charity. Lear is never able to stand abashed and speechless in the dignity of his acknowledged shame as Kent does at the end of this exchange, a dignity so moving it would shame all but the most hardened of hearts to an awakening of mercy. Some generosity of this sort is very likely implied in the deeper wisdom of the Fool's seemingly cruel sexual ridicule at Edgar's expense when Lear asks Poor Tom: "Couldst thou save nothing?" (3.4.65). The Fool replies: "He reserv'd a blanket, else we had been all sham'd" (66). The Fool sees that Edgar, like Lear, is still a "self-covered thing, for shame," whose "presented nakedness" finally comes, like Lear's abdication of power, with a "reservation" for himself. The Fool knows that when anyone suffers his shame nakedly, without brazenness or any attempt to save face, we are all shamed in his shame—the better among us into the action of generosity. Our shame in such moments is not, as one might assume, shame for the person acknowledging his or her shame; ironically, it is a shame for ourselves who are seldom if ever able to follow such a virtuous lead, shed our reservations for ourselves, and openly admit our shamefulness. We know instinctively that, whatever evil the person before us may be acknowledging, his or her admission is pure—in fact virtuous. The confession of one's shame is nothing to be ashamed of. We do not turn away from such a person in shame for him or her, but in shame for ourselves. Only in generosity toward such a person do we gain what he has shown us the way to, a share in the state of grace and the genuine humility that is the first and necessarily ongoing step on the path to restoration. Lear and Edgar, unfortunately, can never bring themselves to suffer their shame nakedly. Surely Shakespeare wants us to ask, for instance, of Edgar's persistent disguise as bedlamite beggar— "Mak'st thou this shame thy pastime?" (2.4.6). And neither Edgar nor Lear is ever, like Kent in the stocks or the tongue-tied Cordelia of the first scene, at a loss for words to "answer" the "extremity of the skies" that they insist, in a desperate attempt to save face, unjustly humiliates them.

Indeed, at the risk of holding Lear's grief for dead Cordelia in blasphemous contempt, we must question whether even in the end Lear has given over reservations for himself. His outraged and accusing tone of voice shows no abashed awareness of his responsibility for Cordelia's death when, bearing her limp body in his arms, he needlessly insults his other faithful subjects:

> Howl, howl, howl! O, [you] are men of stones!
> Had I your tongues and eyes, I'd use them so
> That heaven's vault should crack. She's gone for ever!
> I know when one is dead, and when one lives;
> She's dead as earth. Lend me a looking-glass,
> If that her breath will mist or stain the stone,
> Why then she lives.
>
> (5.3.257–64)

Even in this touching grief for Cordelia Lear unknowingly remains a "self-covered thing, for shame," a voice "bemonstered" into animal howls that merely lacerate his wounds as he continues to alternate between curses and prayers to enforce charity from either men or gods or both. It is true that Cordelia is dead as earth; but that fact should render the king speechless with mortification not encourage his voluble contempt of earth. Cordelia knew that the dead earth still holds "blest secrets" (4.4.15);[7] though herself dead, the earth can miraculously bring forth regenerate life to sustain man if we seek and cultivate her "unpublish'd virtues" (16). Albany is completely correct when he claims "that nature which contemns it origin/Cannot be bordered certain in itself" (4.2.32–33). It is not earth but Lear and the others like him—"idle weeds" earth tolerates and even fosters—who strangle her "sustaining corn" (4.4.5–6).

But Cordelia's care for Lear does not allow us to reduce the tragedy to such simplistic moral judgments. Lear's real failure is not his evil but his unwillingness from the start to acknowledge it and, thus, begin to nurture himself to health. Though Lear should turn inward and acknowledge his responsibility and fault, the last and most central lesson even a dead Cordelia could teach him is not to contemn himself in this shame. For in Cordelia's wondrous scheme of things even the "idle weeds" that strangle her own lovingly cultivated sustenance of men are to be nurtured, given an allowance to grow.[8] The idle weeds have their "blest secrets" and "unpublished virtues" that we must seek to uncover and cultivate despite their apparent worthlessness. In the "art of our [communal] necessities" idle weeds can be transformed to medicinal restoratives, "simples operative, whose power/Will close the eye of anguish" (14–15); the vile can also be precious. Lear should not, in anguished contempt for himself, be so ashamed of his shame he cannot suffer it lovingly—the problem that has driven him into restless hiding from the start, exacerbating his wounds and merely compounding his shame, "killing" his "physician" and the fee bestowing "upon the foul disease" (1.1.163–64). He might have begun to seek the precious in himself by openly looking at and suffering his own vileness; by nursing his deformities, he might have become one of the holy fools he instead betrays, a "simple operative" in his active expressions of love for himself and others in their weaknesses.

The intensity of Lear's grief for the hanged Cordelia clearly overwhelms him. It is completely appropriate to that grief that he look for signs of life in her, that he call for a looking glass out of his desperate need to reject the truth of what he knows only too well—"She's dead as earth." To do otherwise would not be true to life or to his feelings for Cordelia. In another sense, however, to hold a mirror up to Cordelia's lips for traces of her life's breath is to seek a miracle where it may not be found. The looking glass is a traditional symbolic tool of intro-spection and self-confrontation. Rather than hold it up to Cor-delia's face he should, at some point or another, hold it up to his own to discover "Lear's shadow." That may be the more important act because even if he could, by some chance, revive Cordelia, she would live again only to be idly strangled in yet some other way were Lear not also able to confront himself clearly and weep over his sins against her so as to "mist or stain the stone" of the self-protective image of himself with which he has usurped his life.[9] Without a painful self-recognition and a long, difficult submission to himself, having Cordelia alive again would not be the "chance which does redeem all sorrows/ That ever I have felt" (5.3.267–68), as Lear sentimentally be-lieves.

The tragedy is that he has no idea how sentimental he re-mains. Not magical luck but only some genuine act of love on his part could begin to "redeem" him. Without painful recogni-tion and acknowledgment of fault, his redeeming "chance" smacks too much of the gambler's irresponsible bet in the first scene of the play ("I . . . thought to set my rest/On her kind nursery" [1.1.123–24]) for us to feel at all certain their relation-ship would be reestablished on firmer footing were Lear given a second chance with Cordelia.[10] Such gambles that "set" one's "rest" (risk all) on another risk nothing of the self *for* another, exclusively intent as they are, without the generosity of self-forgetful love, on a deliverance not requiring personal conver-sion. The sense of being thwarted in this only apparently unselfish hope informs Lear's "Look on her! Look her lips,/ Look there, look there!" (5.3.311–12). The critical debate about what Lear sees or only imagines he sees here seems superfluous to me.[11] The point is that, as in his reconciliation scene with Cordelia, Lear is "still far wide" (4.7.49) of reality here. If he seeks to see the life-sustaining "breath" or spirit of Cordelia he need not "look there" beyond at it fleeing and run to catch it in death, still coursing his shadow for a traitor as if it had deserted him when, in fact, his shadow has never left his side, fast as he may have fled himself. If, instead, abashed and still, he looked within, he might discover that *his* breath would "mist or stain the stone" of his heart in unselfish regret and sensitive respon-siveness to another and thus also discover—because she is both these things—that Cordelia lives, but in him now where she has always been waiting.

Redeeming the Curse: Cordelia

If Lear refuses restoration to self-empire and the majesty of love, the simple cure for the disease of his sophistication, if his heart does ironically "break into a hundred thousand flaws" before it ever softens to "weep" (2.4.285–86) a confession of its shame or to share Cordelia's living and contented peace,[12] these facts do not so much undercut or subvert pastoral norms as they suggest that we can fully comprehend the tragedy's meaning only in terms of pastoral conventions and metaphoric values needlessly violated. Court "sophistications," warring "contention," and mercantile "busy-ness" of movement have always opposed and threatened the "better way" of Arcadia's fragile peace. When pastoral has not fallen into a decadent, self-indulgent parody of its own highest virtues, it has represented preeminently an idealized social vision in which men do not live preoccupied by fear of nature or one another but in a mutual confidence in the good and goods held in common and more than adequate to their needs.[13] Even farming, Renato Poggioli tells us, is too defensively fearful an occupation for the pastoral shepherds' time and energy.[14] Theirs is a common peace bred of simplicity, gentleness, and mutual enjoyment of themselves and each other in abundant grace. All else is superfluous. This can, of course, prove a deceptive simplicity. Its impulse seems little more at times than nostalgic longing for and subliminal indulgence of gratifications forbidden by hard adult realities, its geographical remoteness a symbolic retreat into self-protective sanctuary from adult cares.

But such a view fails to recognize or sympathize with the way traditional pastoral has voluntarily assumed the rather formidable cares of *eros* and *thanatos,* elegy and love lament. It is a curious form of retreat that bids us confront the things we most fear—death and the human betrayal by those we would most prefer to feel incapable of such treason of heart—and find even there our deepest fears eased, ourselves restored comfortingly. But this is a pastoral commonplace: no sanctuary from death and betrayal *(et in Arcadia ego)* but an affirmation of the possibility of genuine happiness and joy nonetheless. Pastoral's nostalgic cast, then, need not in its essence imply self-indulgence or regression but can symbolize the self-accepting trust that the need we recognize through memory for time's redemption can be fulfilled, that we must and can patiently seek to find the time again to enjoy ourselves and those we love.

This restoration of strength in atonement with self and others at our ease, the appreciative delight in one another celebrated in simplicity of heart can distinctively harmonize, in pastoral's synthesis, two extremes of human conduct whose singular virtues betray each other's limitations; similarly, pastoral is able to integrate nature and civilization, taming nature of its viciousness and civilization of its vices. In its grandest synthesis, pastoral simplicity transcends the Stoic's rigorous discipline of the self to nature's law just as it transcends Epicurean self-indulgence, the paradoxical discipline of the self to the self's licensed arts. Both the Stoic and the Epicurean "stand/ Aloof from the entire point" in standing alone, their hearts inexorably hardening, whether they seek to endure or enjoy. Pastoral, aware of death, suggests in laughing ease that we hang together. Rather than make the Stoic's "best of it" or the Epicurean's "most of it," pastoral would simply accept it gracefully and share it happily. Pastoral's *natura paucis contenta* simplicity does not breathe a hint of the defensiveness in the Stoical spirit of *contemptus mundi* or its consolation prize mentality; it celebrates the miraculous discovery of ease and exalted pleasure in loving lowliness and song. Renaissance pastoral generally ranges between two limits: Tasso's Epicurean *s'ei piace, ei lice* (if it pleases, it is lawful) and Guarini's more Stoical *piaccia se lice* (if it is lawful, it pleases).[15] Within this harmonic range, pastoral resolves all its most threatening internal discords: nature and nurture, personal freedom and the boundaries of self-containment, spontaneity and orderly purpose, personal happiness and charity's call to community. The comfortable home in a grace-bearing world offered to each of us by these wondrous pastoral harmonies is "as you like it," both because it presents us with an idealization worthy of our grandest hopes but also because, like grace itself, it does not force itself on us. In this wondrous order and design, we are yet given our freedom, the final pleasure to realize and choose to enjoy a life too good to be true as well as the opportunity to refuse it, as Lear does, for precisely the same reason. Our only problem is his only problem—to take it or leave it.

The foregoing account obviously does no justice to the varieties of pastoral treatments and perspectives; it is, in fact, an idealization of pastoral idealization in as much as it takes pastoral at its highest harmonic range for the norm, but such ethereal music is, in fact, the norm guiding us through the island wastes of *King Lear*. For, though Cordelia remains one of our literature's most successfully "realized" ideal heroines—an even more incredible achievement when one considers Shakespeare's extreme economy and indirection in dramatizing her for us in the psychologically powerful and subtle scenes with Lear—she simultaneously comes to stand as a richly stylized symbol of pastoral grace. Certainly that is the unmistakeable suggestion conveyed through her own speeches and the emblematic effect of second-hand descriptions of her when she reappears in act 4. A gentleman tells a fleeing Lear, for instance:

> Thou hast [one] daughter
> Who redeems nature from the general curse
> Which twain have brought her to.
>
> (4.6.205–7)

Whether we agree or not that there is a glancing allusion to Cordelia's imitation of Christ in this description,[16] the ambiguity about whether "her" refers to nature or Cordelia insists, at least, on the intimacy of the kinship between nature and her, both innocently and unnecessarily cursed by men who compound their initial shame by continuing to hide from it in it.[17] If we take "her" as a reference to Cordelia, then we see that Lear's initial and unrevoked "curse" upon Cordelia is merely a fevered outburst symptomatic of his succumbing to the "general" disease that Cordelia, in loving subjection of herself to suffering and death, shows redeemed, a human nature at its ease, no longer cursing itself or its fate. If we take "her" as a reference to nature, and the "twain" then as an allusion to the biblical story of the Fall, Cordelia becomes synonymous with the pastoral ideal of the restoration of a prelapsarian realm in which nature is a place of peaceful recreation that is without fear of death or insufficiency of goods. As we noted earlier, even "dead as earth" Cordelia redeems death's "curse" by offering continuing sustenance for life. Moreover, in pastoral's harmonious fashion, she likewise transcends the other significant portion of the curse of the Fall—the strain of work, the labor in pain and grief to bring forth life. Cordelia does labor and abortively so; yet she does so always in the accord between the spontaneous impulse of her natural passions and the studious observance of her responsibilities of civility, restraint, and right conduct she announced as the civilized nature of her "bond" to her father in act 1, scene 1.

Nothing of pastoral's accord between nature and civilized merit claimed by her "bond" in the first scene has altered with Lear's alteration by the time of her reappearance in act 4. Though Lear is as changeable as the moon, she remains an ever-fixed mark, steadfast as the sunshine and steady as the rain the Fool knows "raineth every day." "No blown ambition" urges her return "but love, dear love, and our ag'd father's right" (4.4.27–28), the gracious harmony of her natural feelings for her father and the civilized respect for "right" embodied in his cause. Later, after praying that the physician's efforts will harmoniously tune Lear's "jarring senses" (4.7.15) so that he might once again sound the music of himself, she provides the physician with the prescription for Lear's cure: "Be govern'd by your knowledge, and proceed/I' th' sway of your own will" (18–19). It is a Platonic version of Augustine's "Love God and do what you will," knowledge not purchased at the expense of power or vice versa. Only Lear's reservations are impotent; Cordelia always holds untold power in her quiet and loving reserve. In a play filled with the discords of characters who presume upon what they know, pretend to what they do not, and insist impotently upon what they will, Cordelia offers humble and orderly service to civilizing reason at one with the potent "sway" of a patiently expectant will hoping for a natural birth. She plays a resolving chord joining the individual ("your own will") to a social order ("govern'd"); the self's freedom, to the self-containment necessary for freedom to act with the possibility of power; spontaneity, to orderly purpose; the will's urges, to reason's harness.[18]

Much of the point of the gentleman's lyrical description of Cordelia as the pastoral miracle of "sunshine and rain at once" (4.3.18) lies in confirming her peaceful reconciliation of natural openness to feeling and the civilized dignity of self-restraint. "She," not her "passion," though she feels that openly and fully, is "queen" (13–14) in self-empire and the majesty of love. As in pastoral's playful competitions of song, "patience and sorrow

[strove]/Who should express her goodliest" (16–17). Sunshine·
and rain, two simple, potentially fruitful goods miraculously
blossom, like all pastoral's complementary pairings, when
peacefully married. The "happy smilets" (19) that welcome the
discovery of Lear alive and Kent's faithful ministrations to him
play on her face as if they do not recognize the grieving
"guests" (21) in her eyes weeping over Lear, Kent, and the
Fool's great pain and suffering. Even her grief so "become[s]"
(24) her that while standing still in her grief she is transfigured
into a vision of ease, astonishing beauty, and playful joy. "If all"
of us "could so become" (24) vile sorrow in the precious way
Cordelia does—so becoming sorrowful that it becomes her—
"Sorrow would be a rarity most beloved" (23), not fled or
hanged.

Before our bewildered eyes Shakespeare presents the apparent violation of pastoral peace and ease in Cordelia's martial
invasion of England and the aborted issue of her labors to
deliver Lear; yet he magically turns them to pastoral's greater
and still unflawed advantage. The allusion to the gospel story in
Cordelia's speech about the invasion—"O dear father,/It is thy
business that I go about" (4.4.23–24)—has often been remarked, with an appropriate sense of the wholly flattering effect on Cordelia's worth and virtue in her venture; but it should
also be noted that the phrase has idealizing relevance in the
context of pastoral norms as well. Cordelia goes about Lear's
business because she has no busy-ness of her own in her own
life, no curse of hard labor. The only work Cordelia performs
lies well within the accepted range of conventional pastoral
pieties. Unwilling as she was to take seriously the warring "challenge" of nature and merit Lear demanded at the outset, in act
4 she reveals an eagerness for friendlier contention. Obviously
generalizing from her own eager and loving response, she is
shocked that an old man's frailty, let alone a father's, had not
"challenge[d] pity" of her sisters (4.7.30). And when she is
reunited to Kent she vows to "work" at a friendly challenge with
Kent to "match thy goodness." It is an especially moving vow
given the dramatic irony it hides.

> O thou good Kent, how shall I live and work
> To match thy goodness? My life will be too short,
> And every measure fail me.
>
> (4.7.1–3)

The dramatic irony converts a friendly competition begun in solidarity and love into a terrible prophecy of failure and premature death. A life "too short" in the joys of friendly challenge to outdo one another in good; every gesture made to redeem Lear failing her, just as every measure Lear took to evade her fails her and her hopes for him. But even in this, "sorrow" is not the last word for Cordelia—"waste" is. For, paradoxically, even as we lament her unnecessary loss we also come in wonder to realize that "every measure fails" to hold the plenitude of grace overflowing.

To Cordelia neither the earth nor her labors on it are cursed. She creates and loves in a pastoral gracefulness in which "labor is blossoming or dancing." Like the natural world she so praises, but more superfluously, her own "unpublish'd virtues," without bitterness or strain in her labor and grief, simply "spring with [her] tears" (4.4.16–17). That, like overly abundant fruit rotting unused, Cordelia's easy labor to deliver Lear proves abortive, that her virtues "spring" only to remain "unpublished" does not lessen the wonder; such facts only intensify our regret. For herself Cordelia has no regrets. In fact, had she not experienced her own joy as a sacrilegious offense to the child-changed father she still hopes to deliver to manhood, even the seemingly abortive nature of her labor on his behalf would have blossomed into open delight. Immediately previous to her final, still gently hopeful suggestion that in the bravery of manhood Lear stand to see his daughters rather than refuse her again and thus hide from his own image and cure in them,[19] Cordelia makes a speech that, in the "art of its necessities," strangely masks its cheerful and cheering essence.

> We are not the first
> Who with best meaning have incurr'd the worst.
> For thee, oppressed king, I am cast down,
> Myself could else out-frown false Fortune's frown.
> (5.3.3–6)

Though Lear's "let's away to prison" reply has gathered far more critical attention—perhaps in part because it sounds so much more selfless and philosophically "wise"—Cordelia's speech proves by far the more important and wise consolation because it does not offer consolation at all, as Lear's speech does, but a cure, a restoration. By contrast, Lear's reply is yet another abdication and willing confinement to exhibition.[20]

Cordelia's speech acknowledges her worst fears but also affirms her transcendence of them in the generosity toward her father it hides. Lear's reply—giddy rather than playfully at ease; unconsciously autocratic and patronizing rather than secretly generous—by denying there is anything to fear only reveals a man who is, even now, utterly imprisoned by fear.

Despite the sentimental charm of Lear's speech, when Lear patronizes his weeping "child," Cordelia, then banishes her tears, and dispatches the bogeymen to deal with all who would dream they could harm them (5.3.23–24), we ought to recognize a false note of desperate, jesting bravado blocking from consciousness the mortifying humiliation Lear fears. He, not Cordelia, is the childish one here if he can imagine, in his apparently untroubled, even giddy fantasy, that Cordelia and he can live insulated from the consequences of his sins against her. If there is nothing to weep about, why does Lear need to "catch" Cordelia or speak of their going to prison as "sacrifices" upon which the "gods themselves throw incense"? (20–21). It appears Lear would have Cordelia believe that the only sacrifice burned in prison would be one made in thanksgiving for its safety, a safety so godlike in its imperviousness that the gods themselves would bow in obeisance to it. We know better.

By contrast, Cordelia's speech is "sunshine and rain at once." Her remarks affirm a sadness and depression Lear's giddy reply cannot appreciate and fails even to acknowledge. More important, her speech simultaneously reveals the sunshine of an easy and playful joy overflowing in liberating love and even now living in her raining grief, whereas Lear's gaiety is only an idle promise of a benign future in a fool's paradise. Hers is an expansive sense of an open and classless community of "noblemen" who have suffered fatality in a good cause to which she and her father are now about to be initiated—"We are not the first/Who with best meaning have incurr'd the worst." Lear's reply, however, when examined without sentimentality, reveals itself as a desperate and pathetic fantasy of intimacy, a dream of an ideal society that, in practice, would become not an open and classless community of virtuous men but a privileged exclusion, a decadent nobility unconcerned with questions of right or of society's destiny. If her speech had ended after its first three lines, we would have primarily had the rain—a Cordelia "cast down" in her own personal fortune as a result of her commitment to her father and depressed over her father's

equally disastrous fate. However, the fourth line transforms
everything utterly. If Cordelia felt free to do so (had only herself to think about), she would treat us to the thoroughly
charming spectacle of a whimsically high-spirited parody. She
would look false fortune right in the eye and "outfrown" her
frowns, making such innocent fun of fortune's scowls that even
false fortune would turn true and smile. What keeps her from
the freedom of such antic playfulness and transcendence is
only Lear himself or, rather, something locked in about the
"oppressed" king that imprisons them both, something her love
for him must regret yet accept. But love cannot merely rest
content with acceptance; it must also encourage growth, wish
well and better. So, even as Cordelia tolerates Lear imprisoned
she feels she must, for his own good, try to coax him into
freedom, though indirectly to avoid humiliating him. In other
words, she feels she must do for him what she cannot do because of him. She must manage the difficult task of making
ridicule gentle, try to "make fun" of Lear's false frowns by
parodying them and, thus, turn his oppression to laughter.

> For thee, oppressed king, I am cast down,
> Myself could else out-frown false Fortune's frown.
> (5.3.5–6)

If the "oppressed" king would step out of his solitary
confinement long enough to listen disinterestedly to how his
caged bird sings, he would realize that what appears to be a
song of devotion from his vantage point is, from her point of
view, though still devoted, a hidden plea for liberation—not
from him but for them together. Their "false fortune" is not
military defeat but that even in mutual defeat he forbids himself the available fullness of Cordelia's joy. Cordelia's subtle and
yet forgiving jest suggests, if only to us, that if Lear will not
triumph over his oppression for his own sake he might at least
do so for hers. But he, in his "let's away to prison" reply, as on
the heath with the Fool, "runs,/And bids what will take all,"
however much Cordelia, following like the Fool, but with mild-
er manner, "labors to outjest/His heart-strook injuries" (3.1.14–
15, 16–17). Self-directed laughter would imply the saving
acknowledgment that he is worthy of ridicule for taking advantage of Cordelia if for nothing else.[21] Lear should know that
there is a certain nobility in accepting ridicule that hits the

mark. But the risk involved in that discovery he will not take. He will not be coaxed from his cage; so with a shrug of devotion Cordelia remains with him in solitary confinement but this time in a literal prison. Given the only important choice—take him or leave him—she has always taken him for better or worse or, rather, for the better in the worse until death parts them.

Playful parody, consummate tact, and secret generosity are likewise the identifying hallmarks of Cordelia's controversial behavior in the first scene of the play, the keys to any vindication we may feel she needs there.[22] Since Coleridge, a number of critics otherwise baffled by Lear's irrational outburst have naturally assumed that father and daughter's initial interaction must contain some hint of an explanation for Lear's furious curse that routs the apparently judicious proceedings up to that point. In poring over Cordelia's speeches for hints of self-incrimination that might make Lear's rage slightly more understandable, at least in psychological terms, many have been content to interpret the tone of Cordelia's speeches at face value and to conclude from them that her initial acts are unnecessarily tactless, blameworthy in fact in the sullen self-righteousness presumed to be motivating her.[23] Despite the difficulty of reconciling this selfish obstinacy with her later, mature generosity of spirit, the tendency to fault her in some way for the initial catastrophe has actually increased of late, presumably as part of the reaction against redemptionist readings of the play that tend to lift Cordelia out of her very human predicament and place her safely in an allegorical heaven. But, ironically, even among those who disdain allegory in favor of the subtle psychological analysis necessary to explicate complex realistic characterization, a full appreciation of Cordelia's human predicament at the outset is still lacking. There is, of course, nothing wrong with probing psychological analysis; indeed, we will be turning to that task in a moment. But I think that speculations about Cordelia's hidden motives should be deferred until we make a more careful examination of the dilemma she faces.

Although the *argumentum ad ignorantiam* that follows obviously cannot prove the appropriateness of what Cordelia does say here, nonetheless, it is certainly curious that among those who fault Cordelia for her behavior in the first scene, only one I know of has managed or at least thought to offer a constructive answer to Cordelia's own alarmed question—"What shall Cor-

delia speak?" (1.1.62). Professor Goldberg's suggestion—
Antony's "There's beggary in the love that can be reckoned"—
even if it could be leavened with humor in the telling, would be,
as we shall see, boastful, self-regarding, and unkind in ways
that should only make us marvel all the more at the generosity
with which Cordelia miraculously manages to resolve her dilemma.[24]

And dilemma it genuinely is. Anything Cordelia can seemingly do will misrepresent her true relationship to the king. She
cannot take her initial promise to herself to remain "silent"
literally (though metaphorically, throughout her relation to
Lear, she never violates her vow to "love, and be silent"), because to do so would be to refuse to acknowledge a human
voice calling out its need to her and a father's right to be answered by a dutiful daughter. She cannot in some well-
intentioned parody of her sisters' falseness simply and
unobtrusively play along with Lear's little game, not only because, given the false position Lear has forced upon her, including its competitive, comparative terms, nothing she could
say could be simple and unobtrusive, but also because to "play"
with Lear in that way would defile the love she bears him; to do
so would be to trade her modest hope that he might be led to
see himself and others better for a despair that would settle for
merely humoring his delusions. Love forbids tact when tact
becomes mere flattery, licensed by social convention but unconcerned with deserted truth's absolute right to our fidelity. The
genuine tact Cordelia's speeches embody is, as we shall see, a
far greater accommodation of and accord between fidelity to
truth and love's unwillingness to give offense even when it must
speak the truth. If she cannot remain silent or play along without doing evil, neither is she able to say what she says without its
resulting in evil. Her very obedience to a higher tact honoring
the truth that she cannot marry a husband "to love my father
all" is an equivocation that her willingly sacrificial part in the
progress of the action repeatedly confirms beyond doubt. Her
privately declared love's reluctance to speak, fearful—at least in
part—that it will only offend in obeying truth, has nothing to
show for its trouble but failure. Lear is all too quick to take the
anxious care with which she serves him as a wanton offense.
But if we freely admit that Cordelia's speech results in evil, we
need not necessarily fault her for it. Given the fact that Cordelia is in no way responsible for the false position Lear has put

her in, and given the disproportion between her remarks and his terrible replies to them, as well as the difficulty of demonstrating a better way out of her quandary, it does seem like moralistic quibbling for critics to suspect Cordelia of a hidden self-righteousness, to convict her in fact of it, and to condemn her for doing evil, as if she could do otherwise. If we cannot answer her troubled query and show her a better way in this moral dilemma, we should at least suspend judgment. We should "love, and be silent" rather than accuse her and thus defend ourselves from her and her predicament on the grounds of an assumed moral superiority.

Ultimately, however, we do not have to settle for a merely suspended judgment. Shakespeare gives us ample evidence of Cordelia's essential innocence, even moral heroism, in her action at this point. Though we will necessarily make the final test of the extent of her moral grandeur the generosity of her speeches themselves, much else in the dramatic contrasts of character and image in the first scenes suggests Shakespeare's care in guiding us into admiration for Cordelia. Her behavior gets quick defense from Kent, winning from him, as from France, unqualified praise that she "justly think'st and hast mostly rightly said" (1.1.183). Even Goneril and Regan comment upon Lear's "poor judgment" in casting her off.

More important, Cordelia's manner of risking and then facing parental displeasure is repeatedly and diametrically contrasted in a series of mirroring scenes that follow and set off her distinctive virtue. Rather than risk a recurrence of parental displeasure, this time turned on them, Goneril and Regan plan to "do something" to prevent it—"and i' th' heat" (308). Then in the next scene, Edmund voices a debased parody of Cordelia's initial declaration of love's accord between the liberating bonds of natural affection and dutiful respect, nature and law:

> Thou, Nature, art my goddess, to thy law
> My services are bound.
>
> (1.2.1–2)

In proclaiming the freedom of his devotion to nature's law, however, Edmund does not seal his "bond"; he only proves he is "bound," living out his own "plague of custom" even as he refuses to do so.[25] Given the fact that nature's charms prove only a masquerade for the individual will's autoerotic drive, his declaration of love only serves to prove the self's lust.

Moreover, in a deeply hidden sense, even Edmund's lust hints
at nothing more than impotent bravado. So shamefully and
subconsciously linked is his crippled identity to his bastard
conception that he can only pretend he will not accept society's
conception of him as a merely sexual being and "perform" for
them when he says he will not "stand in the plague" of their
custom and curiosity. Though he claims he will perform only
for himself (his phallic god will serve him: "I grow, I prosper:/
Now, gods, stand up for bastards" [1.2.21–22]), we know, however, that in Edmund's insistence "shame itself doth speak/For
instant remedy" (1.4.246–47). The truth that we learn from the
rest of the play is that, for all his virility, Edmund is lying, even
to himself. He cannot even "stand" for himself without impotently standing in their plague and shriveling before them in
shame. He cannot produce healthy issue because in the
crippled alienation of his autoerotic will there is really no goddess to "service," no one he would gladly serve.[26]

Such is not the case, of course, in Cordelia's loving service.
Faced with a father's displeasure and contempt, Edmund refuses to continue to stand in Gloucester's plague; Cordelia not
only quietly stands in Lear's curse during the first scene, but at
the end of it she reveals she would gladly risk it again were the
father who has just stormed out, leaving her, he pitilessly assumes, to stand in the cold, again to permit it. When she speaks
to her sisters before leaving she does not even hint a complaint
about Lear's disproportionate rage, the injustice done to her;
she speaks for him and for her continuing desire to be near
him.

> Love well our father;
> To your professed bosoms I commit him,
> But yet, alas, stood I within his grace,
> I would prefer him to a better place.
>
> (1.1.271–74)

Nothing can finally defend Cordelia here from anyone who
wishes to impugn her motives, to accuse her of a smug self-
righteousness toward her sisters. But then perhaps we should
not disconcert ourselves since Cordelia, in risking herself to
save Lear, remains at ease, neither troubled to defend herself
nor fearful, except on Lear's account, that what she says or does
will be taken in the wrong way. Whereas Lear and the play's
other tragic fools live in the solitary confinement of their

guarded reserves, her reserve is a hospitably open plenitude so measureless it remains at ease with its vulnerability to plunderers.

If there is no adequate defense for Cordelia here, there is much, nonetheless, that is uniquely praiseworthy. Her eager desire, if only Lear would allow it—a forbearance he may always learn from her—to stand once again with him, facing the risks of again offending him and of his betrayal in another pitiless storm of rage, her eager desire to suffer her fool gladly, contrasts sharply with the preventive guard of Goneril and Regan, the defensive rebellion of Edmund, and Edgar's fearful refusal to risk facing his father's displeasure and possible wrath. But, in a supreme irony, her forbearance also presents a stark contrast to the behavior of Lear himself who, without knowing it, by making his daughter Goneril his "mother," faces a situation analogous to Cordelia's initial one when he confronts and reacts to Goneril's parental reprimand in act 1, scene 4. Like Lear himself in the theatrical charade he tries to pass off in act 1, scene 1, as an actual competition over the division of a kingdom, Goneril orchestrates in act 1, scenes 3 and 4, what purports to be a spontaneous or, better, a contingent event. Like her father earlier with his daughters, she unnaturally "breed[s] . . . an occasion" (1.3.24), forces an issue through Oswald's "negligence," not in order to communicate openly with another human being to air grievances or express real fears in cooperative trust, but in hidden mistrust to manipulate and control, to put her child, Lear, in his place, a place from which he cannot hurt her. Like the bribe that is Lear's division of his kingdom, her little playlet is merely a pretext masking her hidden fear and "darker purpose"—terror at her own vulnerability to her distrusted child, the desperate hope to prevent his power to harm. More detailed examination of these claims can wait until chapter 3; what is important for us to note here is how Lear, now placed in an essentially false position as Cordelia had been, put upon and offended by a Lear-like Goneril, reacts. Because he is not able or willing to see himself in the emblematic mirror of Goneril's behavior here (we should recall that what brought Lear's rage and violence down on Oswald's head was merely the mention, albeit contemptuously expressed, that Lear was "my lady's father" [1.4.79]), he can do nothing to emulate or rival the dignity and serene grace of Cordelia's demeanor in the first scene. Instead, a caged bird having unknowingly stared at himself in a mirror, he is immediately all rage and flight, squawking vengeful curses upon the traitor that will only and literally redound upon his own weak head. If Cordelia, even after being banished, would stay if she were allowed the opportunity, Lear would futilely try to flee from a Lear-like Goneril as he calls to horse in the belief that the more distance he can put between himself and her the better off he will be, sharing the mistaken notion with Goneril that there are safe places for the self and places where we can place others so they cannot hurt us.

Cordelia knows better and desires differently. She "prefers" to put herself again in what she knows to be an unsafe place and Lear in a place where he might hurt her—with her in utopia, the "no place" that is anywhere they might be together. Cordelia knows that utopia is not a safe hiding place in the child's game of "bo-peep" (1.4.177), a version of hide-and-seek the Fool rightly accuses Lear of playing;[27] it is rather a maturely playful, pastoral habit of mind that knows its cost and rejoices. The dense ambiguities of "stood I within his grace/I would prefer him to a better place" richly convey both this clear-sightedness and its joy. There is here a true, though what may sound like a self-righteous claim for the superiority of her love to that of her sisters; but there is also much more. Knowing there are "better places" to be, she would still prefer to be with Lear at whatever cost, though her hope remains for the mutual fulfillment of a better place. Examine the phrase in one light and we see what Cordelia is willing to sacrifice of her own well-being in order to bear Lear to a better place; turn it ever so slightly and the self-sacrificial stance miraculously becomes "no trouble at all," a loving hope for his and their well-being in which self-sacrifice has disappeared into her pleasure and hope for their mutual joy.

This pleasure and hope for the two of them is not a sentimental self-indulgence on her part. Knowing how much Lear needs to grow and grow up, she would urge him to a better place than his cage, even though such urging may involve on-going conflict and pain for each of them. That is a true utopian habit of mind, the active communal preference for a better place: not some other place arrived at by visionary dreams that fill the future's void but embodied "quick, now, here, now, always" in pastoral's playful competitions, wishing each other well and better in healthy striving during our time's being. Edmund is symbolically on the wrong track when he claims:

> the best quarrels, in the heat, are curs'd
> By those that feel their sharpness.
> The question of Cordelia and her father
> Requires a fitter place.
>
> (5.3.56–59)

Cordelia knows from experience that the "best quarrels" are not made "in the heat" but are long and leisurely competitions, not "cursed" in uncontrolled rage but urged in loving restraint. Though herself condemned to feel the sharpness of Lear's initial curse and the curse of the war fought in his name, in both cases she does not curse the quarrels but calmly urges that they continue, hoping to stand again before him risking further offense and condemnation and urging Lear to "see these daughters and these sisters" (5.3.7). The matter of Cordelia and Lear is a question not of justice demanded but simply delayed to a "fitter" time and place that will never come; Edmund's preoccupation with justice ("I shall study deserving" [1.1.31]) is properly answered by Hamlet—"use every man after his desert, and who shall scape whipping?" (*Hamlet* 2.2.529–30)—and by Kent—"to be acknowledg'd . . . is o'er-paid" (4.7.4). The matter of Cordelia and Lear is not a question of justice but one of grace freely given and refused. Cordelia's loving and humble sense of community that would sacrifice to "prefer him to a better place" does not demand anything or even settle stoically for its own abnegation; it offers better, probably in allusion to the host in the wedding feast parable who urged his humble guest, "Friend, go up higher," to richer satisfaction and enjoyment.[28]

When Kent wishes Cordelia to the "dear shelter" (1.1.182) of the gods, his remarks are usually taken as a terrible irony. They *are,* of course, a terrible irony; but they are not simply that. They are true prophecy in one sense, not because they foretell the future correctly but because they tell the truth about her continuing present, herself sheltered and sheltering dearly, at terrible cost and in joyful love. Lear may think that in walking out with Burgundy at the end of the first scene he leaves her standing in the cold. In fact, she stands with warmest regard for Lear and in the shelter of France's arms, which she subse-

quently freely risks, hopeful of yet sheltering Lear again in a
better place. Throughout, even when she follows Lear to
prison, unconvinced by his logic but proving once again that
her love has no regard for its cost, she lives as his shelter from
himself, herself yet more dearly sheltered in the clothing of her
mercy. The utopian "no place" and everywhere that is Cordelia's "dear shelter" is suggested most clearly in the dramatic
irony of one of Lear's heath speeches. Moved to pity, though
not the appropriate sort that would in kindness to himself admit that he has now become one of the wretches he still thinks
himself rich enough to patronize, "shak[ing] the superflux to
them" (3.4.35), Lear melodramatically proclaims the need for
charity for

> Poor naked wretches, wheresoe'er you are,
> That bide the pelting of this pitiless storm.
>
> (3.4.28–29)

By the time Lear makes this remark Kent and the Fool have
already tried several times to get Lear to take shelter. We also
know from Kent that they are the only living things crazy
enough to be standing in the rain.[29] The only storm, then, from
which there is no relief is Lear's, not nature's; for even in the
hovel they must worry over him raging outside, then, subsequently, within as well. There is thus a ludicrous irony in Lear's
grandiloquent gesture of addressing the naked wretches
"wheresoe'er you are" when those who "bide the pelting of this
pitiless storm" are so near and wedded to Lear they should be
called Lear's shadow. Kent, the Fool, Cordelia, and Lear himself consistently suffer the pain of Lear's pitilessness; but while
Kent and the Fool share Cordelia's "dear shelter," "biding" or
dwelling with patient hospitality and at ease in the paradoxical
punishment and protection of the storm's very "pelting," Lear
suffers naked and alone, impatiently and absurdly insisting he
will "punish home" (3.4.16) rather than seek one with those
who love him.

Before we turn to Cordelia's speeches themselves in the initial confrontation with Lear, one other juxtaposition of characters reacting to a similar situation ought to be considered as
evidence of Cordelia's special merit. In the first scene, Kent, in
defending Cordelia, answers Lear rage for rage. It is not, ironically, one of his better moments:

be Kent unmannerly
When Lear is mad. What wouldest thou do, old man?
Think'st thou that duty shall have dread to speak
When power to flattery bows? To plainness honor's bound,
When majesty falls to folly.

(1.1.145–49)

Because Kent speaks for Cordelia's right we may wrongly tend, with him, to overlook how insulting is the lash of Kent's "plainness" on Lear's back. Just as when he was rightly reprimanded for his plainness by Cornwall, here, too, his behavior is profoundly "unmannerly" and self-righteous as he mimics Lear's rage while simultaneously condemning it.[30] In answering Lear's rage, he, also, "amplifies too much and tops extremity." Not only does he publicly call his king and friend a madman and a fool and his daughters, flatterers; but, if we look carefully at the phrase "power to flattery bows," we see that the possibility of an even more humiliating insult presents itself. Kent is also accusing Lear of "flattery," of stooping to the folly of the kept whore or, at best, to the crawl of a trifling beggar. The fact that these accusations are just does not, however, excuse their being used as clubs. Contrary to what Kent claims, duty should at all times "dread to speak" because of concern for the person in the wrong. Duty should not, of course, at the other extreme, so dread to speak that it says nothing at all, as in the case of Gloucester, who remains safely silent about Lear's banishments though we later learn of his disapproval of the king's actions (1.2.23–26, 109–17).

Cordelia ploughs the fertile middle ground. Shakespeare is at pains to highlight for us Cordelia's "dread of speech," her anxiety not to betray duty or her gentle feelings for her father. One of the two primary functions of the introductory conversation between Kent and Gloucester is to reveal to us that the ceremonial interchanges to follow are a mere formality, speech that purposes not. Everything has already been settled; Cordelia, though in a more fundamental way the only member of Lear's family who is rooted and at ease with herself, is here the only person unsettled by the "glib and oily art" of this meaningless ritual. Like trained circus animals answering the crack of the master's whip—the repeated "speak"—Goneril and Regan perform their set pieces for the tidbits of land that are their father's only acknowledgment of them. Nothing he says after their speeches in any way acknowledges what they have said or the persons saying them in a more human, less peremptory and demeaning way. Cordelia's troubled asides contrast sharply with the smooth flow of rhetoric from Lear and his other daughters, also assuring us that, unlike Kent, she dreads telling the truth because of her concern for the person in the wrong. And when, breaking her vow of silence, she does speak, not only does she transcend Gloucester's self-protectiveness, but she shows us the risks and liberties love can innocently take with the self.

For Kent is mistaken when he claims, "to plainness honor's bound/When majesty falls to folly." Honor is always free in itself, even when it allows its own majesty to stoop to an innocent form of folly to parody majesty's sinful folly. Honor need not be "plain"; it can masquerade in parti-colored motley, even, as in the case of Cordelia, disguise its honor as dishonor for love. Kent himself proves honor's loving folly almost immediately when, with a gesture and speech that redeem his insulting outburst in act 1, scene 1, he enters disguised as Caius. Honor may innocently stoop to what seem folly and deceit if its purpose is to help majesty in his folly and deceit up off his knees.

> If but as [well] I other accents borrow,
> That can my speech defuse, my good intent
> May carry through itself to that full issue
> For which I raz'd my likeness. Now, banish'd Kent,
> If thou canst serve where thou dost stand condemn'd,
> So may it come, thy master, whom thou lov'st,
> Shall find thee full of labors.
>
> (1.4.1–7)

It is a wonderful redemption. Sandwiched between petty shames that "speak/For instant remedy" (1.4.246–47)—a Goneril who will "not endure" Lear's antics, who would instead, by means of Oswald's insolence, "breed from hence occasions . . . /That I may speak" (1.3.24–25) and a Lear who enters demanding that he "not stay a jot for dinner" (1.4.8)—Kent enters disguised, freely offering the grand yet simple remedy of standing in the instants as they "come," "now" and as long as it may take to "carry through" this baby to "full issue," patiently hoping for Lear's delivery into healthy life. The metaphorically sexual "service" Kent humorously offers "thy master whom

thou lovest," in its pleasure and potential fruitfulness, answers
Edmund's autoeroticism, offering delight in another for Edmund's onanistic demands, potential birth of healthy issue for
impotent bravado. Similarly it contrasts with Goneril and Lear's
willful "breeding" of occasions that in forcing issue can only
mutilate and deform. Kent's high-spirited jesting makes vile
things precious, transforming the indignity of his disguise into
the mirth of an expectant mother humorously regarding how
her pregnancy has "raz'd my likeness." Moreover, his sexual
punning even allows Kent to transcend the endurance that
faces banishment to "stand condemned." By virtue of the sexual metaphor, to "stand condemn'd" simultaneously becomes
the precious anticipation of pleasure and fulfilling completion:
"If thou canst serve where thou dost stand condemn'd,/So may
it come." (5–6)

But given our present purposes, the most significant feature
of Kent's speech is how perfectly it also characterizes Cordelia's
speech and behavior in the first scene. In resolving her dilemma there, Cordelia also must "other accents borrow/That
can my speech defuse," razing her "likeness" in order to carry
through "good intent" to "full issue." We have already seen that
Cordelia's secret peace deliberations to reconcile her love for
her father and her devotion to the truth present a difficult
dilemma requiring extraordinary tact. She cannot remain silent, she cannot play along, and she cannot speak what she
speaks—dividing her kingdom—without equivocation. Moreover, now that we have looked at Kent's brutally direct speech
to Lear defending Cordelia, we can easily surmise why she
cannot say something more direct to Lear, even something
along the matter-of-fact lines of Professor Goldberg's suggestion. Even if she could insure that such righteous truth saying
would have no hint of Kent's self-righteous tone, Cordelia
would decline such speech because in serving truth it would
neglect the other-directed mercies of the heart. It would not
happily reconcile but disproportionately prefer duty to affection. She fears that the naked truth would be brazen, cruelly
shaming yet further the old man she loves even in his flight
from shame. She knows she must speak the truth, but she also
knows that the truth cannot be spoken plainly because, in this
case, the truth is not plain. So, in order to attempt to do justice
to the truth's complexity, she disguises herself for embarrassed
love, trying by indirection to tell a higher truth in her equivocal

division of her kingdom of love. Rather than risk humiliating
Lear with the naked truth, she would cloak herself, risk being
mistaken for an ungrateful and dishonorable daughter and,
thus, raze her "likeness" but also lovingly refuse to insult Lear's
dignity in his shame. By dressing herself in motley and "making
light" of her "ponderous" (1.1.78) love, Cordelia risks making
herself look bad in order to allow him a dignified exit from this
exhibition of himself, an easier choice of the hidden but genuine good she declares here.

Given her previous and repeated "dread of speech," Cordelia's first "nothing" (87) is very likely as much a plea to stop
the performance, as much a mortified hope that father and
daughter might understand one another without—for both of
them—more and more embarrassing words, as it is a
straightforward attempt to respond to Lear's question and
command. But if Lear must go on with it, her evasive refusal
does generously answer Lear's question, if with oracular indirection.

LEAR: What can you say to draw
        A third more opulent than your sisters'? Speak.
CORDELIA: Nothing, my lord.

                                          (1.1.85–87)

What may seem a smug rejoinder, indicating a refusal to go out
of her way to accommodate her father in his demands is, upon
more careful inspection, another "dear sheltering" of Lear, a
scrupulous attempt to be at once just and merciful. In truth,
Cordelia "can say" nothing to "draw a third more opulent than
[her] sisters'" not only because she does not desire such a third,
materially measured, but, more important, because nothing she
can say would "draw" the portions any differently from the way
Lear himself has already parceled them on the map. It has
already been drawn beforehand and two of the thirds already
given. Nor can Cordelia say anything that could "top the extremity" of her sisters' hyperbolic professions of love. They
have said it all. So, obscured in her seemingly smug refusal to
answer is a forthright and just response to his question if Lear
has ears to hear.

But even this blunt-speaking justice gives way on another
level to a voice speaking the mercy of her loving heart: "Nothing, my lord." In this sense, her "nothing" represents genuine
humility, a dreadful acknowledgment of unworthiness and vul-

nerability that should communicate to Lear how a similar admission about himself would be the appropriate alternative to his present behavior. Like Cordelia, Lear should acknowledge that we cannot by any means "enforce charity," either by winning it in a fair competition with sisters or by buying it with a bribe from daughters. It can only be freely given in trust, like Cordelia's gesture here, often at the greatest risk to the giver, but also with anxiety for the person receiving the gift. In saying what she does, Cordelia stands exposed in shame at her nakedness before him and ashamed at her impotence to help him without his cooperation, yet hoping to inform him that his charity is not something she can in any way secure for herself any more than he can secure or insure his daughters' love in the verbal transaction he has staged. Their charity is theirs alone to determine; it is alone in his power to recognize love when it has been given and to return the favor. Whether he gives love to Cordelia or withholds it from her, the choice is one burden of power he cannot throw off nor Cordelia assume. Nothing she can say will necessarily affect the terrible freedom he possesses either to embrace her or turn away from her. She knows that gestures of love are not made as a matter of deserving's just pay but are always contingent, ultimately discretionary. Her "nothing" confirms her wholehearted agreement with Kent: "To be acknowledged . . . is o'erpaid." Love cannot be earned or purchased. What can one say to win love's preference, "the third more opulent than sisters'?" Nothing. No one deserves love; yet everyone has a profound need of it except those like Cordelia who, though themselves also in need, risk giving it away, preferring Lear to a better place in hope's only possible triumph over our tendency to make demands for love our sole, if hidden, preoccupation.[31]

What Cordelia would have Lear learn through the example of her speech is that while we are powerless to demand or insure love, we can accept this weakness with dignity—without self-contempt—because it always remains in our grand human power to give love. Her speech is a tactful effort, using her own act of speaking it as an abject yet loving lesson, to wean Lear of his obsession with being loved since in her own words she risks not being loved to offer love instead. Utterly self-absorbed emotionally, Lear focuses on other people not as others but as objects by which he can and must capture love. What must underlie such an attitude and, specifically, the motivation for

the love auction here, is not vanity but very nearly its opposite—a dreadful insecurity about intrinsic worth, a shame for
the self's insignificance that in its despair seeks in the obeisant
eyes and acts of others a glimmer of affirmation of the value it
fears may be lacking within. Lear does not give his daughters
his regards because he is too obsessed with seeking and discerning their regards in tendering his, just as Goneril and Regan
are not solicitous of him but of his regards in tendering theirs.
And "love's not love when it is mingled with" such "regards that
stands/Aloof from the entire point." Just as much or more than
Goneril and Regan, Lear, too, implicitly stands accused when
Cordelia speaks of not having the "still-soliciting eye" that "hath
lost me in your liking" (1.1.231, 233). Having banished Cordelia by the time she makes that speech, Lear has unknowingly
"lost" her in "liking" Goneril and Regan's identity with him in
the "still-soliciting eye's" prostitution of love.

But before that, Cordelia had attempted as inconspicuously
as possible to aid Lear in getting up off his knees and thus to
transform the false beggar's pleas for charity into a dignified
man's standing in love's potency. She did so by refusing to love
in the name of a higher love, greeting his "still-soliciting" gaze
and speech with innocence's downcast eye and voice of shame:
"Nothing, my lord." What more can one do when someone one
loves makes a perverse solicitation rather than a request or
offer of love? Only endure shame for and with him and refuse
to love in the name of a deeper love. "Love compels cruelty,"
Eliot tells us "to those who do not understand love."[32] In the
shame with which she offers her "nothing" to Lear, Cordelia
paradoxically presents him with the gift of an ideal image of
what he could yet be, as in a mirror; for, if Lear is ever to attain,
like her, to his naked manhood's possible dignity he must recognize and acknowledge in her downcast eye and voice of
shame the face of *his own* suppressed shame hiding in fear of
discovery behind the still-soliciting mask of brazenness he presents to her and the world.

Because Lear is obsessed with being loved, he does not
understand love's true nature nor recognize it when it has been
proffered. He does not even realize, for example, what subtle
insult is involved in the demand for open declarations of love
from his daughters. Such a demand implies a distrust of their
free commitment to ongoing love and a failure to appreciate or
perhaps even recognize love's past efforts to please. One could

never successfully reassure him. If in the wound of his doubt about his worth, he distrusts the love of others, then reassurances that he always knows deep within were begged for or prompted will not heal but only confirm his obsession. Nor, if one genuinely loves, is it even appropriate to reassure the beloved who looks for the cure of his wounded self in another; for that only exacerbates the disease of self-absorption in the beloved and perhaps insidiously hides the solicitous lover's mirroring obsession with being loved as well, though the lover kindly assumes the flattering if ill-fitting mask of savior. Reassurance is, ironically enough, the last thing those who are preoccupied with doubts about their own worth need. They need to be made aware—sometimes gently, at times not so gently, but always in a loving spirit—that they are not the only people in need and that the doubts about worth that do us such human credit can only be "made good" by our loving actions, not by begging more credit from others.

Cordelia does what needs to be done. In her first reply she lovingly refuses to love on Lear's corrupted terms. Then, basing her justification on the reconciled peace of "love . . . according to my bond" of duty and affection (1.1.92–93), she declines to compete with her sisters in any "challenge" between nature and merit. Finally, in dividing her kingdom and suggesting that her sisters have also implicitly done so in marrying, she makes a claim for a just distribution of available goods, not because she is seriously concerned that justice will not be served in her love for father and husband, but in order to awaken Lear to the reality and needs of others—her own included. For when she articulates her hope that the "lord whose hand must take my plight shall carry/Half my love with him, half my care and duty" (101–2), she is not simply asking Lear to share her fair-mindedly. No doubt she does want Lear to see in her would-be husband's hope that Cordelia's love would fulfill her contractual vow a reflection of his own hope that he will not be betrayed by his daughters' defaulting on their vows of love. But it is not so much that she wishes Lear to be sufficiently just to allow another man to carry off from him half her love, care, and duty toward him. She hopes as well that both Lear and her husband, each and together (since she is plighted to them both), will "carry" half the burden of her "ponderous" love *for her* and thus all together live out the joyous relief of bearing's good fellowship. Making light of her love, she hopes that with the two men she loves each carrying half of her love she will not have to carry anything at all and her ponderous love will turn to unabashed lilt and buoyancy.

If, then, Cordelia is compelled to speak in refusals and restrictions, her manner can hardly be called sullen or self-righteous. One could more convincingly claim she willingly risks being mistaken as sullen in order to allow father and sisters the opportunity of a dignified retreat from their shameful behavior with minimal embarrassment. One cannot deny, of course, the possibility that Cordelia's words—

> Good my lord,
> You have begot me, bred me, lov'd me: I
> Return those duties back as are right fit,
> Obey you, love you, and most honor you.
> Why have my sisters husbands, if they say
> They love you all? Happily, when I shall wed,
> That lord whose hand must take my plight shall carry
> Half my love with him, half my care and duty.
> Sure I shall never marry like my sisters
> [To love my father all].
>
> (1.1.95–104)

—can be read as biting sarcasm. But a more sympathetic and at least as defensible a reading is that, as in act 5, before going to prison with him, when she chides Lear in order to coax him out of his cage, Cordelia's jesting, if perhaps desperate, is not embittered but eager to forgive. She is "sure my love's/More ponderous than my tongue" (1.1.77–78) not simply because speech can be glib and insincere but also because jesting can mask great anxiety. In order to point up the absurdity of the proceedings and thus allow father and sisters to laugh at themselves and stop, she parodies Lear's foolish and futile division of his kingdom by jokingly dividing hers to his consternation. She makes Lear out to sound as if he would preempt husbands, render them superfluous, by himself marrying all his daughters; and she catches her sisters up as plighted bigamists while exonerating herself on the same charge.

The jest, like all else but Kent and the Fool, fails her badly. Though she did "other accents borrow" to "defuse" her "speech" and raze her "likeness," she was not able—any more than Kent was—to "carry through" her "good intent." Lear instead explodes into rage and flight, to which, as always, she

responds graciously. To return to the quotation used earlier in
the chapter to describe Lear and Edgar in hiding, Cordelia, too,
has been a "self-covered thing, for shame," shame for herself
and her compromised part in the false position Lear forces on
her but also, and more significant, in loving shame for him; but
unlike Edgar and Lear, who are in flight from the shame they
suffer, her disguise does not "bemonster" her "features" in
whining or curses. She does not top extremity with her own
answering thunder, neither immediately with Lear nor later
with her sisters. Instead, like the Fool and Kent, in biding the
pelting of the pitiless storm in Lear and yielding to the peaceful
rain of her own ample tears that follow she makes it possible for
pastoral aid to spring. Her masquerade does not distort her
features; it becomes, instead, pastoral's nature to advantage
dressed in the unassuming grace of her honor and generosity.
The truth may be naked, but mercy is clothed.

It is futile to seek an explanation for Lear's outburst in the
dynamics of the exchanges between Lear and Cordelia; there is
none. His outrage is meant to strike us as inexplicable and thus
hint at a cause deeply hidden from surface view. In telling Lear
that one can say nothing to insure love's preference, Cordelia
has, however indirectly, symbolically held up a mirror to his
humiliating behavior. In trying to cure him by gently probing
and exposing the weakness at the center of his being, she
touches a nerve; he recoils, howling his pain. From his self-
absorbed point of view, her "nothing" labels him a worm un-
worthy of respect, exposes his theatrical pretense of "crawling
toward death" as the frightening reality it is. Because the child
he doted upon has become an emblem of his shame, he must
banish her from sight, as Gloucester had banished his bastard
son, Edmund (1.1.31–32). It is a perfectly apt touch that Shakespeare makes such a trifle as Cordelia's early speeches the spur
to such outlandish rage because it is always trifles, these "nothings," that prove our humiliation. We are not ashamed to die
vanquished by epic antagonists, but to have a mere child, and
one pampered at that, prove in a moment our impotence and
absurdity simply by opposing our will, refusing a challenge
when summoned—that is a humiliation not to be endured. The
final irony for Lear is that whether he likes it or not, knows it or
not, he tragically suffers this humiliation even as he refuses to
do so. If he successfully flees Cordelia, he cannot flee himself.
Symbolically, he is his own humiliation, proves his own impo-

tence. Ultimately, he, not Cordelia, is more truly the obstinate child who will not stand to fight to better himself by means of the increased share of a sovereign's love Cordelia repeatedly urges him to take.

This cowardice is even apparent in Lear's reconciliation with Cordelia in act 4, one of the more mistakenly sentimentalized scenes in Shakespearean tragedy.[33] Redemptionists use its apparent contrast to the degenerational spiral of the action to this point as the foundation of the higher wisdom that in some way transcends Lear and Cordelia's deaths. The absurdists, though similarly convinced of its meaningful human accord, discuss it as a human harmony that cosmic disorder mocks in a conclusive reversal. But, if Lear's touching bewilderment and, then, growing wonder that he has been spared, his distressed paranoid fears of further abuse, and his frank and helplessly pathetic self-pity move us deeply, numerous signs throughout the encounter nonetheless forbid the conclusion that father and daughter have attained a genuine reconciliation. The usual interpretation concludes that the old king, having now been stripped of all the external trappings of his identity and having suffered titanically, finally finds peace, renewal, even restoration in Cordelia's arms, a cure for his feverish disease in Cordelia's loving care and in his sadder but wiser welcoming of her rather than, as initially, her banishment. But Shakespeare's language makes it clear that the changes—extremely favorable, even seemingly miraculous—are, nonetheless, merely external, not intrinsic to Lear's character or involving a psychological and moral transformation of his behavior.

To his own amazement and skepticism, Lear awakens to hear soft music instead of howling storm, torturing human voices, and his own answering curses. He sees "fair daylight" (4.7.51) shining and feels himself soothingly rested, not harried and hurrying through repeated and sleepless night journeys and the storm's dark buffeting. He finds himself in fresh, possibly regal garments, not the tattered remnants and bitter weeds he had put on in his despairing cynicism to mock himself, the humiliated carnival king. Instead of daughters who revile and contemn a useless old man, he awakens to a heavenly vision of a woman whose angelic face clearly expresses her devotion to and fear for him as a man and who keeps insisting on formal acknowledgment of and reverence for his social identity as king. The conventions of miraculous romance transformation extend even to Lear's amazed *Quis hic locus* query (65). It is as if the old king had literally awakened from a nightmare. So sudden, unanticipated, and complete is the change, in fact, and so paranoid has Lear become from his buffetings, that the chief undertone in all of his reactions to Cordelia from the beginning to the end of the scene remains one of suspicion. At first he doubts the very reality he is experiencing; then he begins to suspect the likelihood that this woman's signs of respect are merely some trick meant to lull him into trusting her avowals of his kingship so she may then mock him. Finally, as he exits with Cordelia, he reveals a lingering fear of the punishment awaiting him from which, in open self-pity, he hopes to excuse himself by begging mercy upon his age and debilitated condition. However true to the reality of his weakened and abused condition, this final appeal has too much in common with Lear's theatrical ploy in act 1, scene 1 to avoid the pains and responsibilities of kingship and prevent future harm with a similar excuse of aged incapacitation to make us altogether comfortable with the notion that Lear has developed a new psychological and moral maturity.

Continued suspicion and fear do Lear little credit here. They might have meant more had his suspicions in the scene begun to center on anxiety about his deserving forgiveness. Lear does not put himself at Cordelia's mercy; he presumes upon it. His suspicions eschew introspection or self-criticism for paranoia and self-pity; his self-absorbed and distrustful fear preempts the loving fear a genuine apology to Cordelia would involve and instead holds to the attempt to manipulate and enforce her charity. Superficial reunion and reconciliation hide the continued and profound self-exile of "father against child"; the appearance of contrition masks the repetition of insult to and imposition upon his loving daughter.

Let us look more carefully at the extent of this imposition in Lear's speech and behavior throughout the scene. In act 4, scene 3, we learned from Kent how Lear's "sovereign shame" for his "unkindness" to Cordelia so tyrannized the old king that even in the lucid moments when Lear "remember[ed]/What we are come about," he would "by no means . . . yield to see his daughter" (4.3.39–41). The seemingly paradoxical point of the reconciliation scene is that he continues to refuse to do so. Lear, the usurping pretender, "sovereign shame," will not "yield" to restore the rightful king to himself by recognizing in his daughter his own best image and likeness. He continues to presume command, defeating himself by attacking the mirror image he will not "yield to see." Only complete physical collapse, not a yielding will, has forced shame's subject into Cordelia's presence, though their behavior once together seemingly reverses these respective identities. Cordelia, who moments previous to Lear's awakening had eloquently spoken of the profundity of her care for her father, nonetheless finds that when she must speak to Lear her apprehension for his sanity is so great she can only find the words of the humblest petitioner seeking the recognition of her ruler. In her trepidation of spirit and tongue-tied anxiety, she is reduced to impersonal formulas of respect. Her request for recognition and its attendant anxieties do not really diminish her majesty because her anxieties about being recognized do not reflect a concern for herself but a wish for Lear's restoration to sanity. In contrast, the Lear whose flight from shame so hindered him earlier that he would not willingly face his abused daughter and who, therefore, might now be expected to stand so abashed and inhibited that he would be humbled into hesitant petitioning for forgiveness instead grows surprisingly voluble. In fact, he is unabashedly willing to try for the dramatic lead in the scene's dialogue and take the metaphorical center of stage in the unconscious self-importance of the imperial "I" at its repeated assertions of self. (The personal pronoun and its variations occur forty-one times in Lear's thirty lines of dialogue in the scene.)

It comes as a shock, for example, that the first words out of Lear's mouth upon awakening to see Cordelia would be:

> *You do me wrong* to take me out o' th' grave:
> Thou art a soul in bliss, but I am bound
> Upon a wheel of fire, that mine own tears
> Do scald like molten lead.
> (4.7.44–47; emphasis mine)

Even if we allow for a certain distracted irrationality in Lear's speech, given his physical and mental condition, there remains a significant if unflattering coherence in it. If he is genuinely not able to recognize Cordelia or truly cannot tell whether he is on earth or somewhere else, it is clear that he is lucid enough to know she is not Goneril or Regan and that the world she has

awakened him to is for him purgatorially painful in a way that
he is somehow certain hers is not. On first reading, this speech
and Lear's next—"You are a spirit, I know; [when] did you
die?" (4.7.48)—may together suggest Lear's indirect attempt to
convey his regret for what he has done to Cordelia by referring
to his purgatorial agony and lavishly praising her. But the hidden meaning in these words is ultimately less flattering. For one
thing, the distinction between Cordelia and himself that Lear
claims is accurate enough but not the sense Lear makes of it.
Though it is not true that Cordelia is a departed spirit, she is a
kind of "soul in bliss" because she has been reunited with her
father; and even her grieving so becomes her that, as we saw
earlier, "Sorrow would be a rarity most beloved/If all could so
become it" (4.3.23–24). Moreover, it is also true that Lear's own
grief is completely unlike hers because the tears of pain he has
been shedding for himself in his tortures and for his impotence
to revenge himself upon his ungrateful daughters, unlike the
"pearls" she drops for others, have only served to intensify his
agony, scalding his own flesh as they fell back upon him, bound
and turning on his wheel of fire.

In his bewildered agony Lear obviously does not realize the
reason her tears beatify and his scald, however, because he
scalds himself again by waking to weep for the renewal of his
torture, not hers, and in his self-absorption even blames her as
his torturer. He should rejoice to see her; and if he wakes to
suffering, he should welcome it as an opportunity for expia-
tion, not continued self-pity and a refusal to acknowledge that
he has himself had anything to do with his wretched condition.
The confessional aside Lear speaks early in the play while Fool
ridicules him—"I did her wrong" (1.5.24)—he cannot nakedly
repeat to Cordelia's face; instead, he can only express self-pity.
The seeming praise of the angelic "soul in bliss" and departed
"spirit" is at best hidden flattery intended to manipulate Cordelia into charity. At worst, it is a direct, if unconscious insult to
Cordelia's burdened love. In either case, it represents a mistaking rather than a recognition of the daughter who literally, and
for us symbolically, has asked her father: "do you know me?"
(4.7.47). Why is it that the distracted old king is so certain that
Cordelia must be dead? Is it simply that he mistakenly believes
such loveliness and grace "require a fitter place" than sullied
earth? Or is it also implied that he cannot believe that anyone

would be good enough to come back, to return love for injury, since he could not, and so he assumes that if he sees Cordelia again he must be in another world.

To imagine and, even worse, assert that Cordelia could be a "soul in bliss" while Lear suffers in agony shows that he is tragically unconscious of her love, neglectful of the possibility that genuine love may suffer for another, not only for self. We have seen and heard Cordelia's anxiety over Lear in this scene—her fears for his physical and mental health, her outrage at her sisters' behavior, her efforts to make up for what has befallen Lear now that she is again with him. But for his part, Lear insists on claiming that she is in heaven and that, by awakening him, she has reawakened him to the torments of hell: he is "still far wide!"

The pity is that he does not suspect she is suffering for him. This is confirmed in the most heartrendering terms when, after having several times begged not to be mocked or humiliated (58, 67) before he finally, if hesitantly, names his child, Lear next takes note of her tears.

> Be your tears wet? Yes, faith. I pray weep not.
> If you have poison for me, I will drink it.
> I know you do not love me, for your sisters
> Have (as I do remember) done me wrong:
> You have some cause, they have not.
>
> (4.7.70–74)

Lear's moving speech has the look of mortified apology; but if it is an apology, it is so poorly made and unknowingly insulting that Lear needs to offer another and a better one to make up for it. It is not remorse, but despair or worse—a half-conscious and melodramatic pretense of despair put on by guilt to flatter her out of really poisoning him, just as calling someone a "soul in bliss" might perhaps convince her to be an angel of forgiveness rather than the demon of revenge one fears. This speech does not recognize Cordelia but unwittingly proves that he does not imagine she may be suffering for him because he assumes she cries for the same reasons he does. Cordelia is weeping for joy that Lear has regained enough mental clarity to identify her by name and for sorrow over his brutalized, still endangered condition and paranoia. But Lear imagines she is weeping because she wishes to kill him. Why would Lear assume that weeping would attend the desire to kill? It is clearly not that he thinks she regrets having to do such a thing to him because immediately thereafter he himself claims, with a certainty perhaps exaggerated by a contrary hope: "I know you do not love me." It is rather that he assumes she weeps—like him before Goneril and Regan—to lament her inability to revenge herself upon him. As we saw earlier, on several occasions Lear, though disdaining tears, found himself unable to suppress them when he realized he could not summon the immediate means to reestablish his presumed power. Here he tries to comfort Cordelia by assuring her she possesses the power to avenge herself; in fact, he will help her by means of a melodramatic gesture against himself—a gesture whose incongruous relation to reality is underscored by our knowledge that Cordelia has already given Lear poison to heal him. Though Lear has nearly been able to admit his guilt ("you have some cause") and though his offer to drink poison may even suggest a degree of self-reproach for his wrong-doing, Lear's primary concern here is to coax Cordelia into forgiveness and thus find security for himself from himself. He has not nor will he declare his own evil nor regret his actions because he is completely absorbed in an attempt to find relief from his feeling of being in the wrong.

Throughout this scene Cordelia's only hope is to be properly recognized, not for her own sake but for Lear's—"O, look upon me, sir,/And hold your hand in benediction o'er me" (4.7.56–57). She keeps directing Lear's distracted attention to herself, hoping that Lear will not again mistake her, in order that Lear might bless her at last by rightfully assuming his identity as father and king. She hopes he will address her in a "benediction" reserved for one beloved and so wish her well, not cower in accents of suspicion or fear. But Lear disregards her request and insists on kneeling to her instead. One could assume that this, too, is a positive sign of remorse and repentance were it not for the self-absorbed expressions of Lear's fear of mockery and humiliation and his offer to drink poison that follow. Because they do follow, however, we must suspect that Lear's kneeling is another and even subtler repetition of "power to flattery bowing." Were it not for the pitiful state of his mind and body, we might more accurately indict this act of his as an "unsightly trick" (2.4.157) (in the way Regan accused him when he knelt theatrically before her pretending to beg forgiveness of an absent Goneril) than identify it as genuine remorse. Cordelia has from the first not desired to bring Lear to his knees but to raise him from them to stand and walk in the dignity of his manhood, though the first step of such a restoration would indeed demand a confession of his own insignificance and sinfulness. She is mercifully alarmed here by his attempt to kneel to her because he is so weak and ill but also, one might suspect, because she is ashamed to have the father she loves cringing before her in a parody of real humility. When Cordelia asks Lear a little later if he would like to "walk" back into the tent, Shakespeare invites us to take the request in a symbolic sense not necessarily intended by Cordelia but confirmed by Lear's reply.

> You must bear with me,
> Pray you now forget, and forgive; I am old and
> foolish.
>
> (4.7.82–83)

Even if Lear is not literally borne off stage but walks off with Cordelia, he does not do so under his own power but asks to be carried, presuming again upon her overburdened love, gambling again that he can "set his rest on her kind nursery." The sense of his avoidance of the central issue is reinforced by the inappropriate order of events in Lear's atonement. The victim cannot forgive nor the sinner feel the saving grace of forgiveness if the crime has been forgotten. To do so is but to trifle with the need to redeem lost time.

An amazed and suspicious Lear has indeed wakened from a nightmare; but the more certain he grows of the waking reality of his safety and escape from the nightmare's bewildering humiliations into the sunshine of Cordelia's respect and affection, the more eagerly he plunges into the vain daydream that through Cordelia's forgiveness he can forget his sin and that Cordelia and he, insulated from harm, can simply pretend that his humiliation has been but a bad dream from which he has awakened to begin again where they left off. For Cordelia, that is not the father's blessing she had asked but another, if subtler tragedy than the first. For there is an effect of déjà vu in the symbolic dimension of Lear's exclamation here: "Would I were assur'd/Of my condition!" (4.7.55–56). Just as at the beginning of the play, when he sought to assure himself of Cordelia's love, throughout this scene a doubtful Lear persists in seeking some proof adequate to confirm Cordelia's love and respect. He does

not realize that the terms in which he makes such a request do
not begin the interior quest that can eventually, as in Cordelia's
case, assure one's condition; they merely presume upon the
future, seek a fugitive safety from life. If Cordelia's love cannot
be "assur'd," neither can her forgiveness; and surely Lear's sole
object should not have been the desperate gamble upon obtain-
ing Cordelia's forgiveness—a false security at best. The only
genuine assurance of love is loving. Lear would be mistaken if
he confused his condition with Cordelia's. Though he is once
again sheltered in the safety of her protection and love, he
remains profoundly ill. The moment of reconciliation between
father and daughter is not a cure but merely a remission of
fever allowing the old man within whom the disease still festers
untreated the hope that he has recovered. His delusion develops into the giddy sense of imperviousness of father and
daughter together in the "Come, let's away to prison" speech
before it is suddenly shattered when the illness breaks out in
the paroxysm of rage that kills the old king, his daughter's
unacknowledged executioner.

Biding the Pitiless Storm: Kent and the Fool

At the beginning of act 4, just before seeing his blind father
being "poorly led" overturns his self-consoling logic, Edgar
makes a speech whose dramatic irony also serves to summarize
the chief wisdom of the pastoral vision by which Cordelia, Kent,
and the Fool live.

> To be worst,
> The lowest and most dejected thing of fortune,
> Stands still in esperance, lives not in fear.
> The lamentable change is from the best,
> The worst returns to laughter. Welcome then,
> Thou unsubstantial air that I embrace:
> The wretch that thou hast blown unto the worst
> Owes nothing to thy blasts.

(4.1.2–9)

In self-defense, Edgar is attempting to make the best of a bad
situation. Gloucester's entry, however, by making an ironic devastation of his son's position, reveals Shakespeare's indictment
of the folly of Edgar's stoical endurance and its pretense of self-
sufficiency.[34] Bravery such as Edgar's here is only a shield

guarding his vulnerability to being wounded. In his dream of self-sufficiency Edgar may claim he "embraces" the "unsubstantial air" he takes in; but it is hardly a hospitable welcome that embraces air, then condemns it in the same breath as responsible for one's homelessness and alienation. His embrace, then, becomes a hypocritical mask for his contempt of the gracious breath that has come to him despite his misfortunes, only to be presumed upon and abused for its trouble in bearing obviously necessary gifts. The hope Edgar takes aim at fatally wounds a deeper hope; the forced laughter with which he hunts it down destroys pastoral's helpless mirth and communal joy for the corrupt design upon his own last laugh of triumph, fortune's wheel come full circle. The only reason Edgar is still expectant is that he neither understands nor possesses the courage and self-assurance necessary to "stand still," like Cordelia in her dignity, fidelity, and silence, in genuine hope's reconciliation to the world and time. Paradoxically, Edgar "stands still in esperance" to flee into a delusive hope that merely betrays him further—both in the explicit sense that a mutilated Gloucester makes a mockery of his brave words but also in the morally more significant, if merely implicit, sense that his behavior continues to betray the self-involvement that confirms his exile from others.

The special agony of Edgar's situation here was properly identified when Kent mysteriously proclaimed—"Nothing almost sees miracles/But misery" (2.2.165–66). Only great suffering—like Edgar's, for example—can awaken us to our need for a cure; but not all great suffering finds its possible cure if, again as in Edgar's case, in our heightened awareness of need we fly to seek a hope that violates abiding hope, a specious hope that seeks to escape suffering rather than to transform it. But those who together abide in enduring hope are permitted to see and enact genuine miracles. This vision and reality are not some impossibly miraculous last laugh, insulation from the pain of the world's "strange mutations" (4.1.11), or even the easy and subtle evasion we noted earlier when Edgar remarked upon Lear's departure to Dover: the "mind much sufferance doth o'erskip" when it sees "that which makes me bend makes the King bow" (3.6.106,109). The enacted miracle "o'erskips" no suffering but finds rather that the more profoundly and generously one willingly engages the suffering of self and others the more complete is the living soul's "return to laughter."

We have already seen Cordelia, "the lowest and most dejected thing of fortune" when her attempt to save Lear has
failed and left him oppressed, nonetheless "return[ing] to
laughter" to make her gentle fun of Lear in the hope of awakening him yet to her joy. The Fool, whose witty labors throughout to "outjest" Lear's "heart-strook injuries" (3.1.16–17) will
become the focus of our attention in a moment, comes to share
with Kent in Cordelia's "return to laughter" by welcoming Kent
to the select company of fools, offering Kent his coxcomb for
"taking one's part that's out of favor" (1.4.99–100). When the
Fool tells Kent that if "thou canst not smile as the wind sits,
thou'lt catch cold shortly. There, take my coxcomb" (100–1),
the complexity of his wisdom proves he is not an altogether
bitter fool. At one level his remark does intimate that Kent is a
fool for not currying favor with the powerful; but in another
sense, by offering Kent his coxcomb, the Fool offers him shelter for his head against the storms at which Lear raves "unbon-
neted" because the king, unlike Kent and the Fool, cannot
foolishly "smile as the wind sits"—namely, return to laughter
no matter what may come. In asking Kent to "take my coxcomb," the Fool offers Kent the only thanks he can for Kent's
having taken the part first of Cordelia and now of Lear as well,
but he is also urging him to continue to play the fool, to "take
one's part that's out of favor," and fuse a solidarity of equals
among father, daughter, servant, and fool. For in taking the
"part" of a person out of favor, something Lear is never generous enough to himself to do, Kent also generously extends
himself to take the fool's part Lear ignores and finally forgets,[35]
though the old king ought to have known that to take the Fool's
part would have been to take his own part as well.

That Kent honors the Fool's urging is confirmed by his curious mirth at being made a fool of in being stocked. He tells
Gloucester, "some time I shall sleep out, the rest I'll whistle"
and advises his eyes to take advantage of their heaviness so as
not to see or be offended by the shameful state of their lodgings
since the clear light of day will soon enough reveal it. His worst
has returned to laughter because he genuinely "stands still in
esperance, lives not in fear." In accepting his present graciously
and sharing meager benefits with his weary eyes and a Gloucester relieved of the burden of interceding for him, and in still
holding calmly to modest hopes for the future, Kent betrays no
fear for himself, no impatient desire to "o'erskip" suffering, no

corrupt hope for self-aggrandizing vindication or restoration to former prestige. The miracle Kent believes in is not the sort that will even remove him from the stocks necessarily, let alone restore his position at court or spare the king he loves the grief Kent feels lies in wait for him. The miracle he hopes for and then sees is merely the opportunity to read a letter from Cordelia confirming her commitment to try to relieve Lear's losses, a letter his miseries momentarily prevent him from reading. The "comfortable beams" (2.2.164) that will allow him to see the miracle of Cordelia's words of love do not "o'erskip" suffering; they allow him to see miracles by means of suffering. Kent realizes, for example, that the comfortable beams of light that will allow him to see Cordelia's love are the same beams that will force him to see his shameful lodging and face its humiliation in the morning. They are the same beams of the "warm sun" into which the master he loves must come from the comfortable shade of "heaven's benediction" (161–62). Kent hopes that Cordelia's coming will render his "obscured course" (168) superfluous. The comfortable beams come not to magnify him but to allow him to merge unobtrusively into their grandeur. Just as the sun comes in its glory to efface the "obscured course" of the stars, so Kent hopes that Cordelia's journey of love will efface his own disguised and confused night journeying in love for Lear that he implicitly compares to the erratic journeying and dim light of a star. Unlike Edgar, Kent yearns for a self-effacing joy.

When Lear responds to Kent's "Hail to thee, noble master" greeting from the stocks by asking him, "Dost thou make this shame thy pastime?" we can now see that we should understand Lear's words in a sense Kent—on the surface, at least—does not. In symbolic terms "this shame" more tellingly names Lear himself than it does Kent's present condition. Because Kent does truly respect his "noble master" even in his master's shame, his devotion to him does indeed transcend the labor of love's mere endurance of pain and humiliation for the communal delight of a "pastime's" playful ease.

The security of the pastoral community among Cordelia, Fool, and Kent is bred of their willingness to live and suffer for and with each other; theirs is love's triumph over fear for the self. We know that pastoral's idealized shepherds are not builders of cities. The reason is not that they are unconcerned about the well-being of friends or naively believe fields hide no vipers

but only butterflies, but that the erection of walls hints a self-
defensive fear of the world's space, the withdrawal from the
open acceptance of the inevitability and glory of suffering together. They are not farmers because the storage of food similarly hints a defensive fear of time. As Professor Poggioli has
remarked, the pastoral provider "never saves for a 'rainy day' "
because he trusts in the "self-sufficiency that is the ideal of the
tribe, of the clan, of the family."[36] Pastoral shepherds toil not,
neither do they spin—not from presumptuous naiveté, but in
the profoundest wisdom. They understand the Jewish humor
in the benignity of Providence; the lilies of the field do not toil
or spin because "sufficient to the day are the evils thereof." Or
as the Fool in rueful jest would have it, the "rain it raineth every
day" (3.2.77). Pastoral shepherds are never nomads, as real
shepherds must often be, but "stay-at-homes,"[37] though not because pastoral is an effete mode, an evasion of the strenuous
but bracing "good life." Rather they are stay-at-homes because
they know that nomadic wandering, no less than its apparent
opposite, the erection of a city's walls, is merely a futile and
enervating search for an ideal external environment in the
hope of finding a safer place for the self than among those we
love. Such labors, not pastoral's communal joys, are the true
evasion of the "good life" that "stands still in esperance, lives
not in fear." Kent, a man who is unwilling to wander from
Lear's side, does not "fear" to "lose" his life, "thy safety being
motive" (1.1.156–57). By contrast, Regan closes Gloucester's
gates on an eighty-year-old father because "wisdom bids fear"
(2.4.307). And it is Goneril, her own safety being the motive,
who will not let Lear "keep/At point a hundred knights"
(1.4.323–24), because she mistakenly believes it is safer to fear
too far

> than [to] trust too far.
> Let me still take away the harms I fear,
> Not fear still to be taken.
>
> (1.4.328–30)

Rather than risk remaining "still to be taken" like Cordelia, she
orders Regan by letter into flight from her home and then
herself joins the other restless wanderers in exile, fear's fugitive
refuge.

Over and over, in a variety of parabolic quips and riddles, the

Fool tries to convince Lear he will prove himself nothing but a bitter fool by rushing about seeking an external cure. When about to flee Goneril's palace, for example, Lear asks after the readiness of his horses, the Fool tells him the "asses are gone about 'em" (1.5.34). Just previously he had told Lear he had no brains "in's heels" because Regan "will use thee kindly" (8,14–15). Earlier, in the same scene in which the Fool had offered Kent his coxcomb, he tried to explain to Lear the difference between a sweet and a bitter fool by resorting to an ambiguous riddle.

> That lord that counsell'd thee
>   To give away thy land,
> Come place him here by me,
>   Do thou for him stand.
> The sweet and bitter fool
>   Will presently appear:
> The one in motley here,
>   The other found out there.
>
> (1.4.140–47)

In one sense—the sense in which the jingle has always and exclusively been taken—this is merely an inspired bit of ridicule, asking Lear to pretend to play the part of the stupid, traitorous fool who masqueraded as a privy counselor to suggest the division of a kingdom. The difference between the sweet fool and the bitter fool, then, is that the sweet fool, the Fool himself, can remain safely at court in motley; the bitter fool who gave traitorous advice to his monarch will be "found out there," banished. Of course, since Lear is that counselor, he is the one who shall "catch cold shortly" because he is now out of favor with the powerful. When the Fool taunts Lear—

> If I gave [my two daughters] all my living,
> I'ld keep my coxcombs myself. There's mine,
> beg another of thy daughters
>
> (1.4.107–9)

—he is clearly accusing Lear of having outdone him in folly. The Fool would at least have maintained his Fool's identity at court if, formerly, as king he had given all his lands away. But if the traditional court fool is an "O" with a figure, Lear is now, indeed, a fool without one. Fool has his coxcomb, and he knows what cover for his head Lear will get from his daughters should he "beg another" of them. "He that keeps nor crust [nor] crumb,/Weary of all, shall want some" (1.4.198–99).

But if this were the only possible interpretation of the Fool's riddle, he would prove himself a liar since in smugly claiming he was the sweet fool and Lear the bitter, he would unknowingly condemn himself as a bitter fool. The sweet fool does not, however, cynically relish Lear's being banished, nor does he self-servingly hope to dissociate himself from the foolish counselor, though by staying with him he knows he risks being "whipt out" (112). He does not summon the treasonously foolish "lord that counsell'd thee" to banishment but to the fraternal warmth of his forgiveness: "Come place him here by me." When he requests that Lear "for him stand," he does not finally want him to impersonate himself but to be and accept himself, and, like Kent and himself, "take one's part that's out of favor." He asks him to stand for the bitterness of self-recognition in order also to stand up for himself in the sweetness of the generosity of others and himself toward himself. But what the Fool wishes to call loving attention to, Lear would rather dismiss as another of his jestor's foolish "nothings."[38] In ignoring the Fool's "nothings," Lear only ignores himself. It is Lear, not the Fool, who "speaks to purpose not." By refusing to stand for the foolish traitor who counseled him to give his lands away Lear banishes himself, flees himself, like Edgar, to live out an impersonation in a bitter fool's exile. He continues to "course his own shadow for a traitor" (3.4.57–58) rather than "for him stand" to exercise the opportunity to question "Lear's shadow" to find out who he is: a nothing with a figure, the "sweet and bitter fool" who the Fool tells him "will presently appear" next to him should Lear take the part of the fool who betrayed him. The "sweet and bitter fool" Lear could have unmasked is pastoral romance's long lost twin brother of the Fool, since the Fool is himself always both a "sweet and bitter fool" whether in "motley here" or "found out there." One cannot clearly distinguish the sweet fool in motley here who asks Lear to "come . . . here by me" from the bitter fool who never ceases to ridicule Lear; one cannot clearly distinguish the bitter fool "out there" in the storm lamenting its ravages and counseling the common sense of shelter from the sweet fool who bides with Lear without reservation. Though it is tempting to acknowledge neither and, thus, "ever but slenderly" to know ourselves, the sweet and

bitter fool are together and inseparable in each of us. That the
Fool believes so becomes clear from his response to Kent's
query on the heath: "Who's there?" The Fool replies, ridiculing
Lear, "Here's grace and a codpiece—that's a wise man and a
fool" (3.2.39–41). But, in another sense, he is merely speaking
for himself, the contradictory self of every man when he claims
to be both grace and shame, a wise man and a fool. The man
who realizes that "our shadow" is the only thing that can tell us
what we are knows how tantalizingly insignificant our "little tiny
wit" is, what a foolish figure we inevitably cut searching in our
grand and wise quest for knowledge of ourselves. Only a fool,
albeit a wise one, would proclaim that man is what he is not. But
it is both true and ridiculous enough that every time we think
we have located *homo viator* he has moved on, since our essence
is to outpace ourselves, whether in the direction of smug self-
knowledge's hideaway for fugitives or toward the innocent risks
of the open way.

Both the wisdom of making *homo viator*'s open way our home
and the folly of the fugitive's flight to safety coalesce in the
Fool's witty prophecy whose riddling and enigmatic future
proves to be the most matter-of-fact present.

"When priests are more in word than matter;
When brewers mar their malt with water;
When nobles are their tailor's tutors;
No heretics burn'd, but wenches' suitors;
Then shall the realm of Albion
Come to great confusion.
When every case in law is right;
No squire in debt, nor no poor knight;
When slanders do not live in tongues;
Nor cutpurses come not to throngs;
When usurers tell their gold i' th' field,
And bawds and whores do churches build;
Then comes the time, who lives to see't,
That going shall be us'd with feet."
This prophecy Merlin shall make, for I live before his time.
                                                         (3.2.81–96)

As Professor Danby has convincingly argued,[39] the prophecy
begins simply enough as a utopian vision in which the corrupt
present of the first four lines is neatly displaced by the flawless
future (7–10). But in lines 11–14 the clear vision clouds, and

everything "comes to great confusion." It is impossible to tell, as Danby remarks, whether the usurers and whores of this muddled millenium have been converted from their sinful ways or merely live in the brazenness and hypocrisy they always have. It is impossible to determine whether the "confusion" of the realm of Albion is the cleansing prelude to a glorious peripatetic future in the academy of philosopher kings, a regressive decline from Albion's legendary golden age to England's barbaric march into iron, or merely a description that collapses present, past, and future into the "always" when the "going shall be used with feet." Like Cordelia, with whom he shares the utopian "no place" and everywhere that is her dear shelter, the Fool knows that the millenial time is never and always;[40] and we in it still and ever retain the full range of moral choice. Our "going shall be used with feet" either to stand and walk together to progress along the open way or to desert it and others to seek a fugitive safety.

The Fool is not about to desert Lear. He "will tarry, the fool will stay" with him. Rather than "pack when it begins to rain,/ And leave thee in the storm," he tries to take Lear home to stay in his hovel because he knows "the rain it raineth every day." When Lear, after much thundering at the heavens in the rain, momentarily stops,[41] acknowledges a need for shelter, and agrees to look for "your hovel," the Fool replies in a song:

> He that has and a little tine wit—
>   With heigh-ho, the wind and the rain—
> Must make content with his fortunes fit,
>   Though the rain it raineth every day.
>   (3.2.74–77)

Our first reaction to the song may be surprise at its uncharacteristic tone. If, as we may, we read a "little tine wit" as the Fool's reference to himself, the song sounds a note of embarrassed self-deprecation and sweet resignation, not the Fool's usual assaulting and corrosive wit. This is a far cry from the seemingly cynical, self-serving humor of his exhortation moments earlier to Lear: "O nuncle, court holy-water in a dry house is better than this rain-water out o'door" (3.2.10–11). What explains the distinctive change is an act equally uncharacteristic—a momentary expression of concern for another from Lear: "I have one part of my heart/That's sorry yet for thee"

(72–73). As long as Lear thinks of no one but himself, the Fool feels constrained to sing "for sorrow" (1.4.176) his derisive songs; but when Lear seemingly heeds the Fool's own plight, the Fool shows he is not an arrogant or embittered martyr on Lear's behalf. He is, instead, sweetly self-effacing, as if being acknowledged in this way were to be embarrassingly overpaid, his comfort not something Lear should worry himself over.

But we should not make too much of Lear's generous gesture or of the Fool's reply. To the extent that it is generous, the Fool bows to it; to the extent that its generosity but parenthetically interrupts his continuing delusion, the Fool holds it up to ridicule. As Lear momentarily seeks the hovel's shelter claiming, "the art of our necessities is strange/That can make vild things precious" (3.2.70–71), he remains unconscious of his ingratitude for the benefice. For Lear the hovel represents the temporary value of any shelter in a storm. "*Our* necessities" for Lear are but *his* necessities, *his* temporary mishaps and discomfitures. If the vile hut is momentarily precious under the circumstances, it still remains vile; and when circumstances change it will subside again to its unambiguously contemptible status. The Fool's jingle, like the prophecy that follows, insists by contrast that our necessities never change. The vile hovel is intrinsically precious under all circumstances. In fact, any "little tine wit" lucky enough to have it—Lear himself in this case—should have the sense of humor to appreciate the "fit" fortune of a little tiny hut to house it.

What keeps Lear from the familiality that can make the meagerest accommodations home on the open way is, as we have already noted, the self-absorbed conception of love that has grown out of his profound personal insecurity and keeps him restlessly on the move, seeking the regard of others. The Fool tries to communicate this to him in his densely symbolic "codpiece" song.

> The codpiece that will house
>   Before the head has any;
> The head and he shall louse:
>   So beggars marry many.
> The man that makes his toe
>   What he his heart should make,
> Shall of a corn cry woe,
>   And turn his sleep to wake.

(3.2.27–34)

But for the telltale phrase about the "heart," the song might be taken solely as ridicule of Lear's past and present behavior or else as a pragmatic warning for the future addressed to Lear's addled "head," that is, to self-serving common sense.[42] One's first inclination is to see the song as a warning to seek shelter since the Fool has just been urging Lear to take cover, telling him that the man "that has a house to put's head in has a good head-piece" (3.2.26). But if the song is such a warning, it is a strangely negative one since it implies only that Lear will not find the shelter he needs by begging from door to door, especially at the doors of these daughters. The song makes more sense as ridicule of past and present than as advice for a happier future. The Fool knows Lear is an exposed fool, a head without a house, if he thinks or thought he could find shelter from these daughters after resigning his only power over them. More significantly, the Fool may be implying that profligate fathers like Lear, who engender but for sport, without ongoing concern for their progeny, are fools to expect ongoing concern for themselves from that same progeny. When the Fool refers to Lear as a "codpiece" and a "beggar,"[43] he has not randomly chosen to combine these epithets merely because they are convenient or traditional terms of derogation. They come aptly to mind because, as we have already seen, they accurately define Lear's prostitution of the meaning of love and charity. Profligate or beggar alike, each with "still-soliciting eye" makes his "toe" (the beggar's foot, the libertine's phallus) "what he his heart should make," moving restlessly from person to person and house to house, serving only where he can "seek for gain." When the Fool claims that beggars, like libertines, "marry many," he is not simply referring to their literal tendency to pick up lice, he is also indirectly indicting Lear's repeated infidelities to his vows to be faithful to each of his daughters when he finds she will not pay his asking price and accept him as a beggarly dependency.

The Fool's dissecting ridicule is not, however, without its merciful grace. The head can wisely abide in a healthy house and the codpiece thus transform sexuality without love into sexuality with it if the heart, rather than the toe, becomes man's instrument of feeling. The libertine-beggar who feels with his "toe" can only grow calloused—brazenly offensive or defensive in manner, hard on others and himself. There is no cause in nature that makes hard hearts. When Lear repeatedly rushes

about questioning the heavens about his inexplicably cruel
daughters, he is really crying woe of his own corns. The loving
heart can endure repeated abrasion without hardening or
growing calloused. It is the restless motion of foot and phallus
where only the heart should have been moved that has pro-
duced Lear's painful plight. Though corns seemingly develop
as a defensive protection from suffering, ultimately they only
increase and intensify our sensitivity to pain. If Goneril and
Regan behave heartlessly, rather than taking his plea to heaven
Lear should take it to heart and inquire there where they could
have learned such manners.

The same lesson about the loving heart's miraculous capacity
to respond to suffering with perpetual freshness, without hardening into calloused defensiveness or cruel retribution, is the
purpose of the distinction the Fool made earlier between an
oyster and a snail in the midst of several unmistakeable references to Cordelia while ridiculing Lear. Critics have ignored
the Fool's inconsequence about not knowing "how an oyster
makes his shell" (1.5.25), concentrating instead on the ridicule
in his claim that the snail has a shell "to put's head in, not to give
it away to his daughters, and leave his horns without a case"
(1.5.30–31). But if Lear is seemingly not a very clever relation
of the self-protective snail, it would be a mistake to imagine that
the Fool would like him to try to become one. The snail's
merely self-serving cleverness is clearly transcended by the
motionless oyster. It is true that the Fool cannot tell how an
oyster makes its beautiful shell of pearl. It is not, however,
because he does not know that the oyster openly exposes itself
to irritants and gradually fashions its beautiful shell from
them, but because no one can explain the miraculous construction of a beautiful shelter out of the pain of the flesh's vulnerability willingly and patiently suffered. The snail is, by
comparison, a perfect emblem for unregenerate man: a relatively worthless animal whose hard shell hides a pathetic vulnerability deep within, a vulnerability that in its effort to deny
itself only serves to trail slime in its crawling wake. The Fool
ridicules Lear for being more foolish than a snail not to convince him to continue to seek the protection of a hard shell but
to expose him in his pathetic vulnerability so Lear will admit the
painful fact of what he is and thus begin to fashion the oyster's
dear shelter for himself.

The gnomic wisdom we have uncovered beyond the surface

ridicule in the Fool's quips and riddling songs suggests the
misguided nature of readings of his character that would reduce his role in the play into purely functional terms of embittered choric commentary. His full comprehension of the tragic
significance of Lear's agon transcends any exclusive
identification of him with a hardheaded, self-serving common
sense and hardhearted ridicule incapable of broader moral and
emotional concerns or heroic dimensions of character.[44] But
proof of the underlying reality of his comprehension of and
love for Lear in words that match his deeds does not completely
explain and justify the seemingly cruel manner in which this
love consistently expresses itself. Stanley Cavell reveals something of the way in which we should interpret the Fool's verbal
turns of the screw if we are to resolve how the cruel words that
seem, if anything, only to intensify Lear's agony can still remain
the expression of a compassionate heart taking one's part that is
out of favor—out of favor even with the Fool himself.

> It is agreed that the Fool keeps the truth present to Lear's
> mind, but it should be stressed that the characteristic mode of
> the Fool's presentation is ridicule—the circumstance most
> specifically feared by shame. . . . Part of the exquisite pain of
> this Fool's comedy is that in riddling Lear with the truth of
> his condition he increases the very cause of that condition, as
> though shame should finally grow ashamed of itself, and
> stop. The other part of this pain is that it is the therapy
> prescribed by love itself.[45]

Substantiating the Fool's sense of ridicule as a therapeutic
necessity and, moreover, explaining how such a drastic cure
works are the keys to a complete understanding of how his
bitter words are fitting for a sweet fool. There is no real division, as is often claimed, between the Fool's heart and his head;
the codpiece song proves that conclusively enough. It is simply
that ridicule is the only language he can use to get through to
Lear. As Cordelia had remarked to her sisters: Time at last
"with shame derides" those "who cover faults" (1.1.281). And
Lear, we know, must at all costs cover faults. In fact, that is one
reason why the Fool calls him an "O without a figure." We have
already seen that this expression can refer to the fact that Lear
is a fool (in the Renaissance an "O with a figure") who has given
his "figure" (position at court) away. But, more significantly,
Lear is also an "O without a figure" because he is a man who in

the depths of his soul doubts he is anything but a cipher, a ludicrous beast fearful of the treatment he deserves, who therefore tries to hide his suspicions of his absence of worth. So shame must deride him. Though ashamed to do it, the Fool derides Lear because it is the only instrument he can use to drive Lear's shame out into the open and free him from its stranglehold. We must, I think, give him the benefit of the doubt and take the Fool at his word when he answers Lear's question about how long he has been "so full of songs" of ridicule.

> I have us'd it, nuncle, e'er since thou mad'st
> thy daughters thy mothers, for when thou gav'st them
> the rod, and put'st down thine own breeches, [sings]
>   "Then they for sudden joy did weep,
>   And I for sorrow sung,
>   That such a king should play bo-peep,
>   And go the [fools] among."
>   (1.4.172–78)

The last two lines of his song clearly convey the Fool's disappointed shame for Lear; the first two, as we shall see, implicitly convey his shame for himself for having to do what he is doing to Lear.

The Fool knows appearances are deceiving: if Lear's daughters have already indicated they are not what they seemed, neither will the Fool prove so. He may sound cynically delighted when he ridicules Lear, but actually he regrets the need to do so. He knows he does need to do so, however, because even with him the old king continues to play a childish game of hide and seek—hiding his shame as he seeks sympathy from him or anyone else who will listen. Since the Fool does love Lear he wordlessly sympathizes with him, but he realizes it would be utter folly to express open sympathy for the old king in his humiliation when it is Lear's own doing that has brought his miseries down on himself. The alternatives to derision are indifference or some expression of sympathy; and neither of them would do anything but encourage Lear to indulge his self-pity. So derision it must be. Unlike Goneril, Fool can innocently give "offense/Which else were shame, that then necessity/Will call discreet proceeding" (1.4.212–14). He cannot openly sympathize with Lear for being spanked but must make fun of him for pulling down his pants to offer a temptation his daughters cannot refuse. He is not upset that Lear has abandoned common sense; nor does he even believe that Lear has forsaken the self-serving wisdom of calculation. He simply hopes to make it difficult for Lear to indulge himself and, thus, ignore his true condition.

The central point, in fact, of many of the Fool's sardonic quips is not so much that Lear has violated practical wisdom as it is a counsel of moderation against further self-indulgence, against a melodramatic egoism intent on eliciting sympathy for its suffering. The Fool mocks Lear as a man who has gluttonously overindulged: he who "keeps nor crust [nor] crumb/ Weary of all, shall want some" (198–99). When Lear begins to tear off his clothes after the unaccommodated man speech in act 3, the Fool undercuts our sympathetic horror at this act of self-laceration by properly identifying it as one of self-indulgence, telling Lear "'tis a naughty night to swim in" (3.4.110–11). He warns Lear about exaggerating when he says Edgar "reserved a blanket, else we had been all shamed" after Lear had asked: "Couldst thou save nothing? Wouldst thou give 'em all?" (64–67). And he deflates Lear's theatricality when he refuses to take a joint stool for Lear's daughter, Goneril, on mock trial. When early in act 3 Lear urges the heavens to "spout/Till you have drench'd our steeples" (3.2.2–3), the Fool refuses to take the bait and return solicitude for solicitation. Instead, he pretends to react to Lear's urging at face value and quips that such a storm would be too much of a good thing. Even the meager and tainted relief of "court holy-water in a dry house is better than this rain-water out o'door." The Fool's method and purpose in this regard is most completely revealed when he makes yet another mockery of one of Lear's moving rhetorical appeals. Responding to Lear's resentment at being kept waiting by Regan and Cornwall, the Fool subverts the intended effect of Lear's pitiful lament, "O me, my heart! my rising heart! But down!" Instead of some gesture of sympathy or concern, he baits the old king, pretending to urge him on.

Cry to it, nuncle, as the cockney did to the eels when she put 'em i' th' paste alive; she knapp'd 'em o' th' coxcombs with a stick, and cried, 'Down, wantons, down!' 'Twas her brother that, in pure kindness to his horse, butter'd his hay.

(2.4.122–26)

The Fool is drawing a distinction here between the cockney (appropriately enough, the original meaning of this term, the *OED* tells us, refers to a spoiled child, one too tenderly nurtured) and her brother—two kinds of fools. Having given away power to his daughters, Lear has become the cockney in the Fool's eyes. If we see her as a promiscuous young lady, her cry of "down, wantons, down," like Lear's cry to his rising heart, incurs the Fool's mockery as a form of theatrical protest not to be taken too seriously since she is herself wantonly responsible for her present situation. If we see her merely as a foolish cook, the Fool feels our response to her ought to be, as to Lear's present horror at his daughters' snappishness, that she should have known what would happen. Her brother in folly, the loving Fool himself, however, differs radically from his wanton sibling. Though in terms of common sense, he is even more addled than his sister, buttering his horse's hay for love, there is a superior human method in his form of madness. Like the Fool who plays his distasteful jokes on Lear—distasteful both to him and to Lear—the fool in the story greases his beloved horse's hay so that the horse, disliking its taste, will not overindulge and make himself ill.

Early in the play the Fool makes a catalogue of commandments worthy of Polonius in order to conclude that the crafty wisdom of self-protection and calculation will yield "more/ Than two tens to a score" (1.4.126–27), namely, nothing. His subsequent quibbling on Kent's reply—"This is nothing, Fool" (128)—is in all likelihood meant only to force Lear to recall Cordelia's initial speeches. Both Cordelia and the Fool make the same plea to Lear's love, finally: "Can you make no use of nothing, nuncle?" (130–31). Both believe Lear's void can grow fruitful but only if, instead of armed self-defense and militant aggressiveness, he exposes his weakness and tries to love others. The pastoral possibility the tragedy uproots is the social vision Thomas McFarland has asserted about the enchanted locale of *The Tempest*, a world in which "no crime is more than the fault of a willful child, which, after reprimand and immediate but tempered punishment, can be forgiven."[46] If we preface what follows by saying that it may well imply a historical diminution of the starkness or purity of the tragic sense, it may be fair to say that Cordelia and the Fool are a possibility of grace Aeschylus would not have dreamed of, and that Sophocles may have dreamed but could not or did not embody in his version of the

Oedipus legend, but that Shakespeare dressed for sacrifice as
Abraham dressed his son. Cordelia and the Fool represent,
then, failed Prosperos who try to bring grace to fallen "hard
nature" on the heath, but, even more important, to the hardhearted nature of man. In the place of the epicure's self-
gratification and enervating self-indulgence they offer self-
acceptance and the acceptance of suffering; for the stoic's self-
defensive abdication from involvement with others and his
brute endurance, they offer the folly of human love.

Their grandeur is symbolically epitomized by the samphire
gatherer whose risk of life for the community of man goes
ignored or, at best, unappreciated both by Gloucester and Edgar when Edgar imaginatively fabricates his cliff scene at
Dover. Gloucester and Edgar stand poised on the presumed
heights from which they would, like gods, dispose destiny—the
one by disposing of himself in a suicidal flight, the other in an
artistic flight of his own fantasy to refashion his father's life.
Below them, Edgar points to the crawling depths where crows
show "scarce so gross as beetles," fishermen "appear like mice,"
and the samphire gatherer himself "seems no bigger than his
head" (4.6.14, 16, 18). Midway between god and beetle, the
samphire gatherer inconspicuously and calmly goes about his
"dreadful trade," the risk of his own life to gather the medicinal
herb of St. Pierre along the face of the only cliffs where it is
found so that others can extract its "unpublish'd virtues."[47] Renaissance physicians believed that this bitter tasting medicine,
fashioned in the arts of their necessities, melted or cured the
stone, eased the pain in the gall. Nothing more succinctly describes the efforts of Cordelia and the Fool to restore their
beloved king to health.

The Player King

The king's a beggar, now the play is done.
                    Epilogue, *All's Well That Ends Well*

Shame would have it hid.
                              Gloucester, *King Lear*

From a study of the contrasts between the first scenes of *The True Chronicle History of King Leir* and Shakespeare's spare, truncated adaptation of them in the first half of scene one in *King Lear,* we can better inspect several related elements in Shakespeare's design. For one thing, it appears Shakespeare took great care to keep Lear's psyche cloaked, unavailable to immediate inspection, as if our bewilderment—a sense of something hidden in Lear's motives—was a necessary first step toward understanding him. In Shakespeare's source both the abdication and the love test are far more comprehensibly motivated than in *Lear.* In the old play the death of Leir's beloved wife, his impotent old age, his lack of a son for heir, his own death which he imagines imminent, and, above all, his self-sacrificial concern for the safety of his nation are all discussed before his counselors as elements in his decision and combine to convince him he must reluctantly "resign these earthly cares" to his daughters and "thinke upon the welfare of my soul" (1.1.28).

Leir dreads having to shift the heavy burden of rule onto daughters he would prefer to dote upon; but because he cares so much for the future welfare of Britain, he decides he must

118

divide the kingdom impartially among his daughters and
marry each to a "neyghbouring King" so that the "State/May be
protected 'gainst all forrayne hate" (1.1.55), an idea conveniently encouraged by the fact that neighboring Cornwall and
Cambria have already "motion[ed] love" toward Gonorill and
Ragan. The king is not suspicious of any of his daughters nor
does he seem to have a favorite. He does not reveal any fear of
dissension among his daughters, let alone the prospect of civil
strife. The only difficulty he seems to consider is a Cordella
who wishes to marry for love but who fancies none of her
suitors. The love test—whatever private psychological purposes
it may also serve—is consciously and clearly designed as a
public, politically motivated trick, a practical "stratagem"
(1.1.78) by which the king can manipulate Cordella into a pa-
triotic marriage of his choosing with the king of Brittany as a
proof of her anticipated verbal claims to outdo her sisters in
love for the king. Though the trick is obviously wrong-headed,
it is nonetheless a comprehensibly motivated gambit that explains the love test in a way nothing in Shakespeare's *Lear* explains Lear's.

In *King Lear,* on the other hand, with no prior discussion or
even mention of the political wisdom of Lear's decision, no
considered rejection of other alternatives or doubts expressed
about the dangers of abdication and succession without a male
heir, Lear makes but a brief public announcement of what he
has already decided to do. Lear may "express" his "darker purpose" (1.1.36) straightforwardly enough; but we who must try
to understand it without any sense of familial or political context or familiarity with Lear's character do not thereby find the
darkness grow luminous. Not only does the only prior reference to Lear's political decision—Kent's introductory exchange
with Gloucester—fail to enlighten us about the political thinking underlying the decision; but because Lear's plan, even in its
details, is indicated to be general knowledge at court,[1] the reasons why Lear would therefore stage the seemingly empty,
ritualistic love auction are even more puzzling. In Shakespeare,
of course, there is no hint that this love test is any kind of
stratagem to trick Cordelia into subordinating personal happiness to political necessity. Nor in the source, conversely, are
there previously outlined maps or imperial claims to have already "divided/In three our kingdom" (1.1.37–38) to call into
question the seriousness with which that love test may be taken.

In fact, the pretense that there is to be a connection between
the love test and the allotment of portions of the kingdom is
itself a Shakespearean departure from the source. In the earlier play, the audience is aware from the outset that Leir's "zeale
is fixt" (1.1.40) to be impartial and divide the kingdom into
three equal portions. He does not even mention the division of
the kingdom at the love test when he hopes merely to

> Resolve a doubt which much molests my mind,
> Which of you three to me would prove most kind;
> Which loves me most, and which at my request
> Will soonest yeeld unto their father's hest.
>
> (1.3.232–35)

He is not aware that Gonorill and Ragan have meanwhile been
willfully misinformed by his messenger who told them there
would be a *quid pro quo* relationship between flattery and reward. His daughters thus find it an easy matter (since they, like
Cordella, are as yet unmarried) to place Cordella's anticipated
refusal in a bad light by insinuating into their praise of Leir the
promise that "should you appoynt me for to marry/The mean-
est vassayle in the spacious world,/Without reply I would accomplish it" (1.3.248–50; cf. 1.3.269–72).

   Whereas the earlier play, which concentrates our attention
upon Leir's well-intentioned political concerns, creates for us
the sense of Leir as a very good man and king who makes a
foolish mistake, but who, once he has learned a simple lesson,
can very likely recoup his losses and recover both his moral
dignity and stability, Shakespeare's treatment of Lear assures
far less. The absence of carefully defined and presented political motivation in Lear is only one element of our confusion
about the king. Though Lear presumably loves his children,
when he expresses his darker purpose he does not express any
reluctance to burden them with the cares of state. In the source,
by contrast, the central psychological crisis in deciding upon
abdication explicitly involves the conflict between the king's desire to favor his children and indulge their protected lives of
ease on the one hand and the nation's need for orderly succession and responsible rule on the other (1.3.202–211). If Leir is
utterly unsuspicious of his children, Shakespeare's Lear is apparently troubled by doubts. He does not even mention foreign
invasion or the need for a Britain united against its enemies
without; but he does say he wishes

                                                              to publish
Our daughters' several dowers, that future strife
May be prevented now.

                                                  (1.1.43–45)

The decision to initiate the "challenge" that the love test involves would seem to undermine his purpose by encouraging
his daughters to think of conflict as a proper means of settling
questions of jurisdictional power (if we take what he says about
"future strife" seriously). In any case, Lear seems rather boldly
to allude to the fearful possibility that his own daughters or
their husbands could be brought to attack one another. That
same fear may also be intimated by the scrupulous equality of
the portions, despite the likelihood Lear "more affected the
Duke of Albany than Cornwall" (1.1.1–2); it may be hinted at
again when Lear addresses Cornwall before Albany and the
assembled court, despite the fact that Goneril is his eldest child.
   When Shakespeare's Lear speaks of an "unburthen'd crawl
toward death" (1.1.41), he seems momentarily to recall Leir's
spiritual turn to the contemplative from the active life; but by
the end of act 1 it has become clear from Shakespeare's portrait
of the king as a holiday-licensed lord of misrule that his turn is
more spirited than spiritual,[2] his retirement more a luxury and
an impatience (in the modern and corrupted sense of the word
"retirement," implying alienation from our labors) than a traditional reflective submission to a solitude that aids us in engag-
ing life more fully and meaningfully. By contrast, the only
"reservation" Leir makes for himself in the source is to "take
me to my prayers and beads." The offense that results in his
allowance being halved and then halved again by Gonorill is,
ironically enough, nothing more than his occasional counsel to
her against extravagance. Even before turning to seek Cordella's forgiveness, Leir bears up patiently under the adversities
imposed by his other daughters, including an attempt on his
life. On the other hand, Shakespeare's Lear—never a model of
patience under siege—rushes to his complete undoing with
frightening rapidity in acts 1 and 2 before daughters much
more indifferently disrespectful to him than Leir's menacing
and violent offspring. Unlike his predecessor, Lear cannot no-
bly right himself after his initial mistake in moral judgment
because his folly in abdication and the banishments is not a
simple error but a symptom that both manifests and conceals a

more profound disease. The inexorability we come to see in
Lear's deteriorating sense of self intimates a more deep-seated
problem than any one or all of his accumulated acts speeding
him to madness and ruin themselves communicate.

When we analyze in what specific ways Shakespeare's Lear
proves himself less readily sympathetic than his model with
regard to the specific acts he performs, the curious result is that
even as we name and catalogue his acts of apparent bribery, his
self-indulgences, his repeated impatience and petulance, and
his cursing rages we do not feel satisfied that we have identified
the motive for his behavior. A survey of the history of the play's
criticism confirms that no attempt to "explain" Lear by any one
or more of his vices has even begun to satisfy a majority of
readers as an adequate delineation of the man. It would, of
course, be unfortunate were that to encourage us to settle for
equally unsatisfactory alternatives: ignoring the riddle Lear
represents by assuming he is either mad or senile from the
outset or holding that the first scene is merely a spectacular
dramatic donnée setting the play in motion.[3] Rather, it should
invite us to explore the intuition that the essence of Lear's
character lies below the surface of his whining and cursing
vices. What Richard claims of himself is equally true of Lear,
though it is Lear's special curse that he does not know it.

> 'Tis very true, my grief lies all within,
> And these external [manners] of laments
> Are merely shadows to the unseen grief
> That swells with silence in the tortur'd soul.
> There lies the substance.
>
> (*Richard II* 4.1.295–99)

Though Lear's alternately vicious and abject "laments" are real
enough and certainly an operative force in furthering the surface drama of the play, in the final analysis they hide more than
they reveal about the man. Something more significant about
him will emerge when we discern the inner urgencies that seem
diametrically opposed to the outer man's behavior in the first
scenes. In his willful, even wantonly senseless imperiousness at
the love auction we will discover hints of the most pathetic
dependency; in the arbitrary power of kingship unleashed
upon Kent and Cordelia, the fear of impotence; in his subsequent and irrevocable commitment to an embattled path of

action, a paralyzing fear that there may be no help for it—all of this in a man unaware of the paradoxical complexity of his acts.

In the first scene Lear places his nation and, more important (relative to the subject at hand), himself at the mercy of daughters he apparently fears. We wonder why anyone would do that, especially a king, a man with every opportunity to act arbitrarily, to exercise power, and to escape censure or humiliation. We know that as ordinary people we grow subconsciously adept at manipulating others, at subtly bribing them to do our bidding, to affirm our value; and we do so with shameful frequency. But, whenever possible, we do so without risking the humiliation of public exposure should the gambit fail or the appearance of brazenness should it succeed. Viewed in the light of our ordinary, self-protective fears, what Lear does makes no sense at all. In fact, it seems utterly foolhardy. In the glaring light of the public eye and without the serpent's subtlety he tries to purchase declarations of love, declarations that, in the very giving and receiving, reveal suspicious hints that even the parties involved may not take the transaction seriously. We may well be shocked by this display of obsessive egoism, by the prostituted nature of Lear's solicitation; but we are also shocked—though not for moral reasons—by its brazenness. We are not ordinarily either so desperate or so honest that we will risk making such solicitations openly in public and in the unflattering light of day—at least not consciously. This would be madness. But this is, as we shall see more clearly in a moment, precisely the form of madness we sense in Lear and that sets him apart even as he condemns himself by behaving as the rest of us ordinarily do. Consciously, and yet unknowingly, Lear lives out before his court and us what we, in our blindness, would like to believe is something that can only occur in our nightmares: our foolhardy exposure of self, naked in its weakness and need, before a world ready to mock us. There is, then, something openly absurd and incommensurable in what Lear does in the abdication and love test, but there is also something that in its very absurdity suggests that Lear's vices are anything but ordinary. Ordinary vice, however shameless, is seldom brazen; it is, in fact, most often quite subtle, so subtle that it knows enough to mask its deceitfulness as sincerity. But Lear's behavior here, as we shall see, is the complete opposite of such duplicity, not because it is forthright or even brave but because Lear's apparent disingenuousness both disguises and reveals a pathetic ingenuousness. His brazenness suggests no simple, self-serving egocentricity but a buried sense of vulnerability and shame for himself. Though Lear may appear to be overtly manipulative and vain in act 1, scene 1, there is nothing trivial or mean about his soul. Only excruciating misgivings about himself, not efforts to patronize or demean others, drive him to act as he does. The unacknowledged but nonetheless desperate suffering we sense in him forbids the release of laughter that his childish behavior here and throughout the first acts otherwise invites.

In the anguished need for love that Lear suffers privately in the "silence" of his "tortur'd soul" but exposes publicly in "speech" that "purpose[s] not," he transcends the mean self-protectiveness that has the seeming wisdom of the snail and knows enough to "put's head in" his shell. The distinctiveness of Lear's journey to ruin could not be made clearer than in the juxtaposition of his last speech to his daughters in act 2 before his banishment to the heath and Cornwall's quintessentially "ordinary" reaction to it. The end of act 2 marks a minor structural climax in the play. Lear "will not trouble" these daughters again except in his imagination; the external conditions of his suffering will sink no lower. He began in a full display of regal power by banishing one daughter; now he finds himself stripped of all external tokens of civilized position and respect by daughters he feels have banished him. His last plea to them, the "reason not the need" speech (2.4.264–86), is a pathetic and yet powerfully moving outburst despite the fact that, as we shall see, its wisdom is misconceived. The sympathy the speech's rhetoric inspires has nothing to do, however, with the truth or falsehood of what Lear says. In fact, it is not even bred of what he says but of what he cannot say—his tortured silence. His inability to speak what he will do to avenge his injuries pathetically transforms a once powerful king into an impotent old man stammering his rage.[4] But even more powerful is the silence following his declaration that he will announce his "true need," one that presumably lies beyond superficial material needs. However, about this true need, we discover, Lear can say nothing at all. It is conceivable, of course, that he can say nothing because he suddenly realizes he does not really know what his true spiritual need is. But it could also be that he cannot speak the true need he feels because he cannot, without a cloaking mediation, declare the humiliating desperation of his need for love. In either case, his silence speaks the agony of the incapacitation he is suffering.

Against that incapacitation and his childish attempt to punish his daughters and awaken their pity for him by fleeing, we must place Cornwall's abrupt shift of subject to the wisdom of the snail: "Let us withdraw, 'twill be a storm" (2.4.287). It would obviously be a mistake to deny that Lear's entering the storm is as much a self-protective act, however unconsciously so, as Cornwall and his daughters' conscious withdrawal from the storm within Gloucester's castle; but to rest content with this likeness without discriminating the torments Lear voluntarily undergoes in his misguided but noble quest for love from the petty fears and mean self-regard of his daughters and Cornwall would be an even more serious error. Though Lear repeatedly behaves with petty spitefulness and disproportionately offended rage, we do not feel he is a mean or petty man because we are always intuitively aware that he consistently chooses to remain heroically open to undergoing an ever-widening and deepening experience of agonized crisis in his quest for love. Irving Ribner has rightly claimed that by the end of act 2 Lear could expect sympathy for nothing he has done. But, paradoxically, Harley Granville-Barker, who feels quite differently about Lear as he enters the storm, is equally correct in his more favorable assessment: "All his errors . . . have partaken of nobility; he has scorned policy." The two seemingly contradictory critical verdicts actually complement one another in enriching our sense of the complexity of the man.[5]

Norman Rabkin's observation that the first scenes of *King Lear* establish several fundamental likenesses and thus force the spectators to "make sense of the play" by analyzing the "principles underlying . . . (these) analogies" is a rich, if unexplored intuition.[6] The symbolic analogies generated by the juxtaposition of character, situation, and plot in the three playlets constituting act 1 confirm that Lear's initial behavior is not beyond comprehension or explanation,[7] though it will become clear that the explanation both begins and ends well below the surface manifestations of Lear's whims and vices. Given Shakespeare's virtual silence about the political considerations and motivations that dominate his source and his seeming dissociation of the love test from the political arena, the most helpful clue for resolving our bewilderment about Lear may lie buried in the extent of the parallel between the two old fathers who so radically mistake their children. Gloucester's conversations with Kent and, later, with Edmund do, after all, serve to frame Lear's initial appearance on stage. Moreover, the second scene is obviously written to invite comparison between Gloucester and Lear's folly. Edmund's response to Gloucester's first speech to him is Cordelia's "nothing," and Gloucester's immediate rage at innocent Edgar baldly mimics Lear's sudden cursing of Cordelia.

Gloucester enters in the second scene of act 1 registering his shocked alarm at the king's erratic behavior in the opening scene. If there had been any doubts in the audience's mind about whether Lear had acted mistakenly or not there, Goneril and Regan's frank remarks at its conclusion about his "poor judgment" (1.1.291) dispelled them. Consequently, as soon as Gloucester laments

> Kent banish'd thus? and France in choler parted?
> And the King gone to-night? Prescrib'd his pow'r,
> Confin'd to exhibition? All this done
> Upon the gad?
>
> (1.2.23–26)

our first reaction is to suppose that here is a man of some good sense and moral sensitivity. Though he is openly anxious (whereas Lear had initially appeared calm before his court), the favorable first impression Gloucester makes is not unlike the one Lear made on us by virtue of his seemingly egalitarian division of the kingdom and care to avoid the appearance of favoritism in his opening speeches. But there is a false note, however, in Gloucester's surprised lament. He is fearful that the king's most faithful counselor has been exiled, that a foreign king has left Britain angered, that the king has suddenly given over power to live in dependent status; but he has nothing to say about the central moral issue—the sin against Cordelia. That it is undoubtedly but an oversight does not make it any the less revealing. All the issues Gloucester remarks upon in consternation concern the king's imprudent exposure of himself to the vulnerability to attack, as if Lear's exposing himself was what was shocking and disturbing to him. The king and Gloucester, as one of the king's chief supporters, are both now imprudently endangered and exposed. Wisdom bids fear.

However, we have no reason to believe that Gloucester is afraid for Cordelia or even chagrined about the offense against her. But then, only fathers, not children, have ever been at the center of Gloucester's reckonings, at least if we take his earlier remark to Kent about Edgar as truthful: "But I have a son, sir, by order of law, some year elder than this, who yet is no dearer in my account" (1.1.19–21). If Gloucester's claim is for the impartiality of his love for his sons, it is impartiality toward strangers, more indifference than virtue. A bit later he unaccountably fails to recognize his own son Edgar's handwriting; and as for Edmund, he "hath been out nine years, and away he shall again" (1.1.32–33). What is more, for the short while we see Gloucester with Edmund initially, the father thinks nothing of making a series of lewd jests at his son's expense.

When banishing Cordelia, Lear speaks of her as "a stranger to my heart and me/ . . . from this for ever" (1.1.115–16). That statement not only speaks the truth about the past and future of his relationship to his daughter with profound dramatic irony, but it also identifies the essence of Gloucester's relationship to his sons. Only with a stranger could one's distrustful fears be so overwhelming that one would cry villain and ultimately try to execute without trial (as Gloucester would Edgar) instead of "suspend[ing] your indignation . . . till you can derive from him better testimony of his intent" (1.2.80–82) than a rumored threat upon one's life. Edmund can probe so penetratingly into the wound of Gloucester's subconscious fear that his sons do not love him because the bastard knows so intimately the distant nature of his father's relationship to his sons. When he falsely attributes to Edgar the declaration of an "idle and fond bondage in the oppression of aged tyranny, who sways, not as it hath power, but as it is suffer'd" (1.2.49–51), he is not merely inventing a falsehood. Edgar has not made the statement, but it is true in the sense that it accurately describes the only seemingly "normal" dramatic interaction between Gloucester and Edmund that we have seen. Gloucester's "idle and fond" treatment of Edmund before Kent does, in fact, sway only "as it is suffer'd."

If that one moment can be taken as a paradigm, it is a profound indictment of Gloucester's fatherhood. When Kent asks, "Is not this your son, my lord?" Gloucester cannot simply and straightforwardly acknowledge Edmund. Instead he calls distracting attention to himself with a jest, a smug admission that he is guilty as charged.

> His breeding, sir, hath been at my charge.
> I have so often blush'd to acknowledge him, that now
> I am braz'd to 't.
>
> (1.1.9–11)

"The quality of nothing hath not such need to hide itself." His speech confirms that Gloucester's sin is not an isolated, fondly remembered act of lust but a brazenly dissolute attitude of being that dogs his every step and reenacts its shame again in this pretense of shamelessness. Gloucester treats his son shamelessly here, as if Edmund were not there before him absorbing the brutality of his "fondness" for him. Knowing little else but this callous, self-absorbed insensitivity, Edmund has found it easy to harden into shamelessness himself, the shamelessness of his outrage. When Gloucester claims—even if with conscious honesty—that the habit of admitting his paternity has inured him to his shame over the sin of Edmund's conception, we are tempted to quote the Fool to him.

> The man that makes his toe
>   What he his heart should make,
> Shall of a corn cry woe,
>   And turn his sleep to wake.
>
> (3.2.31–34)

It is indeed true that Gloucester has become "braz'd" to the necessity of acknowledging Edmund; but far from being the positive development beyond the need for shame he would like to think it is, the very declaration unwittingly reveals him flaunting shameful unconcern for his son.

To have chosen the alternative he has rejected—to have made his heart rather than his toe his instrument of feeling—would have meant acknowledging Edmund as son, not merely "whoreson" and "knave."[8] When he admits to Kent that Edmund's "breeding, sir, hath been at my charge," he does not realize that he is transforming his shame into a pastime. His jesting may cloak his shame for himself from himself and even from Kent well enough, but it also nakedly exposes his most serious crime to us. If Gloucester could hear himself properly he would be mortified to realize that his easy bravado in acknowledging the sinful "charge" of the bastard's idle and fond conception unknowingly flees its weightier "charge"— Gloucester's responsibility as a parent to make of Edmund's "breeding" a fully human affair by laboring to harmonize his natural affection for the boy with all the arts and graces of civilization in order to deliver a well-bred and gentle man, not a maimed and outraged cripple, to his adulthood. Of that responsibility he has been criminally negligent. Gloucester's self-indulgent failure to assume the burden of fatherhood reveals that his life has been ordinary until now, an unburdened crawl toward death, in which the shame originally attached to his own sinfulness has been conveniently transferred to Edmund and, with him, pushed out of sight. Having known the occasional twinges of anxiety we soon bury, wondering when the piper will be paid for our self-absorbed living and our failures to act upon our good intentions, we can appreciate the menace lurking in Gloucester's unknowing prophecy that the "whoreson must be acknowledg'd" (1.1.24). The latent irony in this statement extends even beyond the fact that the name of bastard will necessarily give way in Gloucester's reckoning to the unmasking of a more substantive bastardy in Edmund. The most dreadful sense in which it is fair to say that Gloucester does not know what he is saying is that he should come to acknowledge (though, in fact, he never does so) that Edmund has become a bastard in the moral sense of that word largely because Gloucester has been one in that same sense all along. Like Lear with Goneril and Regan, Gloucester never fully confronts the fact that the Edmund he has helped to create is in a very real sense a projection of his shame for himself: a "disease that's in my flesh," which, though he should, he never does "call mine" (2.4.222–23).

The similarities between the two fathers so unknowingly estranged from their children that they do not recognize them and, so, banish their better parts "upon the gad" are too extensive to be insignificant. The crucial likeness, however, the one that informs and unites these other parallels into a meaning that begins to clarify Lear's enigmatic behavior remains to be discussed. Stanley Cavell's intuition about Gloucester's initial jest has even greater relevance to Lear's more formal address to

the court: "Joking is a familiar specific for brazening out
shame, calling attention to the thing you do not want naturally
noticed."[9] In Lear's first speech to the court announcing both
the abdication and the love test there appear to be a series of
self-conscious attempts at humor and jest, though in some instances the levity is difficult to prove with any conclusiveness
because it is so much a matter of inflection and delivery rather
than any inevitable contextual sense of the lines. Perhaps the
most difficult and debatable instance is Lear's expression of his
hope that "future strife/May be prevented now" (1.1.44–45). If
this remark is delivered unleavened by cajolery or a coaxing,
somewhat whimsical half-seriousness, it clearly risks direct insult to his daughters and their husbands as a bald expression of
the king's distrust. Nothing forbids the possibility of such di-
rectness, of course, or even of a righteously severe royal warning; but several related considerations would seem to make a
severity of tone less likely. Were Lear to be severe or even
merely serious here, his tone would depart jarringly and without warning from the obviously warmhearted and openly affectionate manner immediately preceding and following these
words. Lear has just finished a familiar address to Cornwall as
his "son" and to Albany as "our no less loving son" (1.1.41–42);
and he also seems eager to present the division of the kingdom
in a benign context of paternal largesse ("our daughters' several dowers") in which his only hesitation or mock-hesitation is,
as we soon discover, to whom shall be given his "largest bounty"
(1.1.52). Moreover, the remarks that follow regarding France
and Burgundy's "long . . . amorous sojourn" (1.1.47) at his
court clearly bespeak a tone of high-spirited bemusement in the
king. If we take Lear's hope that "future strife/May be prevented now" with complete seriousness, it also becomes difficult
to reconcile that admonitory charge against conflict with his
hope to resolve the possibility of future tensions with the present strife of his daughters, even if Lear might only be speaking
of "challenge" metaphorically. It would seem at least possible as
an alternative that both the remark about "future strife" and
the present "challenge" are complementary parts of a jest Lear
makes in order to brazen out his anxieties. Perhaps Lear is
aware that the possibility of future strife cannot truly be "ruled
out" of existence by his last royal edict in the present, that if
anyone conceives of dominion over the others that person

could give birth to strife. But perhaps he may feel pacified by speaking lightly of it, as if by making a symbolic mock conflict "now" in the love challenge he can treat the very real possibility of future conflict as something ridiculously remote and unnecessary since each daughter will have already contested for her fair share.

Fortunately, the two more crucial instances of Lear's jesting—one a remark about his abdication, the other about the love test—are not nearly so questionable in tone. Each definitely, if subtly, reveals Lear as at least marginally aware and embarrassed about the absurd figure he may be cutting; and each reveals a man, like Gloucester, who tries to pretend he is not ashamed in order to put both himself and others off his track. Lear's unacknowledged shame, unlike Gloucester's shame regarding Edmund, is not related to any sense of wrongdoing, however; it is, instead, a shame at his need for love and, beyond that, a shame for himself that makes him feel undeserving of the love he feels compelled to seek. In the absence of any evidence for a true spiritual turn to the contemplative life or any indication of aged debilitation, given his later spirited pranks, Lear's remark about an "unburthen'd crawl toward death" (1.1.41) urges us, with Lear's implicit approval, to skepticism. Lear uses the phrase as a daring bluff, a jest meant to fool everyone by fooling no one. If the statement results in his hearers making light of what he says—taking his jest in jest, refusing to concur in his confession of imminent weakness and incapacity, and protesting the opposite—Lear would not, of course, be displeased. But neither would he be anything but superficially annoyed were the statement greeted merely as a self-indulgent pretense of weakness from a still vigorous and capable old man cajoling special treatment from his subjects— as long as those same subjects tolerated his bidding. What he could not abide is that the others or he suspect that he is telling the truth. His jest is a pretense made to convince others and himself that he has faced and accepted what in fact he feels is too dreadful and shaming for speech: his abject status, the wormlike crawl he is making toward death, and his need for support and expressions of love.[10] Though he never can admit to himself that this is his condition, he imagines himself "the basest beggar in poorest thing superfluous" who nonetheless feels compelled by his needs to seek alms and loving tribute for his nothing. Lear jests about himself, the part of himself he is most ashamed of and most fears, so that he will not have to take its reality seriously.

A similarly unconscious masquerade informs Lear's remark about the love auction a bit later:

> (Since now we will divest us both of rule,
> Interest of territory, cares of state),
> Which of you shall we say doth love us most?
>
> (1.1.49–51)

The last line is a curious circumlocution. It awkwardly, but completely, omits any reference whatever to the demand that he is imposing on his daughters, avoids any direct indication, in fact, that he is now requesting that they outdo one another in speaking the extent of their love for him. Instead, his words glide past all that to construe his role as that of the noble and impartial judge who resolves disputes equitably after they have occurred. What he avoids saying or cannot bring himself to say is some indication of the embarrassment and hidden shame Lear feels at himself. The circumlocution thus helps him ignore what he considers his shameful need for love. Moreover, if we shift the emphasis of the sense and delivery of the final line from the imperial "we" to the word "say," we uncover what may be an even more intolerable embarrassment in Lear. Certainly Lear would not mean to imply by the words "we *say*" any openly cynical distrust of his daughters' honesty; but he might suddenly feel compelled to make light of the whole contest at the last minute out of sheer embarrassment at what he is doing now that he is actually doing it. By jesting at himself, lamely insinuating that the whole thing is a joke they may share together, he sanctions speech that purposes not. Only then—when they need not really believe what they say any more than will he necessarily—can Lear find the psychological wherewithal to continue the artifice. Needing their love so desperately he will bribe for it, he cannot bear to face the fact that he is at their mercy begging them; so he sanctions words that are idle and swallows without comment fulsome praise so hyperbolic it contradicts itself in the telling when Goneril declares that she loves him "more than [words] can wield the matter" (1.1.55), with a love that makes "speech unable" (1.1.60), and Regan suggests that Goneril's words only "name my very deed of love" (1.1.71).

Both Gloucester and Lear then are alike in that we first see each of them openly admitting improprieties involving the prostitution of the love relationship (Gloucester's lust for Edmund's mother; Lear's buying his daughters' declarations of love) in order like brazen beggars to enforce charity for themselves (Gloucester from Kent; Lear from his distrusted daughters). To us, their jesting reveals the truth of their shame; but because they prefer to avoid their shame rather than accept it, they merely trifle with the truth. The apparent openness with which they speak about intimate matters is but a "presented nakedness" (2.3.11), a self-deceiving cloak that hides their abiding shame at themselves from themselves.[11]

The estrangement Lear reveals to us is complete. "He hath ever but slenderly known himself" (1.1.293–94), and, indeed, perhaps as a direct consequence, he has ever but slenderly known his children. By merely doting upon the daughter whose love has innocently fostered whatever well-being he feels, a self-absorbed Lear has for so long neglected his daughters' emotional needs and his paternal responsibility to lead them out of themselves that now Goneril and Regan's distrust of him has matured into a familial likeness of his estranged fear of them. If he, in advance of anticipated difficulties, demands from them a contractual assent to their obligation to deliver services for which he will pay in advance, then Goneril, too, can make special arrangements to "take away the harms I fear" (1.4.329). If, in effect, Lear makes fools of his daughters by asking them to compete over their portions of the kingdom when the division has already been made, he should not be so shocked and outraged to find that Goneril has been speaking with him to purpose not about her request to reduce his train when she has already dismissed "fifty of my followers at a clap" (1.4.294). And when, following Lear's threat to "resume the shape which thou dost think/I have cast off for ever" (1.4.309–10), we hear a smugly vindicated Goneril tell Albany, "What he hath utter'd I have writ my sister" (1.4.331), we also recognize her as her father's daughter, hoping that by acting in advance of anticipated difficulties "future strife/May be prevented now" (1.1.44–45). Finally, in the absence of pressing political demands arguing the need for abdication, Lear's resignation of kingship implies an alienation from his public identity as well. His speech and actions in act 1, scene 1, suggest that he has not lived his reign as a sacred bond of devoted service to his people but as a superficial burden of "cares and business" that have kept him occupied and distracted while his hidden self has stood aloof from the performance of his duties, no matter how conscientiously he may have performed them.

The most explicit intimations of Lear's buried sense of himself and his superfluous condition reveal themselves indirectly in his own words to Regan and then to Goneril and Regan in the scene just previous to his exit into the storm. In a theatrical gesture before Regan, as he kneels in mock penitence to an absent Goneril, Lear makes a very real if unspoken plea not to be humiliated by Regan in the way he feels he has been humiliated by Goneril. Although protected by the cover of his mocking pretense and the ulterior motive in this "unsightly trick," Lear nonetheless confesses to us as to his daughter Regan his secret sense of his true condition.

> "I confess that I am old; [*Kneeling.*]
> Age is unnecessary. On my knees I beg
> That you'll vouchsafe me raiment, bed, and food."
>
> (2.4.154–56).

The same despairing sense of his own helpless contingency is symbolically suggested again later when Lear, the beggar-king, speaking of "basest beggars" as if there could be no human creatures further from his royal station, dismisses their needs with contempt.

> O, reason not the need! our basest beggars
> Are in the poorest thing superfluous.
> Allow not nature more than nature needs,
> Man's life is cheap as beast's.
>
> (2.4.264–67)

Despite the *a fortiori* appeal Lear makes here for better treatment than basest beggars receive or deserve, his argument is not as self-evidently compelling as he would like to think it is. Lear counts on impressing his daughters with a clear sense of the distinction between his majesty and the abject lowliness of beggars, but the sense of his own words indicates he is dimly aware that there is no intrinsic or logically necessary difference between king and beggar. Lear's peremptory claim for special treatment subtly exposes his suppressed awareness of identity with the most contemptible beings. Moreover, when we realize what Lear does not—the "basest" beggars are not the ragged, maimed, and helpless creatures whose very appearance makes us ashamed of our not helping them, but those idle men who, like Lear before Goneril and Regan, though capable of giving succor instead demand it from those less capable of giving it— we also realize it is not poverty or even nature but not listening to shame itself that makes life "cheap as beast's."

If there were any question that Shakespeare wishes us to ponder the oxymoron of king as basest beggar, it is resolved by the symbolic import of Lear's disgust with the lackey, Oswald. When Oswald irreverently remarks to Lear that he is "my lady's father" (1.4.79), Lear flies into a rage, striking him and calling him "slave" and "cur" (1.4.81). Then, later, when he realizes that Oswald's earlier arrival may have soured his welcome at Regan's and then Gloucester's, he claims that his disgust with "this detested groom" (2.4.217) is exceeded only by his hatred for Goneril. He cannot stand to look at the self-important valet:

> This is a slave whose easy-borrowed pride
> Dwells in the [fickle] grace of her he follows.
> Out, varlet, from my sight!
>
> (2.4.185–87)

One can understand why Oswald inspires disgust. He is as despicable as Kent's litany of abuse indicates: he is a "brazen-fac'd varlet," a "superserviceable, finical rogue," a "bawd in way of good service" (2.2.18–20). But such abuse is only fair to the "codpiece" half of his story. Like the rest of us, Oswald has his "grace" too. His devotion to Goneril mitigates the hatefulness of his very real vices, just as the same virtue mitigates the same vices in his self-righteous accuser, Kent.

It is true that Oswald behaves shamefully in his first meeting with Lear. Yet Shakespeare symbolically hints at the residual "grace" Oswald will later manifest when he refuses to betray Goneril's trust to Regan. In the first section of act 1, scene 4 (111–94), Shakespeare has designed a curious parody of the initial love test. It is curious especially because, against the grain of our expectations, he has cast Kent in Goneril and Regan's role as flatterer and Oswald in Cordelia's role as truthteller. Shakespeare's calling up Cordelia's likeness in Oswald's reply to Lear seems a puzzling generosity to Oswald, even if we acknowledge that his and Cordelia's motives in truthtelling differ radically. But let us return to that later. For the moment, let us examine the relevant segment of dialogue depicting a still-soliciting Lear and Kent as a flatterer.

> LEAR: Dost thou know me, fellow?
> KENT: No, sir, but you have that in your countenance
>   which I would fain call master.
> LEAR: What's that?
> KENT: Authority.
>
> (1.4.26–30)

Here, as earlier, Lear openly seeks a public recognition of his worth; and when he receives in reply a speech that flatters his sense of himself, even if it clearly seems to strain credulity, he rewards it with an indifferent and therefore nearly insulting approval not very different from the silence with which he had paid Goneril and Regan. "Follow me, thou shalt serve me. If I like thee no worse after dinner, I will not part from thee yet. Dinner, ho, dinner!" (1.4.40–42). But when Oswald replies without flattery to the same sort of question—"Who am I, sir?" (1.4.78)—a question whose tone commands reverence or at least the appearance of it, he is cursed and banished like Cordelia. By identifying the king with insulting carelessness as "my lady's father" (1.4.79) Oswald confirms for Lear what the rogue's first refusal to acknowledge Lear's call had indicated: a valet feels he can insult a king with impunity, can speak of the king as if he were nothing. In his fury Lear is no more capable of responding consciously to the reverberations Oswald's statement carry any more than he was able in his rage to bring to consciousness the hidden depths of Cordelia's "nothing."

But having called up the image of Cordelia in Oswald's reply to Lear, Shakespeare surprises us yet again. Once Oswald has unknowingly delivered his oracle, the symbolic parallel to Cordelia breaks down. Shakespeare is not, however, finished with correspondences. After Oswald has been cursed and attacked for truth telling, he does not react in the way Cordelia had but, surprisingly enough, in exactly the way Lear reacts to his daughters whenever they slight his dignity—with self-righteous but impotent protest: "I'll not be strucken, my lord" (1.4.85). Oswald's pleas of protest, like Lear's before Goneril and Regan, only serve to produce more severe humiliations and then flight. It is little wonder, therefore, that Lear cannot bear the sight of Oswald: to look at Oswald would force him to see himself in the "slave whose easy-borrowed pride lives in the fickle grace of her he follows." As Lear moves from daughter to daughter, his shame wears its easily borrowed pride only so long as the daughters he depends upon are willing in their fickle turns to grant it.

Were Lear truly to recognize his identity with Oswald as the basest sort of beggar, the ultimate effect would mean, as one might suspect, a fall into the depths of despair; but that very process could also lead to healing. To suggest how, we must reconsider Shakespeare's seemingly arbitrary, if glancing, reminiscence of Cordelia in Oswald's part in the parody of the love test. When Oswald calls Lear "my lady's father," Lear takes his remark merely as an unforgiveable insult. It is certainly true that Oswald's speech is meant to insult Lear and that the valet does not love the king. But if Lear could "stand for" Oswald lovingly enough to come to understand him more fully, he would realize that Oswald is, nonetheless, genuinely devoted to Goneril. The basest beggar is capable of love. Consequently, his calling Lear "my lady's father" could never be merely an insult. In a symbolic sense at least, it is a gesture of praise or tribute: the old king is not a vile nobody, but the father of Oswald's beloved queen. The only virtuous transcendence of shame begins with its acceptance. It is a curious paradox that as long as we attempt to flee shame in order to maintain the pretense of our own purity and virtue we can never overcome our self-absorption. But if, in despair, we admit our shame we may also begin to transcend it because we will have given up the lonely exile of the fugitive's flight from his crime and, consequently, will be permitted to enter a community in which reciprocity and love are possible.

If we try to write a synopsis of the first two acts of *King Lear* in order to integrate the scattered observations we have been making about various scenes in this chapter and the last, we could say that acts 1 and 2 are a series of mirroring encounters between Lear and other characters punctuated only by scenes in the subplot involving Gloucester with Edmund and Edgar in soliloquy.[12] Even these scenes from the subplot do not, however, finally divert us from our ever-deepening and more certain sense of Lear in hiding. They, too, like the mirroring encounters, ultimately serve by means of symbolic correspondences to intimate depths beyond the surface of Lear's acts. The juxtaposition of Gloucester and Lear jesting to brazen out their shame and enforce charity prefaces Lear's oracular encounters with Cordelia and Oswald. Then the Fool lovingly confronts Lear with a sweet and bitter image of himself before Lear flees that door to freedom only to rage, like a caged bird, at his own image in the person of Goneril while Albany's repeated offers of mediation go unheard. Edgar's "disguise" soliloquy also emblematically defines the nature of Lear's self-disguise in exile. And, finally, when Lear unknowingly beholds the mirroring humiliation of Kent stocked, we see in small what awaits him before his daughters in the final scene of act 2.

Such a synopsis suggests the bifurcated effect of the play to this point. The difference between the overtly dramatic and the more obscure symbolic effects of the encounters and juxtapositions in these two acts is so marked that it seems as if we are speaking of two different plays simultaneously. Were it not for the more important and serious drama we sense silently developing below the surface, the literal drama would legitimately prove Lear a character unable to sustain sympathy and concern. For in it Lear plays an arrogant, self-important, willfully impatient and resentful part in a ludicrous series of follies and comeuppances until, by the end of act 2, what Cornwall says of Kent's humiliation can appropriately describe Lear as well: "His own disorders/Deserv'd much less advancement" (2.4.199–200).[13] Lear strikes us as more than the sum of his disorders, however, because we sense that he is also the protagonist in the tragic dumb show we have just summarized.[14] The "external [manners] of laments" nearly alienating us from Lear never fully mask from us the strangling shame that "swells with silence in [his] tortur'd soul." Not the security and distance that laughter provides, but only compassion and dread can comprehend the drama of silence enacted on the symbolic plane of Lear's otherwise ludicrous encounters with others (even those we have yet to discuss: one involving Edgar in act 3, the other, Gloucester in act 4). Our compassion for Lear as a figure of tragic stature grows despite the foolish willfulness with which he may behave at any particular moment. At one point, for example, because he is outraged that half his train has been dismissed, Lear threatens to reascend the throne. The threat may seem more foolish than terrible, but in the final analysis that does not undermine a certain tragic grandeur in the man. We know there is little likelihood that Lear will attempt to make good on his threat to "take't again perforce" (1.5.40) from Goneril, but not because Lear is afraid of the attempt or because he does not, realistically speaking, have the power to do so. Lear shows no fear in facing the storm or attacking Cordelia's hangman. Moreover, if he really desired to, Lear could very likely rally enough support in his kingdom to mount a realistic challenge, especially given the way Goneril has repaid his apparent generosity. We sense, rather, that actual violence upon his daughters is unlikely because we know that no matter how imperiously and manipulatively Lear may act, his is not a rage for domination but a rage for acceptance. And because we are at least intuitively aware that beneath Lear's brittle facade of dignity confirmed or denied lies a nearly unthinkable and certainly unspeakable void, we must take these pleas for acceptance with a seriousness they do not seem to warrant, since in repeatedly making them he can tolerate no slight to his superficial but desperately maintained sense of self-esteem.

If recognizing these hidden needs and avoidances arouses pity in us, the way Lear responds to the frustration of his need for acceptance awakens fear at his titanic agony. Like Oedipus, that other great stranger to himself and his people, once Lear's tenuously maintained self-respect has been jeopardized, he, too, commits himself with extraordinary determination to a quest to discover the reality and meaning of his condition, no matter how degrading and convulsive that condition may be for him or what suffering it may demand. Though every action Lear performs reveals him foolishly demanding that his daughters and then the heavens honor and express love for him on his terms, his folly does not efface the terrible strength with which he greets the repeated refusals of daughters and gods to satisfy him. With an ever-broadening and deepening comprehension of his insecure position in the world, he chooses to keep before himself, without mitigation or trivial distraction, what he understands to be the misery he suffers—the deprivation of love. He shuns nothing that threatens to deepen this sense and experience of his or man's condition. He would, in fact, rather "abjure all roofs" than stop attempting to make sense of his experience or passively accept and live on someone else's trivialized terms.

Perhaps the clearest indication of the unrelenting nature of this quest can be seen if we contrast Lear's attitude toward and experience of suffering with Gloucester's after his blinding.[15] In most ways, Gloucester acts as Lear's double, even to the extent

that, like the king, he radically mistakes the source and meaning of his misery, though suffering greatly. But when we compare their fates, Gloucester shows himself the king's foil—
playing a suicidal Jocasta to Lear's Oedipus. If we consider the
reversals that repeatedly humiliate the blind earl's desires, first
to redeem his "abused" life by asserting a commanding dignity
in death and then, when his suicide attempt misfires, his hope
for his own murder or madness as a delivery from the insulting
consciousness of his own fallibilities and degradation, we come
to realize that Edgar is not the only member of his family who
"must play fool to sorrow/Ang'ring itself and others" (4.1.38–
39).[16]

Amplifying too much in the consistently contradictory and
therefore essentially ironic sequence of "philosophical" remarks he suddenly begins making to a disguised Edgar now
leading him, blind Gloucester also "tops [the] extremity" of the
sorrow he has already suffered. Based on the things Gloucester
says and does after his mutilation by Cornwall, it would certainly be difficult to defend a claim for any significant growth in
his understanding of himself and his condition. Indeed, in his
last major speech in which he expresses his envy of the distracted king and, thus, a curious self-pity (given the grotesque
condition of the king he and we have just witnessed), Gloucester seems anything but wise.

> The King is mad; how stiff is my vild sense
> That I stand up, and have ingenious feeling
> Of my huge sorrows! Better I were distract,
> So should my thoughts be sever'd from my griefs,
> And woes by wrong imaginations lose
> The knowledge of themselves.
>
> (4.6.279–84)

Gloucester's unconscious method here—deflecting attention
from the king's greater grief to evoke sympathy for his own
lesser one—is not significantly different from that in his previous encounter with a distracted Lear before his blinding.
There, we recall, a Gloucester similarly absorbed in his own
grief had begged Caius for sympathy while the king raved:

> Thou sayest the King grows mad, I'll tell thee, friend,
> I am almost mad myself. I had a son,
> Now outlaw'd from my blood; he sought my life,

But lately, very late. I lov'd him, friend,
No father his son dearer; true to tell thee,
The grief hath craz'd my wits.

                              (3.4.165–70)

Clearly we should not minimize the heroism in Gloucester's
decision to risk himself to aid the king in act 3, nor his very real
and unselfish expression of sympathy for the king in their encounter in act 4, especially since by then Gloucester has found
torture his only reward for his troubled efforts to help Lear.
Nor should we underestimate or patronize the mental torments
urging Gloucester to make the kind of remarks quoted. But
these considerations do not finally prevent Gloucester's calling
attention to himself before Caius and Lear in act 3 from striking us in context as somewhat melodramatic and less than
generous. Nor does his earlier generosity diminish the foolish
and self-pitying delusion of this speech in act 4. Gloucester is
surely no worse off now than the raving king is. In fact, the
dramatic irony in his words reveals he is more like the distracted king than a man too sane for his own good. Even after
his blinding, Gloucester's "thoughts" remain "severed from
[his] griefs," his woes proving a distraction in which they "lose/
The knowledge of themselves" by "wrong imaginations." As in
Lear's case, his "grief lies all within"; and his philosophical
curses and prayers to the gods—"these external [manners] of
laments"—are merely "shadows to the unseen grief" in himself
he still has not fathomed. Even blind, he is so ashamed of his
shameful acts that he flees from an acknowledgment of their
shamefulness. Because he cannot, like Cordelia, "become" his
sorrow, he only compounds it. In the face of his humiliation—
the shame at having mistaken his sons and the vulnerability his
mutilation keeps before him constantly—Gloucester imagines
he can yet see his dignified way clear to victory. To shield himself from his own misery, he holds to a fanciful and delusive
hope (as against true and generous hope), speciously imagining
he can triumph over the vulnerability he suffers and the catastrophic mistake he has so clearly made. These are the "wrong
imaginations" that forbid knowledge of himself and his true
grief. Whether wrongly fancying he possesses the unhindered
imperial power to execute himself with a dignity and impunity
his life has not provided him (and thus tyrannize over heaven's
tyrannical will), or wrongly calling for murder or madness to

hasten his abdication from the community of man and the hidden reality of his shame, Gloucester persists in trying to "enforce [the] charity" of oblivion for himself rather than accepting charity for himself and giving it to others.

This last contrast between giving and enforcing charity is the burden of the irony in Gloucester's foolish lament about his remaining sane. Regretting the sensitive capacity of "ingenious feeling" clearly undermines any positive metaphorical sense in which we may have been tempted to take Gloucester's earlier remarks about how the "lust-dieted man . . . will not see/ Because he does not feel" (4.1.67–69) and how he himself now "see[s] . . . feelingly" the way the world goes (4.6.149). For here, presumably at the end of his spiritual journey, Gloucester openly condemns any value in feeling. Distraught by his agony and filled with self-contempt, the blind earl's "other senses" do indeed "grow imperfect/By [his] eyes' anguish" (4.6.5–6). No more precious to him now that he is blind, he condemns them as "vild," ironically concurring in this assessment with Cornwall's horrifying contempt for his eyes as "vild jelly" (3.7.83). The most profound irony in Gloucester's words, however, is the truth that he unknowingly speaks: "The King is mad. How stiff is my vild sense,/That I stand up and have ingenious feeling/Of my huge sorrow!" (4.6.279–81) Gloucester "stiff(ly)," that is, stubbornly sins against generous love for the king in his own self-regarding grief. Love is not love that "stands up" for itself to stand aloof from the entire point. He could yield and bow to active care for Lear and himself, not envy the king his madness in contempt for his own suffering, just as he could have sought reparation and atonement rather than suicide after the blinding.

In Gloucester unacknowledged shame itself speaks for the instant remedy of death, not to secure atonement with the community but as a secure abdication from it. Initially it might appear that his remarks to the old man guiding him, his gift of his purse to Poor Tom, and his speech about distribution undoing excess imply a significant new generosity of spirit in the earl; but that first impression will not bear scrutiny. Gloucester may feel that banishing the old man from his sight is a generous gesture made for the servant's own good ("Thy comforts can do me no good at all;/Thee they may hurt" [4.1.16–17]; "Do as I bid thee, or rather do thy pleasure;/Above the rest, be gone" [4.1.47–48], but the tone of his dismissal, imperious and subtly

insulting, hints just the opposite—that the banishment is really
for Gloucester's wrongly imagined benefit, not his servant's. In
the first place, despairing insistences condemn his servant to
impotence by forbidding him the moral dignity of his choice in
the matter. Banishing his servant to stand apart allows Gloucester, even in despair, to nurse the pretense of his own power.
Alone but for a madman, he can subtly anesthetize his painful
shame before others—his sense that he is utterly at their mercy,
weak, vulnerable, and, despite his protestations to the contrary
(4.1.77–78), desperately in need of someone to lead him who
can discern his state better than he himself does.

When Gloucester blindly claims, "I have no way, and therefore want no eyes;/I stumbled when I saw", (4.1.18–19), we
realize that even his despair is a defense against his experience
of fallibility and weakness. He does "want eyes" because, as
Shakespeare's symbolic staging of his suicide attempt confirms,
"our mere defects" are no "commodity" in that sense. Blindness
will not protect us from blindness.[17] Edgar's ruse proves
Gloucester can "stumble" when he is blind as well. As for his
speech about "distribution"—

> Here, take this purse, thou whom the heav'ns' plagues
> Have humbled to all strokes. That I am wretched
> Makes thee the happier; heavens, deal so still!
> Let the superfluous and lust-dieted man,
> That slaves your ordinance, that will not see
> Because he does not feel, feel your pow'r quickly;
> So distribution should undo excess,
> And each man have enough.
>
> (4.1.64–71)

—the obvious irony bred of the fact that Edgar is the man
whom Gloucester's first two declarations wrongly describe
should awaken suspicion about the remainder. What Gloucester does not realize in beseeching the gods to punish on is that
he is only calling further punishment on himself and those
close to him. The difference between the "lust-dieted" man and
the loving one is the difference between willful self-gratification
and real generosity. His attempted suicide is no generosity to
himself or to others but a willful "excess," a superfluous misery
conceived to gratify his self-contempt. When Gloucester is
dead, or even when all the "lust-dieted" men suffer as he has
suffered, each man will not have enough. That kind of distribu-

tion is not pastoral's sharing of the good and goods in common joy; it is torture that tops the extremity of woe.

The way in which Gloucester greets his failed suicide attempt—

> Is wretchedness depriv'd that benefit,
> To end itself by death? 'Twas yet some comfort,
> When misery could beguile the tyrant's rage,
> And frustrate his proud will.
>
> (4.6.61–64)

—gives the lie to his pretense of patience and renunciation in the suicide prayer made moments earlier.

> O you mighty gods!
> This world I do renounce, and in your sights
> Shake patiently my great affliction off.
> If I could bear it longer, and not fall
> To quarrel with your great opposeless wills,
> My snuff and loathed part of nature should
> Burn itself out.
>
> (4.6.34–40)

It is no accident that the latter quotation should so remind us of Lear's abdication speech, his decision to "shake all cares . . . from our age," renounce the world, and crawl toward death. Each, pretending dignity, holds himself in contempt. Except for his genuine belief that his is but the "snuff and loathed part of nature," all other claims Gloucester makes here are merely a bewildered pretense.[18] Contrary to his claim, and though suffering mercilessly, there is no question of whether or not he can "bear it longer," but only whether his stiff, unwavering refusal to live since his blinding can imply anything but that he has not been able to bear it at all. Even later, in a seemingly more resigned mood, Gloucester reveals he has never fully internalized his suffering and, in loving pity, learned to tolerate it.

> Henceforth I'll bear
> Affliction till it do cry out itself
> "Enough, enough," and die.
>
> (4.6.75–77)

This is not patience, but an unyieldingly painful confrontation with his own misery in which he will wrestle his way to victory even as he dies, just as previously in his suicide attempt he continued to "quarrel" with gods he did not truly believe "opposeless" at all since he felt that he could "beguile the tyrant's rage/And frustrate his proud will."

The true penitent's renunciation would involve sacrificing something he has wrongly loved; Gloucester only wishes to crush his "snuff and loathed" life to spite his blind eyes. The failure of the attempt does not give him a discerning pause. It is true that he comes to realize he was living in illusion when, first blinded and immediately thereafter, he found life "all dark and comfortless" (3.7.85). Now, he recognizes " 'twas yet some comfort,/When misery could beguile the tyrant's rage,/And frustrate his proud will." (4.6.62–64) Not being the worst stands in some rank of praise to be longed for. The unknowing irony in his words, however, shows that Gloucester is taking paltry comfort from the presumption he will have none. Gloucester intends to speak of the "tyrant's rage" and "proud will" of the gods, but his is the more demonstrably tyrannical and unyielding will at work in the play. His miseries once held "some comfort"; but even after the failure of his suicide has again "frustrated" his "proud will," the resulting misery seduces him into the lonely and vain comfort of this new form of despair. His failure has at least temporarily beguiled his tyrannical rage, but it has not "fooled" him enough to put him at his or pastoral's ease in bearing's fellowship. Without generosity toward himself or another, and thinking himself the "worst and most dejected thing of fortune," he cannot yet, like Cordelia and the Fool, take ease's comfort, "Stand still in esperance," and, like them, "return to laughter."

Lear may ultimately suffer no more wisely than Gloucester does, but he does so much more grandly and terribly as we shall see. If, in the final analysis, Lear's growing miseries, like Gloucester's, are endured in an unconsciously defensive and self-defeating attempt to avoid even greater misery, Lear's avoidance is a far more subtle matter than Gloucester's suicidal flight to oblivion. If Lear flees himself he does so bravely attempting to confront himself. If he persists in abdicating from the community of man, he does so even as he involves himself experientially and conceptually in man's suffering in more profound terms than he had previous to the division of the kingdom. As we watch Lear's miseries deepen and broaden, physically, emotionally, and intellectually, right up to the end, what builds in us is a terrible pity for him as a man who in seeking what he assumes to be the highest good does only evil, who in relentlessly seeking the truth always falls short of it. Watching Lear undo himself and die in agony over Cordelia makes us aware that even the greatest suffering need not purify or make us wise. Because the avoidances he lives are so subtly tempting to us all, the Tantalus vision his fate embodies gives us an inkling of the frightful meaning of Kent's riddle: "Nothing almost sees miracles but misery."

[4]

The Prince of Darkness is a Gentleman

Filths savor but themselves.

Albany

As we trace the increasingly subtle dialectic of Lear's anguish in acts 3 and 4, it is of the greatest importance to keep the fact before us that every bit of his soul-bruising effort to confront the truth of his and man's condition, every obsessive return to his preoccupation with crime and punishment, is an ever more extreme and desperate distraction. The real issue—his alienation from Cordelia, the galling bitterness that plagues him now that he has sundered all ties with his "sweetheart" (3.6.63),[1] and thus with his own sweet heart—remains locked in silence. After the banishment and before the reunion, as Arnold Isenberg remarks, Lear speaks of Cordelia again only twice. ("I did her wrong" [1.5.24] may be a third.) The first compares her "most small fault" (1.4.266) with Goneril's greater one, very likely in order to shame Goneril into compliance with Lear's will rather than as any true sign of repentance.[2] Small or not, the "fault" is still Cordelia's, a verdict confirmed by the severe displeasure that persists in his later reference to her (2.4.211–15). Nor will he tolerate any direct reference to her from others. When the knight links her name with the Fool's pining away, Lear abruptly shears off: "No more of that, I have noted it well" (1.4.75). Considering the Fool's habit of thinly veiled allusions to her and given the fact that Lear "lov'd her most" (1.1.123), his failure to refer to her becomes conspicuous. As Professor Isenberg puts it:

147

His failure to recur to her amid the extraordinary strife within his family, in the utmost bitterness and distraction of spirit, is something not to be expected in the ordinary course of things. But the king who turns this way and that in his disconsolate quest; who can say, "Yet have I left a daughter (Regan)"; who eats crow before Goneril; who fumes and rails in public and in private . . . can never, [with the exception of the times he noted] by way of taunt or reproach, recrimination or petition, mention his third daughter and express, to himself or others, the least regret. . . . The relief of madness, which gives free rein to thoughts hitherto suppressed, does not cut the strangulating cord affixed to the idea of Cordelia.[3]

However mistaken, then, Gloucester may have been about himself, he was correct about Lear when he claimed that in the king's distraction Lear's "thoughts" were "sever'd from [his] griefs" (4.6.282). His "grief" is imprisoned in his continuing silence regarding Cordelia, a silence we come to identify as his unvoiced accusation of himself. His "thoughts" in his distraction are, by contrast, a noisy assault on heaven and earth in curses and laments by which he flees his powers of discretion. Lear may think he knows what such discretion is when he declares he knows how to choose between greater and lesser evils.

> Thou'dst shun a bear,
> But if [thy] flight lay toward the roaring sea,
> Thou'dst meet the bear i' th' mouth.
>
> (3.4.9–11)

But if, facing Cordelia's silence, Lear subconsciously identifies his unvoiced accusation of himself as the greater of two evils, he is sadly mistaken. He may feel that his noisy assault on heaven and earth is a bitter form of prudence—a necessary stand to "meet the bear i' th' mouth"; but, as an analysis of his conversation with Kent before the hovel will show, it is not a "stand" at all. In fact, it is only an unwitting and imprudent flight from one agony into yet greater agony. At the hovel, Lear's agony is both titanic and brave. He clarifies the extremity of his suffering when he tells Kent,

> [this] tempest in my mind
> Doth from my senses take all feeling else,
> Save what beats there—filial ingratitude!
>
> (3.4.12–14)

Nor, like Prometheus, will he beg comfort for his miseries if it means bowing to "the tyranny of the open night" (3.4.2). He will show Kent and the heavens that the storm is not "too rough/For nature to endure" (3.4.2–3) if the nature suffering it is grand. After considering attack on his daughters ("I will punish home" [3.4.16]) he decides instead to "endure/In such a night as this!" (3.4.18–19). When Kent, hoping to proffer peace and rest, urges Lear indoors, the king remarks that going in would only "give me leave to ponder/On things would hurt me more" (3.4.24–25). Consequently, he bids Kent and the Fool indoors to "seek thine own ease" (3.4.23) while he will urge a royal prayer of repentance in the name of the "poor naked wretches" he has "ta'en/Too little care of" (3.4.28, 32–33). The pity is that in doing so Lear paradoxically rushes headlong into yet greater woe.

As he explicitly affirms (3.4.21–22), the "roaring sea" he hopes to shun is madness; but in his attempt to shun it, rather than seek the silent refuge of the hovel, he identifies with the raging tempest without by raging within until we hear from Cordelia in act 4, scene 4, that he was "met even now/As mad as the vex'd sea" (1–2). Obviously, then, though "flight lay toward the roaring sea," Lear has unknowingly taken to his heels. To avoid distraction, he distracts himself in the tempest—without and within—that "will not give me leave to ponder/On things would hurt me more" (3.4.24–25), frightful things in the silence that his brave identification with the storm cowers before. To confront himself in silence would "hurt [him] more," but it might also redeem him. The unwitting flight from that pain insures only that he will suffer and enact yet greater woe.

Lear may subconsciously be hoping to awaken admiration and sympathy from Kent and Fool for his towering suffering in the tempest because they, with minds "free" and bodies "delicate" (as he sees it), will act upon his suggestion and "seek [their] own ease" in the hovel. Even so, in his description of the storm to them it is relatively explicit that he believes the storm will provide him with merciful relief from or avoidance of even greater suffering within the hovel with them. Implicitly, then, his urging them indoors does not so much express a real generosity as it is a reiteration of his earlier request ("Let me alone" [3.4.3]) to be allowed to "seek" his own more subtle form of "ease" in the storm while they seek theirs indoors.

Entering the hovel clearly makes Lear anxious in a way that

suggests a symbolic dimension to his avoidance of the act. Even though Lear had spoken of the hovel as one of those vile things made precious by the arts of our necessities (3.2.70–71), when faced with the reality of entering, he feels that his alchemy has failed him. When Kent first urges him in, Lear laments: "Wilt break my heart?" (3.4.4). The avoidance perhaps nearest the surface of Lear's consciousness in his reluctance to enter the hut is his unwillingness to admit his abject, humiliating condition. Having abjured the comfortable roofs of his ungrateful daughters, why now seek a hovel? As long as he desires to stand up to and "outscorn" (3.1.10) the tyranny of the storm and to pray for "poor naked wretches" in the sincere, if impotent dignity of his royal repentance, his "pomp's" need for "physic," he does not need to accept the comforting relief *he* might legitimately receive by acknowledging that he himself is one of the "wretches" to whom he repents not having shown mercy. Obviously his prayer serves to distract him from a recognition that he cannot bear: he is utterly dependent on his own suffering servant and a fool for their charity and not vice versa. Unable to bear this humiliation, he subtly denies it by assuming a superior position in order to patronize their suffering and lacerate himself mercilessly in the process.[4] In this way Lear subtly manages to distance himself both from his friends and himself. His self-laceration becomes a compulsive means of standing above and apart from himself, numbing any awareness of his freedom to choose another and, perhaps, healing path of action. Lear's question of a literally self-lacerating Poor Tom—though not, of course, his self-pitying sense of it—is our question about Lear: "Is it the fashion, that discarded fathers/Should have thus little mercy on their flesh?" (3.4.72–73). He has "ta'en too little care of this." As we shall see more clearly in a moment, even when Lear "exposes" himself "to feel what wretches feel," he does so in a spirit of torturing self-laceration, not in the loving responsiveness of a king's clemency.

Nothing expresses the continuing paradox in Lear's heroic self-defeat more exactly than his speech in act 3, scene 2, calling down a judgment of the heavens upon the wicked.

> Let the great gods,
> That keep this dreadful pudder o'er our heads,
> Find out their enemies now. Tremble, thou wretch
> That hast within thee undivulged crimes

Unwhipt of justice! Hide thee, thou bloody hand;
Thou perjur'd, and thou simular of virtue
That are incestuous! Caitiff, to pieces shake,
That under covert and convenient seeming
Has practic'd on man's life! Close pent-up guilts,
Rive your concealing continents, and cry
These dreadful summoners grace. I am a man
More sinn'd against than sinning.

(3.2.49–60)

The theme of the speech is, of course, retributive justice, a subject that will become an ever more maddened and maddening obsession with Lear up until and including act 4, scene 6, and that will resurface in the final scene of the play. Righteously enraged by the "sentence" he has suffered or certainly by its disproportionate severity and the lack of equal treatment before heaven's law, Lear calls down even more horrifying torments than the ones he suffers on all the hypocrites and unshriven sinners of this world. When he bids them "cry/These dreadful summoners grace" it is unlikely that he believes that the thunder will "peace at [their] bidding" (4.6.102–3). But from what he has already said earlier in this scene (3.2.19–24), Lear clearly believes and hopes, however, that his is a special case. Certainly that is the implicit reservation for himself he holds to in the last two lines of this speech. Describing himself as a "man/More sinn'd against than sinning" subtly differentiates him from those sinners who must, with however little likelihood of success, "cry/These dreadful summoners grace." If Lear can be said to be begging mercy for himself from the heavens in this speech, it is in a way that yet saves face. He begs mercy by proclaiming his comparative innocence, not in the humbled admission of guilt he summons the hypocrites and unshriven to proclaim. His speech metaphorically reveals that Lear has identified completely with the "dreadful summoners" calling men to answer charges against immorality, thunderously accusing them as sinners. He has nothing in common with those who need beg grace for their sinfulness. The irony in this is by now familiar. It is not simply that in failing to acknowledge his own sinfulness, his plea to the heavens for retribution on sinners amounts to a plea for greater punishment on himself; it is, instead, that Lear is absolutely correct when he maintains he is more sinned against than sinning. Unfortunately, however, he is the criminal sinning against his innocent self, that portion of himself that remains earnestly committed to virtue. There is only one way in which Lear's dedication to righteousness could become meaningful rather than frustrated. He would have to suspect and then discover how wrong he has been even in protesting his commitment to virtue. It is *his* thunder that should peace and he who should beg grace of the "dreadful summoner" in himself that he might show more mercy on the discarded father's poor flesh.

Nor is his flesh all that is in need of merciful care. Entering the hovel would symbolically involve confronting the fact that he is a poor naked wretch, but it would also involve confronting his estranged soul. Just before he tells Kent that he does not wish to enter the hovel because the tempest keeps him from more hurtful things, Lear gives us some hint of what those worse things are in an apostrophe that immediately diminishes into a private dialogue with himself.

> Pour on, I will endure.
> In such a night as this? O Regan, Goneril!
> Your old kind father, whose frank heart gave all—
> O, that way madness lies, let me shun that!
> No more of that.
>
> (3.4.18–22)

The dash in line 20 indicates an unspeakable gap in Lear's reflection, a hiatus opening into a silent abyss. The maddening thought that he must "shun" is not very likely Goneril and Regan's "filial ingratitude" since Lear spoke quite freely earlier on that subject. This appears to be a more profound horror. It may be that he is beginning to suspect that even though he "gave all" his power and property to his daughters, in moral terms he showed no generosity at all. Suspicion of our motives can give us silent pause. But it is more likely, however, given the reiteration of the phrase, "No more of that," from the earlier and explicit reference to Cordelia (1.4.75), that Lear has not so much grown suspicious of his generosity as that he is simply overcome by the irony that he has thrown over the daughter he loved best and with whom he had the greatest hope for happiness to give everything to daughters with whom he was less comfortable in the first place and who now have repaid his generosity of heart with callous disrespect for him. It need not mean that the king is reconsidering his daughter's guilt or beginning to repent his own against her but only that he still loves her best and, especially now, needs her. But though he has turned and will turn every way the wind blows, he will not turn to think of her. He veers away because, given the state of Lear's soul, to think of Cordelia is to confront the betrayal of love by the person he held most dear. It is to acknowledge the utter uncertainty of love in the world if she does not love him and, thus, his vulnerability to love's loss. Most of all, to think of his beloved Cordelia would be to see again the face of shame and refusal with which she greeted his request for love in the opening scene. So, ironically, he again refuses her unvoiced request for love and "must play fool to [the] sorrow" (4.1.38) he is suffering. The avoidance is overwhelmingly sad. In the shame and refusal on Cordelia's face is the face of love and graceful bearing as well; in futilely attempting to turn away from the one, he succeeds only too well in turning from the other.

If Lear's obsessive return to the subject of crime and punishment in acts 3 and 4 is, in the final analysis, but a means of distracting himself, it is so only in that analysis, however. For in a sense only slightly less significant, it represents an awesome attempt to confront himself and his life's meaning. Like Ixion on his wheel, he pursues himself even as he runs away from himself *(volvitur Ixion et se sequiturque fugitque).*[5] And though it is undoubtedly true in a symbolic sense that Lear cannot appeal to Cordelia because she has become synonymous for him with his nothingness and the shame at himself from which he must flee, still, Lear's quest for the truth of his suffering condition does not require us to probe too deeply to understand why he does not revert to her. Lear does not consciously consider appealing to Cordelia, no matter how grotesque the alternatives, simply because he believes she does not love him. If she does not love him, there is no point in thinking of her as his salvation. Since Lear does not care about mere comfort, he can only look elsewhere for recognition or endure the absence of love. And he does both with a terrible vengeance on himself, as we have already begun to see.

Certainly we can speak schematically of a coherent progress (if such a word may be used to describe Lear's glacial slide downward to darkness) in his efforts to examine and resolve the problem of evil he confronts. At first, of course, betrayed by one daughter, he seeks the compensatory devotion and respect of his other daughters to heal his wounded sense of self. When they in turn betray him, he takes his case to the heavens, but not before he curses his daughters to a damnation he feels fits their crime. Perhaps the most savagely vindictive speech Lear makes in the first two acts is his condemnation of Goneril to sterility or worse.

> Dry up in her the organs of increase,
> And from her derogate body never spring
> A babe to honor her! If she must teem,
> Create her child of spleen, that it may live
> And be a thwart disnatur'd torment to her.
> Let it stamp wrinkles in her brow of youth,
> With cadent tears fret channels in her cheeks,
> Turn all her mother's pains and benefits
> To laughter and contempt, that she may feel
> How sharper than a serpent's tooth it is
> To have a thankless child!
>
> (1.4.279–89)

Horrifying as the speech is, it does not completely alienate us from Lear both because he conceives of Goneril's future sufferings as a just retribution and, more important, because the agonies he wishes upon Goneril even more emphatically inform us of the agonized "laughter and contempt" Lear is already suffering because of her.

Lear's prayer for the "poor naked wretches" in act 3, scene 4, is a major turning point in his quest for justice, or at least for the bottom of the lake of darkness. Here, as before, first with Cordelia and then with his other daughters, Lear burns his bridges behind him. What begins as a prayer ends in his irrevocable, if misguided, identification with the wretched who have been scourged by the heavens and evil daughters, and his repentant commitment to human action to "show the heavens more just" (3.4.36).[6] Because the thunder, "servile minister" of the gods who betray justice, only added insult to his injuries by not halting at his bidding, Lear abjures all heavens and turns to himself, the most highly authorized representative of human civilization, in order to redress mankind's and his own just grievances. Never again will he pray to the heavens or bid the thunder peace. Now he himself will act as "justicer" (3.6.21) and seek the "cause of thunder" (3.4.155) from his natural "philosopher" (3.4.154), Poor Tom, in order to learn to wield it in the name of an unjustly injured mankind.[7] After Lear identifies with the bedlamite by exposing himself to feel what unaccommodated man feels, in hysteria he hallucinates a court-room and attempts to show the heavens more just by trying his daughters for ingratitude; but he finds they escape unpunished because of "corruption in the place" (3.6.55).

In the silent interim between the trial scene and his en-counter with Gloucester in act 4, scene 6, Lear's thinking makes an awesomely embittered yet comprehensible leap. In act 3, scene 6, the king plays a righteous judge thwarted by corrup-tion in the place.[8] His hallucination emerges symbolically, as in a dream, from his real sense of betrayal and impotence before his daughters at Gloucester's castle. But in act 4, scene 6, no longer is Lear's problem restricted to an isolated treason in his own court, real or hallucinated. If justice can fail for one, it may fail for all. Lear's sense of corruption is now general, so general in fact that he no longer sounds completely righteous since he seems to have included himself in his indictment; such a rever-sal of attitude toward himself would suggest that he has dis-covered the reality of evil within himself. He has come to a terrible conclusion about evil and man's hypocritically civilized attempts to purge it: justice enacted by men anywhere is itself a crime deserving punishment, but there remains no one who can innocently administer just punishment for that crime.

As his speeches to Gloucester near the end of this scene sug-gest, the banished king has come to this view by generalizing upon the contrast between his immunity from reprimand when in the king's "robes and furr'd gowns" (4.6.165) ("They flatter'd me like a dog" [96–97]) and the vilification he has fled but had to endure since he gave up the "great image of authority" (158) to run like a "beggar" (155) from the "cur" (157) in power. Lear now believes the evils of arbitrary power and hypocrisy reign absolute, as they always have. Though at the conclusion of this scene Lear's mind does again slip into a violent revenge fantasy, the import of his logic up to that point is clear on the matter of justice. It is but a mockery. So much for man's showing the heavens more just. When he enters to meet Gloucester, Lear is no longer imagining himself a thwarted judge; he has once again assumed power but the power of a curious kingship—rule over a "stage of fools" (4.6.183). Like the mock ruler of the festival of fools whose insistent satiric inversions point to the pervasive corruptions of the civilized order, a Lear "crown'd with . . . idle weeds" (4.4.3,5) and fantastically dressed with wild flowers enters to exonerate Gloucester on charges of adultery because, like all kings in the last and only important analysis, "I lack soldiers" (4.6.117). The point of his sardonic, self-reflexive irony is clear: one corruption feeds another. Adultery can be sanctioned because bastards help fill conscription quotas. The only defense against these pervasively loathesome realities is cynical contempt and a worldly-wise despair's pretense of patience. If justice enacted is itself a crime, the only "decent" thing to do is to stop seeking justice and liberate criminals to act in the unchallenged way the hypocrites and the powerful always have, if more furtively or more cleverly than the poor.

> The usurer hangs the cozener.
> Thorough tatter'd clothes [small] vices do appear;
> Robes and furr'd gowns hide all. [Plate sin] with gold,
> And the strong lance of justice hurtless breaks;
> Arm it in rags, a pigmy's straw does pierce it.
> None does offend, none, I say none, I'll able 'em.
> Take that of me, my friend, who have the power
> To seal th' accuser's lips.
>
> (4.6.163–70)

We can delay until later an examination of the hidden self-righteousness in Lear's cynical "decency" here, even in his attitude toward himself and his kingship. For the moment, it is enough to explore the attitude itself. The lines do not represent the king's clemency staying the executioner's hand for a Gloucester justly convicted of adultery; rather they portray a show of corrupt power or bribery persuasive enough to prevent the accusation of crime in the first place. At best, Lear imagines that as a king whose power is itself absolute pledge against anyone's accusation of him, even if he should act corruptly, he will grant an analogous immunity to a Gloucester who has no power, a man in "tattered clothes," armed but in rags. At worst, he is cynically and arbitrarily proclaiming, in the name of his friendship for Gloucester, his own kingship's absolute power to bribe or threaten into silence anyone who may be accusing Gloucester of crime.

The short history we have been tracing of Lear's decline into utter bitterness and cynicism is not a pleasant one. Nonetheless, in so far as his fall represents at the same time an earnest, if failed, quest for justice and love, an unyielding effort to measure the dimensions of the problem of evil he confronts with ever greater alarm and distress, it also has positive moral significance. In Lear's efforts to determine the meaning of his human condition regardless of the cost to himself, we see a man relentlessly pursuing himself even as he retreats into madness. The grim spectacle is not without its grandeur and majesty. In fact, Alfred Harbage has called the play "Lear's Gethsemane."[9] Even the king's charges of universal hypocrisy in act 4, scene 6, his denial of human responsibility, and his indictment of life itself, continues Professor Harbage,

> cancel their own nihilism because they sound no acquies-
> cence. Lear is the voice of protest. The grandeur of his spirit
> supplies the impotence of his body as he opposes to evil all
> that is left him to oppose—his molten indignation, his huge
> invectives, his capacity for feeling pain.[10]

This observation clarifies an important complexity in Lear's psychic state in act 4, scene 6, 155–87 that critics on one side or the other of the nihilism-clemency debate about the passage have not recognized. Only the most doctrinaire redemptivist (and there have been some) would identify the tone of Lear's remarks to Gloucester about justice and "seal[ing] the accuser's lips" as charitable;[11] but, though Lear's soul is filled with rancor and disgust, to call his tone "nihilistic" is not an exact enough description either, for the very reasons Professor Harbage suggests. If Lear has become cynically embittered, his nihilism, though real, remains grounded in moral outrage at the sight of innocence abused. In himself he has not despaired of a "decency" that refuses to acquiesce to evil.

On the other hand, however, this apparently noble reservation is hardly sufficient cause for the unqualified commendation Professor Harbage seems to award Lear for it. Though we will soon have to return to explain the paradox more completely, Lear's refusal to acknowledge without reservation his inclusion in the world's evil is itself an ironic form of acquiescence in the world's evil. As a number of commentators have remarked, Lear has come, however reluctantly, to the very view of the world that Edmund embraces with enthusiasm in act 1, scene 2.[12] Like Ivan Karamazov whose cynical philosophical position that "everything is lawful" liberates Smerdyakov's butchery, Lear liberates yet another insecure bastard. By exercising in fantasy his kingly power to free ragged criminals ("I'll able 'em") in order to challenge the evil of those in authority who can "plate sin with gold," Lear abdicates once again, this time in

158 THE PRINCE OF DARKNESS IS A GENTLEMAN

favor of Gloucester's bastard son. He "able[s]" him not merely in demented fantasy but also in calmer fact, the "come, let's away to prison" speech in act 5, whose success, as we have seen, allows Edmund the opportunity to make arrangements for Cordelia's execution. The king's imagined idyll with Cordelia follows as a logical consequence of his position about the arbitrary and corrupt nature of human justice in act 4, scene 6. Lear will not listen to Cordelia's plea to "see these daughters and these sisters" (5.3.7), at least in part because in his mind there is no point in seeking justice from them or anyone else in power. Reunited to the daughter he fondly dotes upon, in his secret and giddy wisdom he can now successfully abdicate and disavow any responsibility to a world in which justice is but a mocking sound.[13] If one cannot free the ragged criminals, one might just as well join them in prison. There, at least, one need have nothing to do with the gilded criminals in power. Wrongly imagining he will be able to "laugh/At gilded butterflies" (5.3.12–13), and so, as "jovial" as the "smug bridegroom" to whom he has appropriately likened himself earlier (4.6.198–99), Lear takes Cordelia off to "die bravely" with him, intent only on his own anticipated bliss.[14]

We have reserved extended comment until now on Lear's encounters with Edgar in act 3 and Gloucester in act 4. But nothing in either meeting significantly qualifies the portrait of Lear's quest we have been sketching. In fact, each is a symbolic mirror further clarifying the unchanging image of Lear's soul for us, simultaneously revealing both the grandeur and the meanness of the old king's psychic journey.

Before considering the meeting between Lear and Edgar in act 3 in detail, it would be useful to recall a significant portion of Edgar's disguise soliloquy.

> I will preserve myself, and am bethought
> To take the basest and most poorest shape
> That ever penury, in contempt of man,
> Brought near to beast. My face I'll grime with filth,
> Blanket my loins, elf all my hairs in knots,
> And with presented nakedness outface
> The winds and persecutions of the sky.
> The country gives me proof and president
> Of Bedlam beggars, who, with roaring voices,
> Strike in their numb'd and mortified arms
> Pins, wooden pricks, nails, sprigs of rosemary;

And with this horrible object, from low farms,
Poor pelting villages, sheep-cotes, and mills,
Sometimes with lunatic bans, sometime with prayers,
Enforce their charity.

(2.3.6–20)

As we have already seen, the speech is a mine of metaphors and
symbolic descriptions that illuminate the relationship between
character and theme in the play; but one feature of it is particu-
larly important to the subject at hand. In a symbolic sense that
characterizes Lear perhaps even more suggestively than it does
Edgar, the passage implies that *in extremis* self-laceration might
be the only way to "preserve" a threatened sense of self, to
maintain a self-respect that has been seriously challenged. The
"numb'd" and numbing insistence of self-inflicted wounds distracts us from ourselves and others, from things that would
hurt us more. Certainly that is the case with Edgar before Lear.
Having taken his self-lacerating disguise in a spirit of "contempt of man," the man in himself who might respond openly
and generously to others (specifically to the man before him in
greater need of the charity Poor Tom would enforce from him)
Edgar makes no gesture or even an expression of sympathy to
Lear in these scenes. His "presented nakedness" before Lear
succeeds in its attempt to "outface/The winds and persecutions
of the sky" in a terrible way Edgar had not anticipated; for Lear
takes Edgar's disguised condition at face value and, insisting
that he will feel what wretches feel, concludes that Poor Tom's
is a more significant suffering than his own to this point and
that, therefore, he, too, should present his nakedness to "answer . . . this extremity of the skies" (3.4.101–2).

The fact that Edgar only helps Lear top the extremity of his
sorrow is not, however, the central feature of their encounter.
The crucial ironies emerge from the way he mirrors Lear's
hidden soul and more subtle agony in parody's exaggerated
terms. Edgar enters "disguised as a madman," literally lacerating himself to scratch at the foul fiend and recounting how he
has coursed his shadow for a traitor; and then he persists in
trying to enforce charity ("Who gives any thing to Poor Tom?"
[3.4.51; and again at 60–61, 82–83, 147, 173]) without ever
giving it. In incipient but real madness Lear also remains disguised, even from himself, coursing his shadow for a traitor,
and, if more subtly and more figuratively than Edgar, still
lacerating himself to enforce charity from whatever quarter

might grant it rather than giving it to himself or to Poor Tom.[15] The telltale but unmistakable sign of something wrong with what may appear to be Lear's acquisition of a more tender conscience toward "naked wretches" is that in identifying with one in the person of Poor Tom he does not give him the appropriate charity of a cloak for his shivering body, but instead he scourges himself by stripping away his own in an unwitting act of identification, not with Poor Tom but with Poor Tom's self-laceration.

The perversity of this kind of identification with the poor is reflected in the curious language of the latter half of the "poor naked wretches" speech, a speech immediately preceding Poor Tom's entrance.[16]

> Take physic, pomp,
> Expose thyself to feel what wretches feel,
> That thou mayst shake the superflux to them,
> And show the heavens more just.
>
> (3.4.33–36)

Clearly it is Lear's plan to announce by these words his intention (as if he were king again) to think and feel more responsively toward the poor and at least to make sure that superfluous wealth is distributed among them. But when Shakespeare has Lear use the phrase "expose thyself to feel what wretches feel" in the midst of a trope involving cure of disease, we may suspect irony, especially if we should begin to question how Lear's exposing himself to cold and vermin will in any way remedy Poor Tom's miseries. The suspicion of dramatic irony here is aroused with more definiteness by Shakespeare's choice of the word "superflux" to refer to the good in excess of "pomp's" true need. According to the *OED*, this is the earliest known use of this compound word. The word "flux" refers to a "morbid or excessive discharge" from the bowels, often in a purgative context. The hope of purification through the discharge of excess seems to define the conscious purpose in Lear's figurative use of the term; but Shakespeare apparently means to hint that Lear's new resolution to "shake" this excess to the poor may have an unintentionally vile, "top extremity" dimension of irony. In any case, whatever excess Lear's "superflux" would discharge, Edgar's immediately subsequent remark within—"Fathom and half, fathom and half!/

Poor Tom" (3.4.37–38)—seems to imply that we have already seen enough of flooding in this storm.

When Lear meets the poor, nearly naked wretch, Tom, he identifies with what the wretch feels immediately; but he does so only in terms of the all-consuming egoism of his own experience of misery. The separate, suffering man is simply annihilated by the force and manner of Lear's fellow feeling. Having assumed and then insisted that "nothing could have subdued" Poor Tom's "nature/To such a lowness but his unkind daughters" (3.4.70–71), Lear clears the way for his self-lacerating exposure of himself by speaking most truly of himself when he declares Tom's naked and bleeding body a "judicious punishment! 'Twas this flesh begot/Those pelican daughters" (3.4.74–75). By now we should immediately recognize the all too familiar "top extremity" irony in this. If the king's daughters have indeed fed on his blood, how can his own feeding on now self-inflicted wounds be considered "judicious"?

That Lear is merely adding insult to injury in his obsession with punishment, whether self-punishment or vengeance on his daughters, is communicated by two remarks Poor Tom unknowingly makes to Lear. When Lear discovers that his "learned Theban's" (3.4.157)[17] study is how to "prevent the fiend, and to kill vermin" (159), he will not willingly separate himself from him. Tom may not mean much by the remark, but Lear has in all likelihood taken it in a symbolic sense that fits his obsessions. Perhaps "this philosopher" (154) can enlighten what has been his increasingly dark and fruitless quest to "prevent the fiend" of madness and "kill the vermin" torturing him, his loveless daughters he has thus far been impotent to rid from his tortured flesh and mind. The kindled hope, however, turns into a searing flame. When we next meet Poor Tom and Lear together, we find that far from being prevented, the fiend of madness possesses Lear utterly. Despite Poor Tom's conventional warning: "Pray, innocent, and beware the foul fiend" (3.6.7–8), Lear madly ignores good advice to sound a Satanic claim to vengeance: "To have a thousand with red burning spits/Come hizzing in upon 'em—" (15–16). Poor Tom's reply— "The foul fiend bites my back" (17)—is, if merely an attempt to call attention back to himself, important on a symbolic level. It seems to imply that scratching at the infestation of vermin confirming the fiend's presence only spreads infection and intensifies the agony one wishes to prevent. All attempts to punish the villain intensify the self's own torment.

What has been argued regarding Lear's treatment of Edgar in act 3 can be claimed as well of his reunion with Gloucester in act 4, scene 6, after Lear's long absence from the stage: "Love's not love/When it is mingled with regards that stands/Aloof from the entire point." In act 3 both Lear and Edgar "stand aloof" from one another despite the real availability of relief from their respective miseries in mutual sympathy and generosity. Rather than give charity, each prefers to continue to beg it, directly or indirectly, from the other. Similarly, in act 4, in a scene that should exhibit the king's recognition of his loyal subject maimed in his service, Lear instead stands so far off from Gloucester in detachedly cruel verbal mockery that unless one knew otherwise, one would not suppose that the blind man before him was Gloucester himself. Some simple questions of Gloucester would have revealed that his "squiny" (4.6.137) has nothing to do with "blind Cupid's" (137) invitation to lechery and everything to do with his self-sacrifice for the king that silently calls for an acknowledgment that Lear, thinking himself a clever wit, refuses: "I'll not love" (137–38). A simple query would have revealed that Gloucester, too, is an exhausted old man disgracefully dispossessed by his own children; but Lear does not escape his self-absorbed obsessions to ask. Instead, in what seems to fit the pattern of manic and cynical glee that dominates the entire scene, Lear, like Edgar before him, merely "play[s] fool" to Gloucester's already overwhelming "sorrow" (4.1.38). Nor is his barbed wit at Gloucester's expense mingled with the gentler touches of Lear's own Fool. This is no sweet and bitter fool, one who would take "one's part," like Gloucester's, "that's out of favor" (1.4.99–100) and request to "come place him here by me" (1.4.142); Lear is an utterly embittered fool, a fool not in playfulness but a fool in dreadful earnest who himself acknowledges midway through the scene his need for something to "sweeten [his] imagination" (4.6.131). As Theodore Spencer rightly characterized it, in his bitterness Lear merely "rubs in" his mockery of Gloucester's blindness.[18]

One could argue that Lear's madness mitigates his responsibility for his cruelty, and clearly it does; but were it to relieve him of it completely it would destroy or radically diminish the play's tragic irony. As Edgar remarks in an aside, there is too much "reason in [this] madness" (4.6.175). If Lear is actually beyond the power of discretion, any moral evaluation of his behavior would be beside the point. Critics have not been willing to yield that privilege at other points in the play when Lear is "mad"—such as at the finale; it would be inconsistent to single out this scene for scrupulous qualification.

With his reasons in madness, when Lear first sees Gloucester he identifies him as "Goneril with a white beard" (4.6.96). Though perversely insulting, that epithet is not without its apparently logical appropriateness. To identify Gloucester as Goneril grown old is to accuse him, with her, of perfidious betrayal, of sycophantic hypocrisy that said "'ay' and 'no' to every thing that I said" (4.6.99), only to drive father and king out of doors to his humiliation. In the reference to his "white beard," Lear may also be hinting at the charge of goatish lechery against Gloucester, especially given the king's immediately subsequent speculation that the capital crime committed by the man before him is adultery. Charges of sycophancy and lechery are almost fair to our sense of Gloucester's character before his belated decision to take the king's side. There is enough correspondence between Lear's speech and Gloucester's character to suggest that the fallen king "know[s]" Gloucester "well enough" (4.6.177) from the outset, not merely when he explicitly acknowledges that he recognizes him later in the scene.

But if Lear recognizes Gloucester from the start he does not acknowledge him or his suffering because he is so obsessed with his own grievance and its presumed precedence. (As Lear had argued earlier, "where the greater malady is fix'd,/The lesser is scarce felt" [3.4.8–9].) The images of Gloucester that preoccupy him are not the bleeding blind man before him but the parent whose comparative good fortune—despite his lechery—proves that Lear's is the greater malady ("Gloucester's bastard son/Was kinder to his father than my daughters") and the false counselor whose hypocritical part in the king's abasement Lear has finally "smelt . . . out." Lear has either forgotten that Gloucester came to his rescue in act 3 or perhaps he never even realized what the earl had done in the first place since he was then preoccupied with the trial of his daughters and his interview with his Theban philosopher. One thing is certain: Lear does not here return Gloucester's favor. He does not generously "expose" himself "to feel what wretches feel."

Even when later in the scene Lear appears to soften toward Gloucester, his speech and behavior remain ambiguous. It would appear that the expression, "If thou wilt weep my fortunes, take my eyes" (4.6.176) immediately preceding Lear's open acknowledgment that he recognizes his old friend, is a straightforwardly pathetic attempt at generosity from king to subject.[19] But the matter is not so simple. There may be here, as earlier, a dimension of "greater malady" irony in what Lear says to Gloucester. Perhaps Lear believes that the only way the blind man in tears before him could adequately comprehend his suffering and weep the king's worse misfortunes would be for him to see the king's fortunes and suffering through Lear's own eyes. So he offers Gloucester his eyes on the condition that Gloucester use them to weep in compassion for him. A reading of the line in this self-pitying sense rather than as expressive of a desire to be generous would coincide perfectly both with the way Lear has treated Gloucester up to this point and with the way he does thereafter. Once Lear calls Gloucester by name, he does not reach out to him in fellowship and the compensatory comfort of an embrace; he begins to preach to him his own cynical contempt for the stench of life in the body, whereupon his mind veers almost immediately from Gloucester to return to his obsession with revenge. When Cordelia's soldiers enter, he has no thought for Gloucester whatever but only pity for himself as he deserts yet another faithful servant. Though he had enlisted Gloucester moments ago to "read . . . this challenge" (4.6.138) to his daughters and sons-in-law, now he exits alone bewailing his lack of faithful retainers: "No seconds? All myself?" (194).

Thus, largely because of Lear's manner of treating Gloucester, instead of two suffering old friends reuniting to see themselves "feelingly" in each other's fate, mutual recognition and reunion give way to an emblematic mirroring in which a blind man with eyes gazes unseeingly at his blind shadow and then flees it. Though Lear plays fool to Gloucester's sorrow, the "mock is . . . that a man should have the best use of eyes to see the way of blindness" (*Cymbeline* 5.4.188–90).

Though it is true that for most of act 4, scene 6, Gloucester is the man more sinned against than sinning since, like Fool and Kent in act 3, he bides the pelting of Lear's pitiless storm, nonetheless, at the scene's conclusion he unwittingly mimics Lear's sinful treatment of him by expressing his envy for what he wrongly imagines is the king's lesser malady—the good fortune to be distracted.

> The King is mad; how stiff is my vild sense
> That I stand up, and have ingenious feeling
> Of my huge sorrows! Better I were distract,
> So should my thoughts be sever'd from my griefs,
> And woes by wrong imaginations lose
> The knowledge of themselves.
>
> (4.6.279–84)

It can hardly be accidental that in the scene that directly follows this speech Shakespeare stages an ideally achieved reunion between Cordelia and Kent.

> CORDELIA: O thou good Kent, how shall I live and work
>   To match thy goodness? My life will be too
>   short,
>   And every measure fail me.
> KENT: To be acknowledg'd, madam, is o'erpaid.
>
> (4.7.1–4)

Cordelia's grateful acknowledgment of Kent and Kent's humbled embarrassment before it together constitute so simple and extreme a contrast to the failed reunion and the spectacle of mutual envy between Gloucester and Lear in act 4, scene 6, that the juxtaposition of the two suggests symbolic import, directing us to judge the mutual and unatoned solitude of king and earl by a comparison with the innocent communion and gratification in Cordelia and Kent's fellowship. Lear's embittered assaults on sexuality and justice in act 4, scene 6, may be more conspicuous and, for that reason, more often and fully discussed by critics of the play; but they are no more important than Lear's treatment of Gloucester. No blistering jeremiads on vice and hypocrisy in the abstract begin to atone for Lear's concrete sins against his friend here.

Nor is Lear's cruelty restricted to his treatment of Gloucester. If he willfully plays fool to Gloucester's sorrow, he also unwittingly plays fool to his own. In the recent criticism of the play, it has become more and more commonplace to hear Enid Welsford's observation reiterated that Lear's speech throughout act 4, scene 6, "has something of the wit, the penetration, the quick repartee of the court jester. . . . The King . . . has now himself become the Fool."[20] Except for one very serious qualification, this is a striking and fruitful insight. There is clearly a significant parallel between the Fool's speech mannerisms and Lear's now consuming penchant for quibbling, nonsense riddles and quips, and satirical inversions. And I have already suggested that the Lear who enters crowned with idle weeds to declare himself "every inch a king" before whose imperial "stare" every "subject quakes" (4.6.107–8) may be a Lear presenting himself with self-conscious irony as a carnival king, the mock king of a festival of fools, whose edicts and arbitrations may be satirically acute but lack any real power to effect change. Certainly there is little question about how he sees himself near the end of the scene when he preaches to Gloucester in a bitter tone about "this great stage of fools" (4.6.183). Moreover, a moment later, when the appearance of his unidentified "daughter's" soldiers threatens further humiliation, Lear earnestly laments what he now believes are his ludicrously repetitive misfortunes: "I am even/The natural fool of fortune" (4.6.190–91).

But though there are, then, any number of indications that Lear sees himself in the role of fool in act 4, scene 6, we must still ask in what sense he has actually become one. Critics have not remarked, for example, upon the irony that we learn as much about Lear here by the differences between his behavior and his fool's as we do from their resemblances. We have already seen that Lear exhibits the bitterness but none of the sweetness of his own fool. Lear's loving fool "will stay"; but Lear here proves himself the "knave" who but "turns fool that runs away" (2.4.84–85) from Gloucester and himself to seek a fugitive safety. As in all other things, Lear becomes a fool, too, with a reservation for himself. In act 2, scene 4, before his daughters, Lear had begged the heavens to "give me . . . patience, patience I need," the same virtue he momentarily exhorts Gloucester to join him in; but now, no more than then, does the king willingly become "fool . . . so much/To bear it tamely" (2.4.271, 275–76). He refuses to stand for or acquiesce in his misfortunes because he is so subconsciously terrified of reflecting upon his own responsibility for them. He still prefers to feel he is a man more sinned against than sinning. When he lashes out at sexuality, it is only at the sexuality of women. When, as "justicer," he tries and condemns justice as mere hypocrisy, he does not question his own verdict upon it, its impartiality or its justness. His own cynical decency to Gloucester and others too powerless to act with the greedy and vindictive hypocrisy of the wealthy and powerful is, as Ruth Nevo suggests of all his speeches here, "still spoken by an intellect which will not merely submit to the way the world goes,"[21] a voice that claims a reservation of righteousness for itself. Despite the fact that his mad royal edict—"None does offend, none, I say none, I'll able 'em" (4.6.168)—would legislate a nihilistic riot of appetite and viciousness, Lear believes it would at least do so with virtuous impartiality. When he declares the world merely a "stage of fools," he just as clearly hopes his knowing it to be so exempts him from being one. If he is fool enough to be fortune's whipping boy and dupe, its "natural fool," he is not so much a fool as to refrain from crying out against it. And when he exits the stage, rushing into a fugitive's exile, he does so with a pretense of self-possessed dignity in death: "I will die bravely" (4.6.198). In so doing he remains unable to stand for or generously take the part of the foolish counselor who urged him to give away his lands. He cannot bear his fortunes tamely primarily because he has not been able to acknowledge to himself just how complete a fool he has been and still is. Nor does he love himself enough to forgive and accept himself in his folly as his Fool did when the Fool kindly summoned to his side the fool who counseled Lear to give away his lands. His greatest need is not, in fact, the Stoic's wherewithal to face out the vagaries of his fortune; it is the same one that a wise servant speaks of to Pericles: "To bear with patience/Such griefs as you yourself do lay upon yourself" (*Pericles*1.2.65–66). Only a complete fool can bear them tamely, in humility's bemused acceptance. Lear should go to singing school to the Fool.

> He that has and a little tine wit—
> With heigh-ho, the wind and the rain—
> Must make content with his fortunes fit,
> Though the rain it raineth every day.
>
> (3.2.74–77)

In accepting rather than avoiding being fool enough to bear his own folly tamely, the Fool can then go out of himself in the greater folly of fully human love. He stands still in Cordelia's peaceful accord, exposing himself to help others. The Lear we meet in act 4, scene 6, remains a hounded fugitive: he does not have peace within himself or within the world but a vindictive

spirit of warring challenge designed to protect himself and attack others. Even his royal clemency to those in rags and tattered clothes is, in fact, more properly a war cry or incitement
to riot.

> None does offend, none, I say, none, I'll able 'em.
> Take that of me, my friend, who have the power
> To seal th' accuser's lips.
>
> (4.6.168–70)

Lear does, in fact, possess the power to seal the accuser's lips,
though not in the sense that he fantasizes when he tries to
assure Gloucester he can secure his friend's immunity. The
only dreadful summoner we are certain exists in act 4, scene 6,
is Lear himself. What this lacerated and lacerating fool should
do to exercise his real power as "the king himself," the power
he appears to think he has lost, is to stop punishing home. Lear
cannot make the radical admission about his past and present
behavior that would redeem him and his treatment of Gloucester. Could he acknowledge and accept how much of a fool he
has been, the king himself would be restored, the usurping
pretender banished, because, as was argued in chapter 2, were
Lear to take the fool's part that is out of favor he would be
taking his own part as well.

Only in these terms can we plumb the irony in Lear's remarks
as he enters to confront Edgar and Gloucester: "No, they cannot touch me for [coining,] I am the King himself" (4.6.83–84).
Lear may be making a mockery of himself here, but he may also
be suggesting his paranoia about the real possibility that others
will make more of a mockery of him. Given the precipitous
slide in his fortunes and his sense that his daughters and the
heavens have driven him to his present plight, he may feel
literally hunted, fearful that if his enemies should catch him
now he will be treated to the ignominious mockery and execution afforded pretenders. (Compare, for example, the treatment of York in *3 Henry VI* [1.4.70–108].)[22] Consequently, he
protests with a bravado masking fear that no one has the right
to lay punishing hands upon him or try him for counterfeiting
since he is in fact the king. But even though he is literally the
king, he has metaphorically been a "counterfeit/Resembling
majesty" (*King John* 3.1.99–100). It is the prerogative of the
king to designate the coin of the realm; but even so, Lear was

not free to devalue Cordelia's worth in the arbitrary way he did in the opening scene: "When she was dear to us, we did hold her so,/But now her price is fallen" (1.1.196–97). This is the counterfeit of a pretender. And if we interpret Lear's "coining" in yet another figurative sense, as his fathering of offspring, daughters impressed with the features of the king, we discover another reason why Lear deserves the mockery and punishment he protests. To a significant extent at least, Goneril and Regan are the daughters they are because Lear has been what he has been as their father.[23] When Cordelia offers him the opportunity, the father with "undivulged crimes" against them should have seized it to "cry/These dreadful summoners grace" (3.2.52,58–59). Given their disgraceful treatment of him, it may seem harsh to suggest that he beg *their* forgiveness; but someone must begin and they are not likely to do so. Besides, his is the initiating fault.

The disastrous effect of Lear's "coining" of daughters goes a long way toward explaining the mood in which Lear tries to justify adultery to Gloucester and even his subsequent expressions of utter disgust with sexuality. Sheldon Zitner clarifies much of the reason in this madness.

> Proposition: there is no need to punish adultery.
> Arguments: first, adultery is the norm of nature, viz., the wren and the fly; second, adultery has better effects than does lawful intercourse, viz., the 'loyalty' of Edmund, the 'treachery' of Edgar; third, kings need soldiers; fourth and fifth, amplifications of the first, adultery is the law of human life, viz., yon 'simp'ring dame' and women's centaur nature. And all the arguments are enclosed in the consciousness that they are products of an imagination gone sour, for which, good apothecary, an ounce of civet.[24]

Nonetheless, it remains curious why the full fury of Lear's outrage at the loathesomeness of sexuality should so fixate itself upon the female genitalia.

> But to the girdle do the gods inherit,
> Beneath is all the fiends': there's hell, there's
>   darkness,
> There is the sulphurous pit, burning, scalding,
> Stench, consumption. Fie, fie, fie! pah, pah!
>   (4.6.126–29)

Even if his daughters have behaved despicably, Lear should remember what he had admitted earlier, "'twas this flesh begot/ Those pelican daughters" (3.4.74–75) upon his queen. The fault was obviously not hers alone. Lear's nausea at women, then, suggests an unconscious but characteristic projection of guilt, as if beneath consciousness he feels "not to be worst/ Stands in some rank of praise."

There is certainly more madness than reason in it. We have had repeated glimpses in act 4 of Cordelia's restorative efforts, both literal and metaphorical. Edmund has not been kinder than *all* Lear's daughters. Cordelia's loving character and acts overturn for us the truth and appropriateness of Lear's absolute indictment of womanhood. Moreover, although Lear's attack on sexuality may sound like the Fool's lewd satiric license, it differs significantly in that the Fool's wit scolds men and women impartially; also, the Fool's codpiece song reveals he believes—as Lear obviously does not—that sexuality need not be a defiling thing. It can be innocent if the heart's love replaces the toe's lust. Lear has no faith in the transforming power of love; he merely desires "civet's" sweetness to cloak the body's ineradicable "essence," its stench. But Shakespeare's choice of civet, a perfume fashioned from a secretion of the civet cat's anus, implies his agreement with the Fool, his disagreement with Lear: "vild" can be changed, changed utterly to "precious." The poet may intend a related irony when he has Lear declare: "Beneath is all the fiends': there's hell, there's darkness,/There is the sulphurous pit." In recalling Poor Tom's mad talk as he chases the verminous "foul fiend" vexing him ("There could I have him now, and there, and there again, and there"), the phrase suggests that Lear's present efforts to scratch at his foul fiends may provide immediate relief only at the expense of spreading infection and greater woe. Like Edgar, Lear is still coursing his shadow for a traitor. Lear's fiends are not attacking him from without, offending him with their stench. As Albany rightly declares: "Filths savor but themselves" (4.2.39). When, near the end of his conversation with Gloucester, Lear tells him "the first time that we smell the air/ We wawl and cry" (4.6.179–80), he is mistaken in the most basic of ways. Though the baby's first human act is, indeed, to cry, it is neither because of the "smell" of the mother's womb nor because of the stench in the "air" of a corrupting world. A baby cries for the same reasons child-changed Lear wails—his need in his wounded alienation and utter vulnerability for the comfort and communion of a mother's kind nursery, the need for the "dear shelter" Lear banished himself from when he banished Cordelia.

Perhaps the most compelling suggestion of the madness in Lear's disgust with female sexuality is the way it exemplifies Albany's wisdom: "That nature which contemns it origin/ Cannot be bordered certain in itself" (4.2.32–33). The usurper cannot be bordered certain within himself because from the beginning of act 3 when he bids the thunder "smite flat the thick rotundity o' the world/Crack Nature's molds, all germens spill at once," until, with Cordelia dead in his arms, he claims, "She's dead as earth," Lear persists in contemning his origin. The self-reflexive irony in this is nicely communicated by a remark Gloucester made about Edgar, about himself, or about each of them: "Our flesh and blood, my lord, is grown so vild,/ That it doth hate what gets it" (3.4.145–46). Such, too, is Lear's growing disgust with life in the body on earth. The way in which Lear has "grown so vild" is symbolized in the extent of his likeness to Nero, to whom Shakespeare has Edgar make allusion.

> Frateretto calls me, and tells me Nero is an angler in the lake
> of darkness. Pray, innocent, and beware the foul fiend.
>
> (3.6.6–8)

Much is compressed here. It would seem enough of a shock to realize that Nero is a symbolic prototype of Lear: an intemperate and idle emperor who indulged himself when he should have ruled himself and his kingdom responsibly.[25] But there is more. Nero's angling in the lake of darkness suggests, first of all, something of his sexual promiscuity, his engendering for sport (recall Poor Tom's remarks about doing the "act of darkness" with his mistress and Edgar's later reference to the "dark and vicious place" where Gloucester "got" Edmund). Though this has only metaphorical relevance to Lear's character, it contains a suggestion of his irresponsible, self-indulgent fatherhood. In addition, as Edith Sitwell long ago pointed out, the allusion is almost certainly also a reference to two legendary incidents in Nero's life: his failed attempt to sound the depth of the reputedly bottomless Alcyonian lake and his matricide, when he anatomized his mother's womb to determine his own source.[26] In conflating the image of the bottomless lake and

Nero's mother's womb, the allusion brilliantly implies Lear's relentless but failed efforts to sound the depths of the problem of evil and his increasingly maddened tendency to identify its origin with the womb of woman. In act 4, scene 6, the identification becomes complete, but even in the same scene in which Poor Tom warns Lear about Nero, an idle king self-righteously obsessed by the hideous reality of evil in his world urges an anatomy upon his daughter to find the source of "these hard hearts" (3.6.78).

When Lear sanctions lust and mayhem in act 4, scene 6, he makes vile things precious in a manner even more Satanic than that of Goneril, Regan, or Edmund. In order to act, they must rationalize their evil into good; Lear, who believes he recognizes evil as evil, nonetheless asserts, "Evil, be thou my good." The vile is not changed in a transformation by which even our bodies and souls' shamefulness becomes as precious as the leper's wounds to Damian; rather, the vile is still vile, but it is precious as self-justification. Though outraged and disgusted by lust and hypocrisy, Lear sanctions them in mock royal edict because they guard his fragile self-esteem. As William Chaplin remarks:

> Lear moves toward implicating himself in the world's justice when he comes to feel those in positions of authority are guilty of crimes against which their authority is used. Since all are guilty, and all are animals, Lear pardons them in an act of negation. He has come as far as hysterical consciousness will allow in hypostatizing his symptoms, and his last defense against self-condemnation is a fantasy of power, through which he thinks for a moment that he will lend his authority to the wretches and hypocrites whose actions he condemns.[27]

Thus Lear flees the truth of his condition even as he pursues it relentlessly to its wrongly imagined source in woman. Tragedy exhibits such ironic paradoxes at its core, a man proving his smallness in his very greatness. Lear's grandeur is Pyrrhic; his refusal to surrender, confused. "The prince of darkness is a gentleman" (3.4.143), not a woman at all as Lear prefers to believe. Lear cannot triumph over evil, though he does, in futility, bravely challenge it to the death. The unthinkable alternative that would have redeemed him would have been to suffer his evil willingly, to bear himself tamely, as Cordelia and the Fool bear themselves and others, in laughing humility. "Sorrow

would be a rarity most beloved,/If all could so become it"
(4.3.23–24). Lear willingly suffers everything else in majesty,
even unto death; but all the miseries he endures are subtly self-
glorifying, an indulgence in pain to help him avoid the acknowledgment of his own evil. The suffering that would
redeem him demands more from the self. It demands, for example, that Lear stop pretending to heroism. At each moment
Lear avoids facing what in another sense, and in ever more
distressing dimensions of abasement, he is actually facing at
each moment: loss of respect for his heroic worth.

By way of a conclusion to discussion of the play, let us return
to a short exchange between Gloucester and Edmund in act 2
after Edgar has made his escape.

> *Enter* GLOUCESTER, *and* SERVANTS *with torches.*
> GLOUCESTER: Now, Edmund, where's the villain?
> EDMUND: Here stood he in the dark, his sharp sword
> out,
> Mumbling of wicked charms, conjuring the
> moon
> To stand['s] auspicious mistress.
> GLOUCESTER: But where is he?
> EDMUND: Look, sir, I bleed.
> GLOUCESTER: Where is the villain, Edmund?
> EDMUND: Fled this way, sir, when by no means he
> could—
> GLOUCESTER: Pursue him, ho! Go after.
>
> (2.1.37–42)

The passage at first appears to be nothing more than the most
mechanical bit of stage business in which Edmund successfully
delays his father's pursuit of Edgar in order to prevent being
trapped in his own web. On closer inspection, however, as
Thomas McFarland has rightly observed, it reveals itself as perhaps the most striking and important emblem in the play. The
first curiosity masking symbolic significance is Edmund's first
reply. Of course, the passage most literally refers to Edgar; and
Edmund has made up the account of Edgar's "mumbling of
wicked charms, conjuring the moon/To stand's auspicious mistress" to play upon his father's superstitious nature. But it is
certainly also possible, given Edmund's inventiveness and his
bitterness toward his father, that Edmund intends to make an
unwitting dupe of his father here as well by characterizing

Gloucester himself as the "villain." We have earlier heard Gloucester "mumbling of wicked charms," and there is little question that he is enough of a fool to "conjure" the changeable moon to be his faithful "mistress" in so doing. Certainly he acts the fool here, standing with sword drawn, but "in the dark" (though he has brought torches), not simply because he does not realize Edmund and not Edgar is the villain but also because Edmund may be naming him fool and villain without Gloucester's knowing it. The audience knows, of course, what Gloucester does not—that the villain standing here in the dark, his sharp sword drawn is his son Edmund, too. The literal sense of the exchange, then, gives way to a breathtaking emblem in which villain stares at villain as in a mirror, though neither sees himself.

Gloucester's second request for the villain and Edmund's reply lead us to the unspeakable shame at the center of the play's vision of things. In his own mind, Edmund's "Look, sir, I bleed" is but an attempt to distract Gloucester from Edgar by concerning him with his insignificant, self-inflicted wound. He may even be taunting his duped father yet again by suggesting that his villain is bleeding before his very eyes. But the reply and its effect on Gloucester symbolically speak something far more complex and moving about Edmund. Though he does not know it of course, his wound is neither insignificant nor self-inflicted. Shakespeare gives us a wonderful glimpse of his complex attitude toward Edmund in the dramatic irony of something the bastard says to Cornwall. "How malicious is my fortune, that I must repent to be just!" (3.5.9–10). Edmund's words are but brazen hypocrisy when he says them, but they contain a symbolic sense in which he unknowingly speaks the truth about himself. He is a "villain" who must "repent to be just"; he has committed horrible crimes. But Shakespeare does not overlook the mitigating fact that it is also his "malicious . . . fortune" that he who has suffered long years of laughter and contempt should need to repent his own evil reaction in order to be a just man. In a symbolic sense, then, Edmund's "Look, sir, I bleed" means variously. It confesses villainy, but it also describes the laughter and contempt the bastard has endured. It is an epitome of all his unspoken requests for recognition as beloved son that he has long since despaired of being graced with. Most important, it designates the unspeakable shame at himself that we have inferred he feels. If Edmund is the vicious criminal without whose compensational quest for absolute power Cordelia and Lear would not have died, he is also the play's most crippled victim. The more unspeakable shame is Gloucester's. It is he who, as before, is so absorbed in his own efforts to prevent anticipated injury to himself, he does not even see the injuries his bastard son is already suffering. Consequently, like the Ixionic Lear, he flees himself as he "pursues him" who "fled this way," coursing his shadow for a traitor.

The relevance of this emblem to aspects of the play beyond the characters of Edmund and Gloucester is also crucial. Professor McFarland is, I believe, absolutely correct when he identifies the "search for the villain" as an "index to the true moral fault in the world of *King Lear*." The problem of the play's characters "is not the fixing of just blame, but how to achieve fullness and meaning in life."[28] Perhaps the profoundest tragic irony of the final scene in *Lear*, the scene with which we began this study, is that this "search for the villain" continues unabated as the nearly exclusive concern of the principals there, especially Lear, while the "fullness and meaning of life" lies wasted before us, an unapprehended possibility of a love that "redeems nature from the . . . curse" with which the outraged Lear parts from this world and life.

There is no need to hunt out villains. They brazenly stand wherever fathers, in self-absorbed fear for themselves, look past their children and do not proffer needed love, and in children whose response to their wounded sense of themselves is to lash back at their parents and, thus, perpetuate the vicious circle of mutual recrimination. The villain hidden in shadow stands exposed here in bastard and king, in all men whose defensive responses to their wounded selves, hidden even from themselves in shame, urge them on to pitiless destruction for which they must repent to be just. The way to the fullness and meaning of life lies not in pursuing the villain but in taking "one's part that's out of favor." Cordelia and the Fool, at ease with being nothing, know

> There is some soul of goodness in things evil,
> Would men observingly distill it out.
>
>   (*Henry V* 4.1.4–5)

Notes

Chapter 1. A Tragedy of Fools

1. Both S. L. Goldberg, *An Essay on "King Lear"* (London: Cambridge University Press, 1974), pp. 7–14, and William Elton, *"King Lear" and the Gods* (San Marino, Calif.: Huntington Library, 1966), pp. 3–8, ably summarize the recent history of the critical debate about the play. Carol Marks, "Speak What We Feel: The End of *King Lear*," *ELN* 5 (1968): 169–71, provides a thorough summary of a number of recent pessimistic readings of the finale.

My indebtedness to the previous critical writing about *King Lear* is, of course, incalculable. But I would like to record my debt to the critics whose work this book is largely designed to build upon or, at times, to answer. In addition to the works of S. L. Goldberg and William Elton, I would cite Judah Stampfer, "The Catharsis of *King Lear*," *Shakespeare Survey* 13 (1960): 1–10; Nicholas Brooke, "The Ending of *King Lear*," in *Shakespeare 1564–1964: A Collection of Modern Essays by Various Hands*, ed. Edward A. Bloom (Providence, R.I.: Brown University Press, 1964), pp. 71–87; Maynard Mack, *"King Lear" in Our Time* (Berkeley: University of California Press, 1965); Stanley Cavell, "The Avoidance of Love," in *Must We Mean What We Say?: A Book of Essays* (N.Y.: Scribners, 1969), pp. 267–353; H. A. Mason, *Shakespeare's Tragedies of Love* (N.Y.: Barnes and Noble, 1970), pp. 165–226; A. L. French, *Shakespeare and the Critics* (London: Cambridge University Press, 1972), pp. 144–205; Richard Fly, "Beyond Extremity: *King Lear* and the Limits of Poetic Drama," in *Shakespeare's Mediated World* (Amherst: University of Massachusetts Press, 1976), pp. 87–109; and Marvin Rosenberg, *The Masks of "King Lear"* (Berkeley: University of California Press, 1972).

Citations of the text of the play are based on *The Riverside Shakespeare*, ed. G. Blakemore Evans et al. (Boston: Houghton Mifflin, 1974). References are to act, scene, and line.

2. Stampfer, "Catharsis of *King Lear*," p. 10.

3. Brooke, "Ending of *King Lear*," pp. 87, 85–86.

4. Helen Gardner, *King Lear* (London: Athlone Press, 1967), p. 28.

5. Goldberg, *Essay on "King Lear*," pp. 156, 157–58. The sense of the ironies in acts 4 and 5 that repeatedly undercut the speakers' confident pronouncements and prayers and "top extremity" of their woes has been noted in recent criticism. Cf., for example, Fly, "Beyond Extremity," p. 90; Brooke, "Ending of *King Lear*," pp. 76, 78, 82, 85; Reuben Brower, *Hero and Saint: Shakespeare and the Graeco-Roman Heroic Tradition* (N.Y.: Oxford University Press, 1971), p. 399; N. Joseph Calarco, *Tragic Being: Apollo and Dionysus in Western Drama*

(Minneapolis: University of Minnesota Press, 1968), p. 102; John Holloway, *The Story of the Night* (Lincoln: University of Nebraska Press, 1961), p. 90; John Reibetanz, "Theatrical Emblems in *King Lear*," in *Some Facets of "King Lear": Essays in Prismatic Criticism*, ed. Rosalie Colie and F. T. Flahiff (Toronto: University of Toronto Press, 1974), p. 49.

6. Goldberg, *Essay on "King Lear*," pp. 2–3. Though Rosenberg, in *The Masks of "King Lear*," does not express any similar conclusion about the play, the nature of his commentary implicitly suggests agreement with Professor Goldberg's position.

In *Shakespeare and the Critics*, pp. 193–205, French concludes that *Lear* does not ultimately hold together as a "felt whole." Though the questions he raises about the play's coherence are substantial ones, I also hope that they will be answered in the course of this book's argument.

7. "*King Lear* and the Comedy of the Grotesque," from *The Wheel of Fire* (London: Methuen, 1949), reprinted in *Shakespeare: The Tragedies*, ed. Alfred Harbage (Englewood Cliffs, N.J.: Prentice-Hall, 1964), pp. 124, 137. Two other more recent and very important studies of the comic dimensions of *King Lear* are those of Robert F. Miller, "*King Lear* and the Comic Form," *Genre* 8 (1975): 1–25, and Katherine Stockholder, "The Multiple Genres of *King Lear:* Breaking the Archetypes," *Bucknell Review* 16 (1968): 40–63. As Professor Miller says of the play's tone: "Jan Kott and others are radically reductive when they read it as an example of the Theater of the Absurd"; but, like G. Wilson Knight, "they are surely correct in detecting throughout the play a cruel humor that makes a mockery of human suffering. This is perhaps not everything that can be said about our condition, but any view that leaves this terrible insight out is something less than totally clear-eyed and honest" (p. 21).

8. Gardner, *King Lear*, p. 28.

9. It is possible to read Kent's gesture here not as a sign of friendship so much as an inappropriately self-centered desire for recognition from Lear. See, for example, Michael Goldman, *Shakespeare and the Energies of Drama* (Princeton, N.J.: Princeton University Press, 1972), p. 103; Paul A. Jorgensen, *Lear's Self-Discovery* (Berkeley: University of California Press, 1967), p. 84; Rosenberg, *Masks of "King Lear*," p. 316. However, none of Kent's lines hint at anything but his pain at witnessing what he is witnessing; and, though he does eagerly seek Lear's recognition, it could just as well be for reasons that are not at all self-centered. He could be trying to urge Lear to recognize him so that Lear will realize he is not alone, that he can lean on him for support in his grief. Certainly, when he gets nothing but the most perfunctory sort of recognition, he does not seem spiteful or disappointed over that fact. Cf. Cavell, "Avoidance of Love," p. 299 n9, for a different defense of Kent's behavior here.

10. Someone might object that when Lear finally does recognize Kent slightly later he does not banish him but welcomes him "hither" (5.3.290), even if in doing so he sounds more like a king welcoming a state visitor than an old friend. But the metaphoric context of Lear's remark—its maddening inappropriateness to the dramatic context of the great grief at hand—makes the remark seem dementedly humorous. Kent's reply reinforces the fact that such welcomes are equivalent to exile: "Nor no man else" (5.3.291).

11. Geoge Orwell, "Lear, Tolstoy and the Fool," in *Shooting an Elephant and Other Essays* (N.Y.: Harcourt, Brace, 1945), p. 39.

12. French, *Shakespeare and the Critics,* p. 191, formulates a similar question. In Lear's speeches over the dead body of Cordelia "what we are responding to is the agonised *intensity,* not (or not necessarily) the *disinterestedness,* of the feeling. . . . [Shakespeare] is silent on whether Lear feels it because Cordelia would be *answering his needs."*

13. Cf. Martha Andresen, "'Ripeness is All': Sententiae and Commonplaces in *King Lear,* " in *Some Facets of "King Lear,"* p. 163. "In the play's last dark scene Lear does not recognize Kent, whose sententious voice has marked him as a representative of rationality and communal wisdom. In rejecting Kent with the others, Lear rejects both a community of sufferers and a tradition of consolation. In his madness he suffers alone." See also E. E. Stoll, *From Shakespeare to Joyce* (N.Y.: Doubleday, 1944), p. 116.

14. In *Conceptions of Shakespeare* (Cambridge, Mass.: Harvard University Press, 1966), p. 95, though Alfred Harbage unaccountably argues that the final scene leaves us "in no mood for censure" of Lear, he rightly praises Cordelia, Kent, and the Fool's solidarity in love for the king.

> The focus of their love is Lear, and there is never a moment in the play when one or another of them is far from his side. Kent is beseeching his attention as he kneels by Cordelia's body. Lear dies craving the thing he has always had. It is in this sense that he dies unredeemed: he has *not* learned. An aura of martyrdom surrounds him because his suffering stems from the value he has placed on a thing of value [love], but he dies a martyr without faith.

15. The idea that in this reference to the Fool Shakespeare was merely fashioning a theatrical "in joke" based on the fact that the same actor played the roles of Cordelia and the Fool seems precious to me. (See, for example, Irving Ribner, *Patterns in Shakespearean Tragedy* [London: Methuen, 1960], p. 136.) In *Fools of Time: Studies in Shakespearean Tragedy* (Toronto: University of Toronto Press, 1967), p. 105, Northrop Frye, following Bradley, concludes that Lear's cry suggests a "blending together in his mind of the two people he loves as a father." The more likely claim, however, is George Duthie's in his edition of *King Lear* (London: Cambridge University Press, 1960), p. 274: "Surely the Fool, like Kent, is forgotten." Even if we were to suppose that Lear was consciously referring to his Fool here, we would have to keep in mind what he had just said about Caius's being "dead and rotten" as we evaluated this statement. We could not, of course, distinguish fact from paranoid fiction in it. The discussion that follows is based on Mason's assumption in *Shakespeare's Tragedies of Love,* p. 169, that "nobody . . . can really believe that Shakespeare *forgot* to give the Fool a significant departure from the play."

16. Thus the psychologically symbolic appropriateness in Lear's murdering the scapegoat executioner. As his curses on Kent and Cordelia show, the way Lear deals with those who present an uncomfortable image of himself to himself is to drive them away: "Hence, and avoid my sight!" (1.1.124).

Professor Marianne Novy, who has offered a number of helpful suggestions to improve the argument of this book, has urged me to question whether Lear's "I might have sav'd her" could not be a sudden change of emotion expressing Lear's contrition for his part in Cordelia's death, not a distracting vaunt as I have claimed. If it is so, it could only be the most momentary self-recrimination; the weight of contextual evidence both prior to and immediately after these words when Lear clearly stands in a self-proclaimed role as virtuous defender of his sacred daughter against all violators would seem to favor my supposition of a hint of self-righteousness in Lear's tone, even in these apparently more self-reflexive words. Sudden self-recrimination and assumption of responsibility, especially in a matter of this seriousness, would produce a greater pause, a silencing mortification, not speech that can so easily remind us of the guardian's role Lear self-flatteringly assumed in his "let's away to prison" speech that helped push the action on to the catastrophe.

17. As Cavell puts it in "Avoidance of Love," p. 301: "From the beginning, and through each moment, until they are led to prison, he might have saved her, had he done what every love requires, put himself aside long enough to see through to her, and be seen through." Cf. Rosenberg, *Masks of "King Lear"*, p. 299.

18. I am aware that some critics take this unwillingness on Lear's part to see his daughters as a sign of moral advance, that Lear is now beyond them in a "purer" moral element because he no longer needs to confront them with their ingratitude as he had earlier. See, for example, Dorothy C. Hockey, "The Trial Pattern in *King Lear*," *SQ* 10 (1959): 395; Ernest W. Talbert, "Lear, the King: A Preface to a Study of Shakespeare's Tragedy," in *Medieval and Renaissance Studies*, ed. O. B. Hardison, Jr. (Chapel Hill: University of North Carolina Press, 1966), p. 104; Elton, *"King Lear" and the Gods*, pp. 238–41; Herbert R. Coursen, *Christian Ritual and the World of Shakespeare's Tragedies* (Lewisburg, Pa.: Bucknell University Press, 1976), pp. 288–94. Nonetheless, Goneril and Regan are his own daughters; and when Cordelia asks to see them with him, surely she does not wish to get involved in a shouting match with them as Lear had. Only when her own eyes see it will she believe they are capable of the cruelties she anticipates. She has sufficient hope for them and in them to believe they might respond favorably to their own consciences when confronted with their ravaged father. It would seem that Lear, however, has abandoned them in his despair and elbowing shame.

19. Not only is Lear not forced to choose between two problematic alternatives, he barely acts at all. After his banishment of Kent and Cordelia, he never initiates the kind of activity that would awaken our terrible apprehension for a tragic hero's inexorable march to ruin. As Miller, *"King Lear* and the Comic Form," p. 9, notes, Lear "seems more like someone who foolishly leans against a prop and brings his house crashing down around his head than a [tragic] hero." Cf. Mark Van Doren, *Shakespeare* (N.Y.: Doubleday, 1939), pp. 204ff., on Lear's extraordinary inaction.

20. Cf. Alexander Grinstein, "King Lear's Impending Death," *AI* 30 (1973): 128. "One of the reasons for the partition of his kingdom during his lifetime may be to buy his daughters' affection—to guarantee that they will continue to love him now that he is so old." Though important surely, age may have less to do with it ultimately than his wondering whether he is deserving of the love he so desperately needs.

21. In an important but neglected essay, "Cordelia Absent," originally published in *Shakespeare Quarterly* in 1951 and reprinted in *Aesthetics and the Theory of Criticism: Selected Essays of Arnold Isenberg* (Chicago: University of Chicago Press, 1973), pp. 125–37, Professor Isenberg carefully defends the thesis that

Cordelia "is continuously present both to Lear's mind and our own; and the silence [in Lear about her], the absence, are not only compatible with this visionary presence, they are the positive pledge and proof of its reality" (p. 126). But this subconscious awareness only serves to emphasize how Lear avoids coming to terms with himself or his crimes against Cordelia and Kent. As Warren Taylor, "Lear and the Lost Self," *CE* 25 (1964):511, comments:

> Shakespeare holds Lear's . . . awareness of the fuller and deeper natures of man, father, and king to fitful and transient moments. Those bright lights still flash from the shadowy and deranged awareness of a willful and dispossessed old man. Unlike his handling of Antony and Othello, whom he permits to voice their own errors in judgment, Shakespeare never permits a full sense of his failure to both his family and his kingdom to cross Lear's consciousness.

See also, Levin Schucking, "Character and Action: *King Lear*," reprinted in *Shakespeare: The Tragedies. A Collection of Critical Essays,* ed. Clifford Leech (Chicago: University of Chicago Press, 1965), pp. 63–65; Robert Heilman, "'Twere Best Not Know Myself': Othello, Lear, Macbeth," in *Shakespeare 400: Essays by American Scholars on the Anniversary of the Poet's Birth,* ed. James G. McManaway (N.Y.: Holt, Rinehart, and Winston, 1964), p. 97; and William Empson, "Fool in *Lear*," in *The Structure of Complex Words* (Ann Arbor: University of Michigan Press, 1967), p. 154, who quotes—apparently with unqualified approval—George Orwell's claim that the ending of the play shows Lear "still cursing, still understanding nothing" (from *Shooting an Elephant and Other Essays,* p. 39).

22. James, *The Dream of Learning* (London: Oxford University Press, 1951), p. 76.

23. Rosenberg (*Masks of "King Lear",* p. 321) is the only critic I have been able to discover who calls attention to this central metaphor: "*Usurped:* illicitly commandeered Lear's identity, drove out the rightful self, occupied it by force. . . . The image extends the Ixionic: on his wheel, Lear pursued and fled from himself."

24. Ernest W. Talbert, "Lear, the King: A Preface to a Study of Shakespeare's Tragedy," pp. 87–88, makes a similar point about the first scene. Though James's views on unification could support the notion of the political character of the mistake, Professor Talbert notes that what permeates the text, however, is the "great injustice done Cordelia."

25. Even Iago becomes more comprehensible as a character when we see him as a protean transformation of the clever servant of comic convention "doing in" his supposed master, like Mosca, for example, in Jonson's *Volpone*.

26. Stockholder, "Multiple Genres of *King Lear*," p. 49, speaks of how Lear participates in the "conventional low comedy of servants' brawls."

27. As Roland M. Frye, *Shakespeare and Christian Doctrine* (Princeton, N.J.: Princeton University Press, 1963), p. 123, suggests, in *King Lear* "much can be said of the old king's folly, but that folly never went so far as to justify the inhuman response to him on the part of Regan and Goneril."

28. French, *Shakespeare and the Critics,* p. 166. In some respects related is Stephen Reid's, "In Defense of Goneril and Regan," *AI* 27 (1970):226–44.

29. For corroboration of the point, see Philip W. London, "The Stature of Lear," *University of Windsor Review* 1 (1965):177.

30. Elton, *"King Lear" and the Gods*, p. 329.

31. As Miller, *"King Lear* and the Comic Form," p. 9, states: *"Lear* is not his play in quite the unshakable sense that *Hamlet* is Hamlet's or *Othello*, Othello's." As in the comedies, there is a "societal rather than a personal orientation."

32. I cannot agree with Leo Kirschbaum, *Character and Characterization in Shakespeare* (Detroit: Wayne State University Press, 1962), p. 61, that Edgar is not a "mimetic unity" but a "dramatic device." See also, Harold S. Wilson, *On the Design of Shakespearean Tragedy* (Toronto: University of Toronto Press, 1957), p. 185. The *reductio ad absurdum* of the position is Irving Ribner's defense of Edgar when he insults the mortally wounded Edmund. Though Ribner himself admits Edgar's remarks (5.3.171–74) are in poor taste, he nonetheless justifies them because Edgar is "not a real person; he is a dramatic device" (*Patterns in Shakespearean Tragedy*, p. 135). As Janet Adelman's Introduction to *Twentieth Century Interpretations of "King Lear"* (Englewood Cliffs, N.J.: Prentice-Hall, 1978), p. 10, suggests: "The request that we abandon the psychological mode of inquiry and response at just those moments when the behavior of a character seems unaccountable or bothersome to us is fundamentally a request that we abandon an important part of ourselves; and as such, it will often impoverish our experience of the play." Professor Adelman's own analysis of Edgar's character is a far more satisfactory one, though like Rolf Soellner, *Shakespeare's Patterns of Self-Knowledge* (Columbus: Ohio State University Press, 1972), p. 298; Roy W. Battenhouse, *Shakespearean Tragedy: Its Art and Its Christian Premises* (Bloomington: Indiana University Press, 1969), pp. 294–300; Morris H. Partee, "The Divine Comedy of *King Lear*," *Genre* 4 (1971):61, 69—other recent critics who express significant reservations about Edgar's character and behavior but who also believe Edgar ultimately changes for the better—she, too, believes that after the scene at Dover Edgar behaves admirably.

33. Cf., for example, Mason, *Shakespeare's Tragedies of Love*, p. 218; Goldberg, *Essay on "King Lear"*, pp. 87–88; James, *Dream of Learning*, pp. 112–13. Anthony Dawson, "Paradoxical Dramaturgy in *King Lear*," *Wascana Review* 9 (1974):37, speaks of the building suspense in the "stagey" developments of act 5, scene 3, a scene whose movement and tone suggest the conclusion of a comedy, set us up to expect a reprieve. Cf. Emrys Jones, *Scenic Form in Shakespeare* (London: Oxford University Press, 1971), pp. 191–92.

34. Cf. Kirschbaum, *Character and Characterization in Shakespeare*, p. 48; Warren Stevenson, "Albany as Archetype in *King Lear*," *MLQ* 26 (1965):257–63.

35. Stockholder, "Multiple Genres of *King Lear*," p. 61, points to the comic scuffle here after Albany recalls his intentions for the king and his daughter.

36. Richmond Y. Hathorn, *Tragedy, Myth, and Mystery* (Bloomington: Indiana University Press, 1963), pp. 184–85, quotes John Lothian, *"King Lear": A Tragic Reading of Life* (Toronto: Clarke, Irwin, 1949), p. 98, on Albany's easy, insufficiently reflective optimism at the close, a hint for Hathorn "that he is about to repeat all the errors that the old king had made before him." Cf. Alan R. Young, "The Written and Oral Sources of *King Lear* and the Problem of Justice in the Play," *SEL* 15 (1975):319.

37. The pattern holds true even in Edmund who, at the finale, delays his act of repentance well beyond his initial decision and in the gentleman's

speech to Albany when, having carried a bloody knife onstage, he does not immediately specify who has been killed so that the audience is free to assume it may be Cordelia or Lear before we discover that Goneril has committed suicide.

38. As Nicholas Brooke, *Shakespeare: "King Lear"* (London: Edward Arnold, 1963), p. 36, states, Edgar's truth here "is shrouded in complacency. It *is* true; but it cannot be known smugly."

39. Cf. Cavell, "Avoidance of Love," p. 282; Robert Egan, *Drama within Drama: Shakespeare's Sense of His Art* (N.Y.: Columbia University Press, 1975), p. 25; Elton, *"King Lear" and the Gods*, p. 92; Empson, "Fool in *Lear*," p. 141; D. J. Enright, *Shakespeare and the Students* (N.Y.: Schocken Books, 1970), pp. 25, 44–45, 51; Alvin Kernan, "Formalism and Realism in Elizabethan Drama: The Miracles in *King Lear*," *Renaissance Drama* 9 (1966):61–62. Kernan states: "While Gloucester may be taken in by Edgar's miracle, the grotesque awkwardness on stage of that 'miracle' emphasizes the fact that it is only a shabby theatrical device, imposed on a man of less than first rate intellect to make him go on living some dream of the gods' care for human life which is at odds with what has happened and what will" (p. 62). Rosenberg, *Masks of "King Lear"*, p. 265, suggests that King James and Samuel Harsnett's exposures of "false miracles" may add a further irony to Edgar's behavior here.

40. Edgar does, it is true, reveal himself to Gloucester just before Gloucester dies. But at that point, having led his wounded father on a dangerous chase, whatever joy the revelation brings Gloucester must be weighed against the extent to which it may have helped kill him, assuming Edgar is correct when he claims Gloucester's heart "burst smilingly" betwixt "two extremes of passion, joy and grief" (5.3.199–200). When Albany asks him how he has "known the miseries of your father," Edgar replies, "By nursing them" (5.3.181–82). There is an obvious and richly ironic ambiguity in Edgar's answer.

41. Cf. Goldberg, *Essay on "King Lear"*, p. 116.

42. As Cavell has suggested (in "Avoidance of Love," p. 285), it may be significant that Edgar only summons the strength to reveal his identity to Gloucester when he is armed. Certainly, he has hedged his bets by then; and his means secure him: if he loses in combat, Gloucester will regret his stricken youth; if he wins, he is, of course, a returning hero. In neither case does he risk presenting himself as himself to his father for his father's sake.

43. Kirschbaum, *Character and Characterization in Shakespeare*, pp. 44–45, reads Edgar's behavior here as a "necessity of plot," though he admits Edgar speaks as if a victory of the Albany forces were a necessary preface to his settling his accounts with Edmund.

44. My interpretation of this scene differs radically from the one offered by Andresen, " 'Ripeness is All,' " pp. 145–50.

45. W. B. C. Watkins, *Shakespeare and Spenser* (Princeton, N.J.: Princeton University Press, 1950), p. 83, calls the trial by combat an awkward and unnecessary delay that seems "tedious and questionable [structurally] at such a crisis."

46. Here, as elsewhere, the Gloucester subplot appears to have a simple homiletic clarity. The impression is, of course, misleading, though some critics feel otherwise. See, for example, Howard Felperin, *Shakespearean Rep-*

resentation: Mimesis and Modernity in Elizabethan Tragedy (Princeton, N.J.: Princeton University Press, 1977), p. 92.

47. See Robert Ornstein, *The Moral Vision of Jacobean Tragedy* (Madison: University of Wisconsin Press, 1960), p. 264.

48. Egan, *Drama within Drama*, p. 51, finds Edgar's statement "almost obscenely incongruous; we have watched Gloucester lose his eyes, and we know that while Edmund contributed to and permitted the act, its more direct cause was Gloucester's own moral choice to comfort and save the life of Lear." Egan's objection to Edgar's speech is almost mild by comparison to some others: cf. Mason, *Shakespeare's Tragedies of Love*, p. 222; Rosenberg, *Masks of "King Lear"*, pp. 306–7; Empson, "Fool in *Lear*," p. 150; Brooke, "Ending of *King Lear*," p. 83; R. C. Bald, " 'Thou, Nature, Art My Goddess': Edmund and Renaissance Free-Thought," in *Joseph Quincy Adams Memorial Studies*, ed. James G. McManaway et al. (Washington, D.C.: Folger Shakespeare Library, 1948), p. 338; Adelman, Introduction, p. 15.

49. Enright, *Shakespeare and the Students*, pp. 61–62, speaks of the self-involvement of Edgar here and his tedious and gratuitous moralizing.

50. Though in this instance I use the word "nature" in a totally different sense from that in previous examples, I think the symbolic range of the phrase "where nature doth with merit challenge" justifies the equivocation.

51. In Fly, "Beyond Extremity," p. 96.

52. See, for example, Holloway, *Story of the Night*, p. 76; Stephen Booth, "On the Greatness of King Lear," in *Twentieth Century Interpretations of "King Lear"*, p. 102; Ruth Nevo, *Tragic Form in Shakespeare* (Princeton, N.J.: Princeton University Press, 1972), pp. 304–5; Frank Kermode, "Introduction to *King Lear*," in *The Riverside Shakespeare*, p. 1253.

53. Rosenberg, *Masks of "King Lear"*, p. 322; see also Felperin, *Shakespearean Representation*, p. 95.

54. Sheldon Zitner, "*King Lear* and Its Language," in *Some Facets of King Lear*, p. 4, also takes Edgar to task for his last words, but for different reasons.

55. I owe the clarifying formulation of this distinction between tragedy and melodrama to my friend and colleague, Jerome Miller.

56. As Coursen, *Christian Ritual*, p. 270, rightly states: " 'Thou swearest thy Gods in vain,' says Kent to Lear (1.1.163), and the taunt could be applied to any reference to the gods in the play"—not because the gods do not exist or operate in the world necessarily, but because men are blasphemously presumptuous. See also Mason, *Shakespeare's Tragedies of Love*, p. 170. Contrast the conclusion Brooke draws in "Ending of *King Lear*," p. 85.

57. Of the last scene in which Cordelia is pushed aside by "subordinate issues" and forgotten, Jones in *Scenic Form in Shakespeare*, notes: "Everyone is frantically, or at least busily (even fussily), self-preoccupied" (p. 192). Only "Kent, with his single-minded devotion to the King, jolts their attention to where it should have been all along." Lionel Trilling also argues that man himself might be solely responsible for tragedy in *King Lear* (*The Experience of Literature* [N.Y.: Doubleday, 1967], p. 131).

58. Peter Anderson, "The Fragile World of King Lear," *Comparative Drama* 5 (1971–72):273, quotes Montaigne's *Apologie of Raymond Sebond* (2.12.446–47) on the wise man's pursuit of self-knowledge: "I am perswaded, if he speaks in conscience, he will confesse, that all the benefit he hath gotten by so tedious a persuit, hath been, that he hath learned to know his own weakness."

Chapter 2. The Pastoral Norm

1. *"King Lear" in Our Time,* p. 63.
2. Ibid., p. 65.
3. Cf. Rosalie Colie, "'Nature's Above Art in that Respect': Limits of the Pastoral Pattern," in *Shakespeare's Living Art* (Princeton, N.J.: Princeton University Press, 1974), p. 304. "In *Cymbeline,* wild creatures may have threatened the boys, but they learned to hunt them for food. In *King Lear,* the wild creatures, as Albany says, are all human, and they do the hunting until it seems to Albany that 'Mankind preys upon itself.' Even the "head-lugg'd bear" (4.2.42) is an indictment of man, not nature, since the phrase refers to an animal mutilated by dogs trained by men to kill.
4. Battenhouse, *Shakespearean Tragedy,* p. 297, remarks that when Edgar took his disguise: "He was then thinking of a charity on the part of others than himself; yet his own commitment to humiliation implies on his part a pilgrimage in search of charity. . . . As a beggar he is associating himself with society's outcasts; he is suffering imaginatively their miseries as a way of eliciting fellowship from his neighbors." If Edgar is on a "pilgrimage in search of charity," it is only charity for himself. His selfishly "eliciting fellowship from his neighbors" should not be made to sound as if he is doing them a favor.
5. As we shall see, this description of Edgar symbolically applies to a number of encounters in the play: Gloucester before Edmund in act 1, scene 1; Lear with Goneril and Regan in act 1, scene 4, and act 2, scene 4; Gloucester with Kent before the hysterical king in act 3, scene 4; Edgar as Poor Tom before Lear and then before Gloucester; and Lear before Gloucester in act 4, scene 6.
6. Russell Fraser, *Shakespeare's Poetics in Relation to "King Lear"* (Nashville: Vanderbilt University Press, 1966), p. 14, remarks upon the emblem or "mute figure" in the juxtaposition on the same stage of Kent in the stocks and Edgar in disguise, but only to conclude the two men are alike in being unjustly made wretched.
7. The gentleman's speech at act 4, scene 6, 205–7, explicitly claims that Cordelia redeems nature from death, the "general curse" of the Fall.
8. Contrast Edgar, who, though not self-consciously villainous like Edmund, is like him in persistently manipulating his father, allowing him nothing.
9. Lear is genuinely neurotic about weeping. It is symbolic for him of his womanish weakness (read Cordelia, who is several times described as "in tears") and thus, mistakenly, of his manhood's shame. Though repeatedly overcome by tears, he insists he must avoid womanish weakness at all costs to life. To Goneril he wails: "Life and death! I am asham'd/That thou hast power to shake my manhood thus" (1.4.296–97). To the heavens he cries:

> fool me not so much
> To bear it tamely; touch me with noble anger,
> And let not women's weapons, water-drops,
> Stain my man's cheeks!

(2.4.275–78)

With devastating dramatic irony, given the play's ending, he feigns strength:

                            You think I'll weep:
No, I'll not weep.
I have full cause of weeping, but this heart
Shall break into a hundred thousand flaws
Or ere I'll weep.

                                                    (2.4.282–86)

See also act 5, scene 3, 24–25.

10. Contrast France's response to Cordelia. He will "take up what's cast away" (1.1.253) when he marries the dowerless daughter "thrown to my chance" (256).

11. Phyllis Rackin, "Delusion as Resolution in *King Lear*," *SQ* 21 (1970):29, summarizes the range of critical reaction to Lear's "look there" speech.

12. Hence the dramatic irony in Lear's outraged claim in act 1, scene 1,— "So be my grave my peace" (125)—measured against Cordelia's living ease.

13. For general discussions of pastoral ideals, see Renato Poggioli, *The Oaten Flute: Essays on Pastoral Poetry and the Pastoral Ideal* (Cambridge, Mass.: Harvard University Press, 1975), pp. 1–82; Harold E. Toliver, *Pastoral Forms and Attitudes* (Berkeley: University of California Press, 1971), pp. 1–19; Lawrence Lerner, *The Uses of Nostalgia: Studies in Pastoral Poetry* (N.Y.: Schocken Books, 1972), pp. 11–104. Attempts to relate pastoral conventions to *King Lear* include: Mack, *"King Lear" in Our Time*, pp. 63–66; David Young, "The Natural Fool of Fortune," in his *The Heart's Forest: A Study of Shakespeare's Pastoral Plays* (New Haven: Yale University Press, 1972), pp. 73–103; Nancy Lindheim, *"King Lear* as Pastoral Tragedy," in *Some Facets of "King Lear"*, pp. 169–84; and Colie, "Limits of the Pastoral Pattern," pp. 284–316.

14. Poggioli, *Oaten Flute*, p. 5.

15. Lerner, *Uses of Nostalgia*, pp. 81–104.

16. S. L. Bethell, *Shakespeare and the Popular Dramatic Tradition* (Durham, N.C.: Duke University Press, 1944), pp. 67–68, notes that Cordelia alone among the characters in *King Lear* is associated with Christian language and doctrine. The best general treatment of Cordelia's character remains John Danby's chapter on her in *Shakespeare's Doctrine of Nature: A Study of "King Lear"* (London: Faber and Faber, 1948), pp. 114–50. Surely Dean Frye, "The Context of Lear's Unbuttoning," *ELH* 32 (1965):25, is mistaken when he claims Cordelia is not associated with pastoral. If Arthur Kinney, "Lear," *Massachusetts Review* 17 (1976):684, is correct in his assumption that Shakespeare consciously chose the Spenserian spelling *Cordelia* for the youngest daughter in order to play on the Elizabethan "use of Delia as the sonnetteer's anagram for "*ideal*," we have Cordelia figuring as the ideal heart. See also Joseph Satin, "The Symbolic Role of Cordelia in *King Lear*," *Forum* 9 (1971–73):15.

17. My dear friend and colleague, Jerome Miller, has brought it to my attention that Lear is not the first to compound his shame by hiding from it in it. In Genesis after the Fall, Jehovah pays a visit to Adam and Eve, only to find them turned away from him in hiding, presumably out of a combination of shame and fear. Having confronted them and called them out, his first words to them are not a thunderous accusation of sin or a curse, but a question about the source of their discovery of shame: "Who told thee that thou wast naked?" Given his later decision to clothe them before they leave Eden, the likelihood is that even his tone of voice may have been more alarmed and

grieving than accusational. But when the details of the disobedience become clear, Adam and Eve's shame still keeps them from facing their shamefulness. Rather than admit their offense against God and beg forgiveness, Adam blames Eve and Eve, the serpent for the crime. Who is to say what Jehovah would have done had they stood abashed before him asking forgiveness? He cannot be accused of mercilessness if, having apprised them of their cursed destiny, he clothes them, not as they clothed themselves in their shame, but as Cordelia clothed Lear, in pity for his suffering flesh, and as God marked Cain, not to brand his sin but to mitigate suffering so that anyone finding him would not exact vengeance. Perhaps, then, original sin was not the original sin, but the second.

18. Lindheim, *"King Lear as Pastoral Tragedy,"* p. 177, discusses Cordelia as a perfect balance of feeling and restraint.

19. Lear's refusal of Cordelia's request to confront his other daughters confirms the dramatic irony in an earlier speech, theatrically delivered to Goneril.

> I will not trouble thee, my child; farewell:
> We'll no more meet, no more see one another.
> But yet thou art my flesh, my blood, my daughter—
> Or rather a disease that's in my flesh,
> Which I must needs call mine. . . .
>   But I'll not chide thee.
> Let shame come when it will, I do not call it.
>
>   (2.4.219–26)

20. A considerable number of recent critics agree substantially with Stanley Cavell ("Avoidance of Love," pp. 300–01), about his speech, but none have put it so well:

> Lear imagines that she is crying for the reasons that he is on the verge of tears—the old reasons, the sense of impotence, shame, loss. But *her* reasons for tears do not occur to him, that she sees him as he is, as he was, that he is unable to take his last chance; that he, at the farthest edge of life, must again sacrifice her, again abdicate his responsibilities; and that he cannot know what he asks. And yet, seeing that, it is for him that she is cast down.

Cf. Danby, *Shakespeare's Doctrine of Nature,* p. 194; Mason, *Shakespeare's Tragedies of Love,* p. 223; French, *Shakespeare and the Critics,* p. 186; W. F. Blissett, "Recognition in *King Lear,"* in *Some Facets of "King Lear",* p. 113; Allen B. Cameron, "The Value of Lear's Death," *CEA Critic* 35(1973):17; John E. Van Domelen, "Why Cordelia Must Die," *South Central Bulletin* 35(1975):134.

21. See Knight, "Comedy of the Grotesque," p. 127.

22. Since writing this chapter, I have come upon Duncan Fraser's article, "Much Virtue in 'Nothing': Cordelia's Part in the First Scene of *King Lear,"* *Cambridge Quarterly* 8(1978):1–10, which anticipates me in suggesting the likelihood that Cordelia is using parody "to get the situation treated lightly" (p. 8). Coursen, *Christian Ritual,* pp. 278–84, in defending Cordelia from Roy Battenhouse's accusation of her here (see the next note), rightly argues that Battenhouse does not allow for the possibility of parody in Cordelia's reply to Lear in the love test.

23. See, for example, Brooke, *Shakespeare: "King Lear"*, p. 18; Sophia Blaydes, "Cordelia's Loss of Innocence," *Studies in the Humanities* 5(1976): 15–21; Battenhouse, *Shakespearean Tragedy*, pp. 282–84; G. R. Elliott, "The Initial Contrast in *King Lear*," a supplementary essay in *Dramatic Providence in "Macbeth": A Study of Shakespeare's Tragic Theme of Humanity and Grace* (Princeton, N.J.: Princeton University Press, 1960), p. 243; Enright, *Shakespeare and the Students*, p. 21; Thomas Greenfield, "Excellent Things in Women: The Emergence of Cordelia," *SAB* 42(1977):47; French, *Shakespeare and the Critics*, p. 148; Goldberg, *Essay on "King Lear"*, pp. 20–28; Mason, *Shakespeare's Tragedies of Love*, p. 174; Nevo, *Tragic Form in Shakespeare*, p. 265; Arthur Sewell, *Character and Society in Shakespeare* (London: Oxford University Press, 1951), pp. 62, 112; Wilson, *On the Design of Shakespearean Tragedy*, p. 184.

The most substantial defenses of Cordelia's behavior in the first scene are those of Cavell, "Avoidance of Love," pp. 290–95; Fraser (see the preceding note); Alan Sinfield, "Lear and Laing," *EIC* 26(1976):3; and Ivor Morris, "Cordelia and Lear," *SQ* 8(1957): 141–58. Reibetanz, "Theatrical Emblems in *King Lear*," p. 54, and Zitner, "*King Lear* and Its Language," p. 7, also defend her, but in ways that unnecessarily repudiate psychological realism.

24. Goldberg, *Essay on "King Lear"*, p. 22.

25. Richard Matthews, "Edmund's Redemption in *King Lear*," *SQ* 26(1975):26; Ornstein, *Moral Vision of Jacobean Tragedy*, p. 264; and Paul Siegel, *Shakespearean Tragedy and the Elizabethan Compromise* (N.Y.: New York University Press, 1957), p. 164—all point out the irony that Thomas McFarland, *Tragic Meanings in Shakespeare* (N.Y.: Random House, 1966), p. 144, notes: "Edmund the free, Edmund the maker of his own destiny, is more shackled in human bondage than any other figure in the play." When Edmund declares, "All with me's meet that I can fashion fit," he speaks with dramatic irony. He may mean by it only that anything he can make serve his purposes he will consider suitable behavior; but given the way he acts in the challenge with Edgar in act 5, we know he is also unwittingly desperate to "fit fashion," to stand in the plague of a custom he thinks he has abjured.

For more extended discussions of Edmund's character, see Bald, " 'Thou, Nature, Art My Goddess,' " pp. 337–49; Robert Bauer, "Despite of Mine Own Nature: Edmund and the Orders, Cosmic and Moral," *TSLL* 10(1968):359–66; and, especially, Claude Summers, "Stand Up for Bastards: Shakespeare's Edmund and Love's Failure," *College Literature* 4(1977):225–31.

26. I believe Felperin, *Shakespearean Representation*, p. 94, and Ornstein, *Moral Vision of Jacobean Tragedy*, p. 263, are mistaken when they claim there are no hidden depths in Edmund, that his resentment is more logical than psychological. The sexual implications I have been discussing in Edmund's speech, implications that surely lie deeper than Edmund's consciousness, argue the opposite conclusion, in fact.

27. When Edmund says to Edgar, "Fly this place,/Intelligence is given where you are hid" (2.1.20–21), he formulates an explanatory emblem for Lear's child-changed game strategy. He must "catch" Cordelia in his "away to prison" speech or be caught in the act of his evasions.

28. Cf. Luke 14:10. That parable may be an analogue to the Lear story; for the guest who finds he does not belong in the highest place "begins in shame to take the lowest."

29. Cf. Rosenberg, *Masks of "King Lear"*, pp. 186–87.

NOTES

30. That is the point, I think, of Shakespeare's making Oswald so faithful to Goneril. In a sense, he thus becomes Kent's double. In self-righteously raging at a faithful servant, Kent does not realize he is implicitly condemning himself.

31. Contrast the view of Sears Jayne, "Charity in *King Lear*," *SQ* 15(1964):287, who believes man is "trapped in the paradox of requiring love but being unable to give it."

32. *The Family Reunion*, pt. 2, scene 2, in T. S. Eliot, *The Complete Poems and Plays, 1909–50* (N.Y.: Harcourt, Brace, and World, 1958), p. 279.

33. The only critics I have discovered who note any significant reservations about the reunion are Lawrence Danson, *Tragic Alphabet: Shakespeare's Drama of Language* (New Haven: Yale University Press, 1974), pp. 195–96, and Goldberg, *Essay on "King Lear"*, pp. 28–33, 141–46. But one should also compare Paul Alpers, *"King Lear* and the Theory of the Sight Pattern," in *In Defense of Reading*, ed. Reuben Brower and Richard Poirier (N.Y.: E. P. Dutton, 1962), pp. 150–51.

34. A number of critics have—I think mistakenly—argued the virtues of Stoical endurance in the play's scheme of things. See, for example, Rosalie Colie, "The Energies of Endurance: Biblical Echo in *King Lear*," in *Some Facets of "King Lear"*, p. 136, and her "Limits of the Pastoral Pattern," p. 316; Ornstein, *Moral Vision of Jacobean Tragedy*, p. 272; Holloway, *Story of the Night*, pp. 85, 88, 92; James P. Driscoll, "The Vision of King Lear," *Shakespeare Studies* 10(1977):159–60.

35. I cannot fully agree with Maynard Mack in "The Jacobean Shakespeare: Some Observations on the Construction of the Tragedies," from *Essays in Shakespearean Criticism*, ed. James Calderwood and Harold Toliver (Englewood Cliffs, N.J.: Prentice-Hall, 1970), p. 33, when he maintains: "We are invited to apply the Fool's comments to Lear's inner experience and I suspect that most of us do so. The Fool thus serves, to some extent, as a screen on which Shakespeare flashes, as it were, readings from the psychic life of the protagonist, possibly even his subconscious life." In restricted terms—the bitter terms of ridicule—Mack's suggestion makes a good deal of sense. Lear undoubtedly does reflect consciously or subconsciously about the folly of what he has done. But the sweetness of the Fool's wisdom remains well beyond Lear's reflection. There are many things in the Fool's pronouncements that are not aspects of the king's psychic life in any way. Cf. William Rosen, *Shakespeare and the Craft of Tragedy* (Cambridge, Mass.: Harvard University Press, 1960), p. 13.

36. Poggioli, *Oaten Flute*, pp. 4–5.

37. Ibid., p. 6.

38. Just previously, in response to his Fool's question—"Can you make no use of nothing, nuncle?" (1.4.130–31)— Lear had claimed, "nothing can be made out of nothing" (1.4.132–33).

39. In John Danby, "The Fool and Handy-Dandy," from *Shakespeare's Doctrine of Nature*, reprinted in Calderwood and Toliver's, *Essays in Shakespearean Criticism*, p. 487.

40. The jumbled time relationships in the Fool's speech (3.2.95–96) further undercut the significance of temporal order or any sense of time's progression to a better time.

41. I say "momentarily" because at the beginning of act 3, scene 4, Lear is again resisting the idea that he needs shelter.

42. Cf. Rosenberg, *Masks of "King Lear"*, p. 194.

43. See the references to Lear at act 3, scene 2, 40 and act 2, scene 4, 48.

44. See, for example, Goldberg, *Essay on "King Lear"*, pp. 90–91; Brooke, *Shakespeare: "King Lear"*, pp. 23–24; Mason, *Shakespeare's Tragedies of Love*, pp. 183–84; Empson, "Fool in *Lear*," pp. 133–34; Bernard McElroy, *Shakespeare's Mature Tragedies* (Princeton, N. J.: Princeton University Press, 1973), pp. 188–89; Roger Ellis, "The Fool in Shakespeare: A Study in Alienation," *Critical Quarterly* 10(1968):246–68; Hidekatsu Nojima, "Exit the Fool," in *English Criticism in Japan*, ed. and comp. by Earl Miner (Tokyo: University of Tokyo Press, 1972), pp. 84–100; Donald M. Smith, "'And I'll go to bed at noon': The Fool in *King Lear*," *Essays in Arts and Sciences* 5(1976):37–45; Glena D. Wood, "The Tragi-Comic Dimensions of Lear's Fool," *Costerus* 5(1971):197–226; Zitner, "*King Lear* and Its Language," p. 12; Robert Speaight, *Nature in Shakespearean Tragedy* (N. Y.: Collier, 1962), p. 108; John Danby, "The Fool and Handy-Dandy," pp. 483–92; Larry S. Champion, *Shakespeare's Tragic Perspective* (Athens: University of Georgia Press, 1976), pp. 161–64; Peter Bryant, "Nuncle Lear," *English Studies in Africa* 20(1977):35–38.

45. Cavell, "Avoidance of Love," p. 287.

46. In McFarland, *Shakespeare's Pastoral Comedy* (Chapel Hill: University of North Carolina Press, 1972), p. 28.

47. Cf. Fly, "Beyond Extremity," p. 94.

Chapter 3. The Player King

1. Cf. Van Laan, "Acting as Action in *King Lear*," in *Some Facets of "King Lear*," p. 59.

2. As Soji Iwasaki, "Time and Truth in *King Lear*," in *English Criticism in Japan*, p. 67, states: "To have the nominal authority of a king and a hundred knights for hunting and banqueting, however, is in fact to be a holiday king, or a Lord of Misrule."

3. Both William Frost, "Shakespeare's Rituals and the Opening of *King Lear*," reprinted from *The Hudson Review* in *Shakespeare: The Tragedies*, pp. 190–200 and Elliott, "The Initial Contrast in *King Lear*," pp. 235–50, argue that the first scene is a spectacular dramatic introduction about which we need not raise questions regarding the central characters' motives.

The problem with the ingenious analysis of the first scene made by John R. Dove and Peter Gamble, "Our Darker Purpose: The Division Scene in *Lear*," *Neuphilologische Mitteilungen* 70 (1969):306–18, is that if, as they maintain, Lear's coronet for Cordelia is to be a surprise bequest in exchange for her marrying neither of her suitors, then they cannot logically argue that her replies to Lear are clipped because she realizes that to express her love would be to sacrifice herself to Lear. If his plan is a surprise, she cannot *know* that.

4. Cf. Goldberg, *Essay on "King Lear"*, p. 112: "His speech about 'need' significantly breaks off when it brings him face to face with the utter impotence of his will to *make* the external world yield satisfaction."

5. Ribner, *Patterns in Shakespearean Tragedy*, p. 118, and Granville-Barker *Prefaces to Shakespeare. Vol II*. (Princeton, N. J.: Princeton University Press, 1946), p. 30. See also Sigurd Burckhardt, *Shakespearean Meanings* (Princeton, N.J.: Princeton University Press, 1968), p. 247.

6. *Shakespeare and the Common Understanding* (N.Y.: Free Press, 1967), pp. 32–33; Cf. Champion, *Shakespeare's Tragic Perspective*, pp. 156–57.

7. Cf. Van Laan, "Acting as Action in *King Lear*," p. 64.

8. Cf. "Avoidance of Love," p. 276. Cavell's entire discussion of the Gloucester–Edmund relationship is a profound one.

9. Ibid., p. 277.

10. It is difficult to agree with Cavell (ibid., pp. 288–90) that what Lear really wants is "false love" or that he has a "terror of being loved." If those are his desires and fears, he does not require a love test to gain the former and avoid the latter.

11. If Shakespeare were seriously interested in suggesting that unacknowledged incestuous desires were the cause of Lear's behavior in act 1, scene 1, he would not have found it necessary to develop a subplot. The extensive number of parallels we have just seen between Gloucester and Lear would appear to argue that Shakespeare's vision of things is embodied in the behavior of *both* old men. For claims that an incest theme exists, see Arpad Pauncz, "Psychopathology of Shakespeare's King Lear," *AI* 9(1952):57–78; John Donnelly, "Incest, Ingratitude, and Insanity: Aspects of the Psychopathology of King Lear," *Psychoanalytic Review* 40(1953):149–53; F. L. Lucas, *Literature and Psychology* (Ann Arbor: University of Michigan Press, 1957), pp. 62–71; Mark Kanzer, "Imagery in *King Lear*," *AI* 22(1965):3–13; Jorgensen, *Lear's Self-Discovery*, pp. 128–29; S. C. V. Stetner and Oscar B. Goodman, "Lear's Darker Purpose," *L&P* 18 (1968):82–90; William Chaplin, "Form and Psychology in *King Lear*," *L&P* 19(1969):31–45; Simon O. Lesser, "Act One, Scene One, of *Lear*," *CE* 32 (1970–71):155–71; Leslie Fiedler, *The Stranger in Shakespeare* (N.Y.: Stein & Day, 1972), pp. 209–15; Cavell, "Avoidance of Love," p. 296. Both Stephen Reid, "In Defense of Goneril and Regan," *AI* 27(1970):238 and Alan Dundes, "To Love My Father All: A Psychoanalytic Study of the Folktale Source of *King Lear*," *SFQ*, 40(1976):361, even argue that Cordelia is the one with the hidden incestuous desires!

12. Speaking of the tragedies in general, Mack, "Jacobean Shakespeare," p. 43, insightfully identifies the structural practice in *King Lear:* "During the hero's journey, or at any rate during his over-all progress in the second phase, he will normally pass through a variety of mirroring situations . . . (though it will be by us and not him that the likeness in the mirror is seen)." Cf. Reibetanz, "Theatrical Emblems in *King Lear*," p. 39 and Fly, "Beyond Extremity," p. 109.

13. Margaret Webster, *Shakespearean Tragedy* (London: J. M. Dent, 1957), pp. 216–17; Jones, *Scenic Form in Shakespeare*, p. 181; McFarland, *Tragic Meanings in Shakespeare*, p. 128—all seem to agree with Schucking, "Character and Action: *King Lear*," p. 61, when he claims that until act 3 Lear shows a lack of judgment and immoderation like that in act 1, scene 1. "Nevertheless, the poet evidently does not wish him to forfeit thereby the sympathy of the spectator, though it is put to a very severe test." Cf. Edward A. Block, "*King Lear:* A Study in Balanced and Shifting Sympathies," *SQ* 10(1959):499–512.

14. Cf. Stockholder, "Multiple Genres of *King Lear*," 46–47.

15. Both Jorgensen, *Lear's Self-Discovery*, pp. 92–93, and Norman Council, *When Honour's at the Stake: Ideas of Honour in Shakespeare's Plays* (N.Y.: Barnes and Noble, 1973), p. 153, argue that Gloucester functions as a foil to Lear because of his defeatism.

16. Bridget G. Lyons, "The Subplot as Simplification in *King Lear*," in *Some Facets of "King Lear"*, p. 31, uses act 2, scene 4, 146–50 as an effective emblematic motto for Gloucester's suicide; but I cannot agree with either her or John Danby, "*King Lear* and Christian Patience," in *Poets on Fortune's Hill* (Port Washington, N.Y.: Kennikat Press, 1966), p. 126, that Gloucester finally gains patience and fulfillment.

17. Cf. Rosenberg, *Masks of "King Lear"*, p. 242.

18. Cf. Enright, *Shakespeare and the Students*, p. 54.

Chapter 4. The Prince of Darkness
Is a Gentleman

1. Lear's reference in act 3, scene 6, to his daughters as "Tray, Blanch, and Sweetheart," palace dogs who do not recognize their master—"See they bark at me" (3.6.63), now a homeless exile—is an extremely moving touch. However, I do not think its pathos saves the figure from suggesting Lear's patronizing view of his daughters. A king does not love his dogs; at best he bestows doting favor upon them for pleasing him.

2. "Cordelia Absent," p. 125; cf. French, *Shakespeare and the Critics*, pp. 150–51.

3. "Cordelia Absent," pp. 130–31.

4. Speaking of Kent, Lear mistakenly claims, "When the mind's free/The body's delicate" (3.4.11–12). Lear ironically describes himself—ungrateful for Kent's aid—when he accuses his daughters: "Is it not as this mouth should tear this hand/For lifting food to it?" (3.4.15–16).

5. The relevance of the Ixion myth is developed in Elton, "*King Lear*" and *the Gods*, p. 359; Harold Skulsky, *Spirits Finely Touched: The Testing of Value and Integrity in Four Shakespearean Plays* (Athens: University of Georgia Press, 1976), p. 135; Nevo, *Tragic Form in Shakespeare*, p. 299; O. B. Hardison, Jr., "Myth and History in *King Lear*," *SQ* 26 (1975):227–42.

6. Egan, *Drama within Drama*, p. 33, observes that at the end of act 2, Lear leaves the microcosm of society to take his case directly to the macrocosm; but then he finds "the lesser chaos of society is enclosed by the greater chaos of the heavens themselves." Cf. Calarco, *Apollo and Dionysus in Western Drama*, p. 99, and J. C. Maxwell, "The Technique of Invocation in *King Lear*," *MLR* 45 (1950):142–47.

7. In "*King Lear*" and the Gods, p. 201, Elton documents the fact that Renaissance thinkers were increasingly searching among natural causes rather than in inscrutable divine ones to explain the "cause of thunder."

8. Though Lear had spoken of his having taken too little care of distributive justice and of his own miseries as a "judicious punishment," when he tries his daughters in an imaginary court, he reveals no sign of feeling any guilt.

9. See the Introduction to the revised edition of *The Penguin "King Lear"* (Baltimore: Penguin Books, 1970), p. 22.

10. Ibid., p. 25.

11. See, for example, Susan Snyder, "*King Lear* and the Prodigal Son," *SQ*

17 (1966):367; Peter L. McNamara, *"King Lear* and Comic Acceptance," *Erasmus Review* 2(1971):104; Terence Hawkes, *Shakespeare's Talking Animals: Language and Drama in Society* (Tatawa, N. J.: Rowman and Littlefield, 1973), p. 177.

12. See, for example, Fraser, *Shakespeare's Poetics*, pp. 88–89; Norman MacLean, "Episode, Speech, and Word: The Madness of Lear," in *Critics and Criticism,* Abridged edition, ed. R. S. Crane (Chicago: University of Chicago Press, 1957), p. 100; Felperin, *Shakespearean Representation,* p. 99; Rosenberg, *Masks of "King Lear",* p. 276.

13. Hathorn, *Tragedy, Myth, and Mystery,* p. 181.

14. As A. C. Bradley, *Shakespearean Tragedy* (London: Macmillan, 1904), p. 274, suggests, the Folio stage direction "Storm and tempest," following Lear's "Come, let's away to prison" speech, may hint Lear's presumption in his claim to "take upon 's the mystery of things/As if we were God's spies" (5.3.16–17). Elton, *"King Lear" and the Gods,* pp. 249–53, points out numerous Renaissance instances when the usage, "to take upon 's" connotes presumption. Cf. Young, *The Heart's Forest,* p. 96.

15. See, French, *Shakespeare and the Critics,* pp. 174–75; Goldberg, *Essay on "King Lear",* p. 124. In self-absorbedly identifying Poor Tom with himself, Lear mistakes their truer identity. Having suffered previously as Edgar, Poor Tom's first ploy to preserve himself when threatened is to drive the intruder off ("Away! The foul fiend follows me!"). If the intruder hopes to abuse him, such cries may drive him away; if his intentions are generous, the same words may evoke pity. Tom's technique, then, is not substantially unlike Lear's appeal to Kent and the Fool to "let me alone" and to "seek" their "own ease."

The profoundest irony in Tom's "Who gives anything to Poor Tom?" is not simply that he could ask the same question even after Lear's attempted disrobing but that his question is really Lear's secret question as well. The Edgar who speaks through Tom's pretended self-pity actually speaks as a son unjustly betrayed by his father, just as Lear has been begging charity, a father betrayed by his daughters.

David Horowitz, *Shakespeare: An Existential View* (N. Y.: Hill and Wang, 1965), p. 83, rightly points out that Edgar's disguise is, in another sense, not Lear's mirroring image at all, but an image of his crime against Cordelia since, like her, he was driven out by his father. "If Lear saw truly, he would see in Edgar his own crime, not a sympathetic suffering." But though this is clearly true on a symbolic plane, in dramatic terms it is unreasonable to expect Lear to see through Edgar's disguise. However, it is hardly unreasonable to expect that Lear at least extend his sympathy to the man before him.

16. Several critics have also noted that Lear's words, "And show the heavens more just," do not suggest piety but, rather, the king's radical questioning of the gods' providential operation in the world. See, for example, Brower, *Hero and Saint,* p. 398; Jorgen Johansen, "The Structure of Conflicting Cosmologies in *King Lear," Poetics* 6(1972):97; Empson, "Fool in *Lear,"* p. 137. Dieter Mehl, "King Lear and the 'Poor Naked Wretches.'" *Shakespeare Jahrbuch* (Heidelberg) (1975):154–62, disputes the notion that the speech is crucial for Lear's development.

17. Lear has in all likelihood identified the ragged and ascetic Tom as a cynic; see Jane Donawerth, "Diogenes the Cynic and Lear's Definition of

Man, *King Lear* III. iv. 101–09," *ELN* 15(1977):10–14, and E. M. M. Taylor, "Lear's Philospher," *SQ* 6(1955):364–65.

18. The quoted phrase is from *Shakespeare and the Nature of Man* (N. Y.: Macmillan, 1942), p. 137. Cf. Empson, "Fool in *Lear*," p. 144; Paul V. Krieder, *Repetition in Shakespeare's Plays* (Princeton, N. J.: Princeton University Press, 1941), p. 208; Felperin, *Shakespearean Representation*, p. 98; Alpers, "*King Lear* and the Theory of the Sight Pattern," p. 146; Paul Gottschalk, "The Universe of Madness in *King Lear*," *Bucknell Review* 19 (1971):62; French, *Shakespeare and the Critics*, p. 183; Cavell, "Avoidance of Love," pp. 279–80; McElroy, *Shakespeare's Mature Tragedies*, p. 193.

19. Cavell, "Avoidance of Love," p. 278, is correct when he speaks of everything in the subplot leading to the recognition in act 4, scene 6; but I disagree with him, as I do with Maynard Mack in "Jacobean Shakespeare," p. 43, about whether the recognition is as complete and satisfying as they believe it is. Contrast the view of Rosenberg, *Masks of "King Lear"*, p. 278.

20. *The Fool: His Social and Literary History* (N. Y.: Doubleday, 1961; orig. published by Faber and Faber, 1935), p. 266. See, also, Hathorn, *Tragedy, Myth, and Mystery*, pp. 187–88; Krieder, *Repetition in Shakespeare's Plays*, p. 208; Empson, "Fool in *Lear*," p. 144; Young, *Heart's Forest*, p. 95; Rosenberg, *Masks of "King Lear"*, pp. 274–75.

21. *Tragic Form in Shakespeare*, p. 298.

22. The picture may be complicated by elements of ritual sacrifice as well. See for example, E. K. Chambers, *The Medieval Stage. Vol. I* (London: Oxford University Press, 1903), p. 137; M. C. Bradbrook, *The Living Monument: Shakespeare and the Theatre of His Time* (London: Cambridge University Press, 1976), p. 149; Holloway, *Story of the Night*, pp. 97–98; Chaplin, "Form and Psychology in *King Lear*," p. 44.

23. McNamara, "*King Lear* and Comic Acceptance," p. 97.

24. "*King Lear* and Its Language," in *Some Facets of "King Lear*," p. 20.

25. Debauchery is a perfect metaphor to describe Lear's converting shame into perverse "pastime," the indulgence in sin to anesthetize one's shame over an initial offense.

26. From *A Poet's Notebook* (N. Y.: Little, Brown, 1943), reprinted in "*King Lear": Text, Sources, Criticism*, ed. G. B. Harrison and Robert F. McDonnell (N. Y.: Harcourt, Brace, and World, 1962), pp. 154–55.

27. Chaplin, "Form and Psychology in *King Lear*," p. 43. See also Goldberg, *Essay on "King Lear"*, pp. 135–38; French, *Shakespeare and the Critics*, pp. 179–84; Skulsky, *Spirits Finely Touched*, pp. 133–34; Webster, *Shakespeare Today*, p. 219; Johansen, "The Structure of Conflicting Cosmologies in *King Lear*," p. 99; Ornstein, *Moral Vision of Jacobean Tragedy*, p. 269; Ribner, *Patterns in Shakespearean Tragedy*, p. 128; and L. C. Knights, *Some Shakespearean Themes* (Palo Alto: Stanford University Press, 1960), pp. 106, 113—all of whom, I believe, underestimate the "reservation" for himself Lear holds to even as he denounces the corrupt social order he has been a part of.

28. *Tragic Meanings in Shakespeare*, pp. 146–47.

Selected Bibliography

Adelman, Janet, ed. *Twentieth Century Interpretations of "King Lear."* Englewood Cliffs, N.J.: Prentice-Hall, 1978.

Allgaier, Johannes. "Is *King Lear* an Antiauthoritarian Play?" *PMLA* 88 (1973): 1033–39.

Alpers, Paul J. "*King Lear* and the Theory of the Sight Pattern." In *In Defense of Reading,* edited by Reuben Brower and Richard Poirier. New York: Dutton, 1962.

Anderson, Peter S. "The Fragile World of *King Lear.*" *Comparative Drama* 5 (1971–72): 269–82.

Baker, James V. "An Existential Examination of *King Lear.*" *CE* 23 (1962): 546–50.

Barish, Jonas A., and Waingrow, Marshall. "'Service' in *King Lear.*" *SQ* 9 (1958): 347–55.

Barnet, Sylvan. "Some Limitations of a Christian Approach to Shakespeare." *ELH* 22 (1955): 81–92.

Barron, Frank, and Rosenberg, Marvin. "King Lear and His Fool: A Study of the Conception and Enactment of Dramatic Role in Relation to Self-Conception." *Educational Theatre Journal* 22 (1970): 276–83.

Battenhouse, Roy W. *Shakespearean Tragedy: Its Art and Its Christian Premises.* Bloomington: Indiana University Press, 1969.

Bauer, Robert J. "Despite of Mine Own Nature: Edmund and the Orders, Cosmic and Moral." *TSLL* 10 (1968): 359–66.

Bennett, Josephine W. "The Storm Within: The Madness of Lear." *SQ* 13 (1962): 137–55.

Bethell, S. L. *Shakespeare and the Popular Dramatic Tradition.* Durham, N.C.: Duke University Press, 1944.

Black, James. "'King Lear': Art Upside-Down." *Shakespeare Survey* 33 (1980): 35–42.

Blaydes, Sophia. "Cordelia's Loss of Innocence." *Studies in the Humanities* (Indiana University of Pennsylvania) 5 (1976): 15–21.

Block, Edward A. "*King Lear:* A Study in Balanced and Shifting Sympathies." *SQ* 10 (1959):499–512.

Bloom, Edward A., ed. *Shakespeare 1564–1964: A Collection of Modern Essays by Various Hands.* Providence, R.I.: Brown University Press, 1964.

Blythe, David F. "Lear's Soiled Horse." *SQ* 31 (1980):86–88.

Bowers, Fredson. "The Structure of *King Lear.*" *SQ* 31 (1980):7–20.

Bradbrook, M. C. *The Living Monument: Shakespeare and the Theatre of His Time.* London: Cambridge University Press, 1976.

Bradley, A. C. *Shakespearean Tragedy.* London: Macmillan, 1904.

Brooke, Nicholas. *Shakespeare: "King Lear".* London: Edward Arnold, 1963.

———. "The Ending of *King Lear.*" In *Shakespeare 1564–1964: A Collection of Modern Essays by Various Hands,* edited by Edward A. Bloom. Providence, R.I.: Brown University Press, 1964.

Brower, Reuben. *Hero and Saint: Shakespeare and the Graeco-Roman Heroic Tradition.* New York: Oxford University Press, 1971.

Brown, Stephen J. "Shakespeare's King and Beggar." *Yale Review* 64 (1975):370–95.

Bryant, Peter. "Nuncle Lear." *English Studies in Africa* 20 (1977):35–38.

Bullough, Geoffrey, ed. *Narrative and Dramatic Sources of Shakespeare:* Vol. 7, *Major Tragedies.* New York: Columbia University Press, 1973.

Burckhardt, Sigurd. *Shakespearean Meanings.* Princeton, N.J.: Princeton University Press, 1968.

Bush, Geoffrey. *Shakespeare and the Natural Condition.* Cambridge, Mass.: Harvard University Press, 1956.

Calarco, N. Joseph. *Tragic Being: Apollo and Dionysus in Western Drama.* Minneapolis: University of Minnesota Press, 1968.

Cameron, Allen B. "The Value of Lear's Death." *College English Association Critic* 35 (1973):16–19.

Campbell, Lily B. *Shakespeare's Tragic Heroes: Slaves of Passion.* London: Cambridge University Press, 1930.

Campbell, O. J. "The Salvation of Lear." *ELH* 15 (1948):93–109.

Cavell, Stanley. *Must We Mean What We Say?: A Book of Essays.* New York: Scribners, 1969.

Chambers, E. K. *The Medieval Stage.* Vol. 1. London: Oxford University Press, 1903.

Chambers, R. W. *King Lear.* Glasgow: Jackson, 1940.

Champion, Larry S. *Shakespeare's Tragic Perspective*. Athens: University of Georgia Press, 1976.

Chaplin, William. "Form and Psychology in *King Lear*." *L & P* 19 (1969):31–45.

Clemen, W. H. *The Development of Shakespeare's Imagery*, pp. 133–53. London: Methuen, 1951.

Colie, Rosalie. *Shakespeare's Living Art*. Princeton, N.J.: Princeton University Press, 1974.

Colie, Rosalie, and Flahiff, F. T., eds. *Some Facets of "King Lear": Essays in Prismatic Criticism*. Toronto: University of Toronto Press, 1974.

Council, Norman. *When Honour's at the Stake: Ideas of Honour in Shakespeare's Plays*. New York: Barnes and Noble, 1973.

Coursen, Herbert R. *Christian Ritual and the World of Shakespeare's Tragedies*. Lewisburg: Bucknell University Press, 1976.

Creeth, Edmund. *Mankynde in Shakespeare*. Athens: University of Georgia Press, 1976.

Danby, John. "*King Lear* and Christian Patience." In *Poets on Fortune's Hill*. Port Washington, N.Y.: Kennikat Press, 1966.

———. *Shakespeare's Doctrine of Nature: A Study of "King Lear"*. London: Faber and Faber, 1948.

Danson, Lawrence, ed. *On "King Lear"*. Princeton, N.J.: Princeton University Press, 1981.

———. *Tragic Alphabet: Shakespeare's Drama of Language*. New Haven: Yale University Press, 1974.

Dawson, Anthony. "Paradoxical Dramaturgy in *King Lear*." *Wascana Review* 9 (1974):29–38.

Delany, Paul. "*King Lear* and the Decline of Feudalism." *PMLA* 92 (1977):429–40.

Doebler, John. *Shakespeare's Speaking Pictures: Studies in Iconic Imagery*. Albuquerque: University of New Mexico Press, 1974.

Donawerth, Jane. "Diogenes the Cynic and Lear's Definition of Man, *King Lear* III. iv. 101–109." *ELN* 15 (1977):10–14.

Donnelly, John. "Incest, Ingratitude, and Insanity: Aspects of the Psychopathology of *King Lear*." *Psychoanalytic Review* 40 (1953):149–53.

Donner, H. W. "'Is This the Promised End?': Reflections on the Tragic Ending of *King Lear*." *English Studies* 50 (1969):503–10.

Doran, Madeleine. "Command, Question, and Assertion in *King Lear*." In *Shakespeare's Art: Seven Essays*, edited by Milton Crane, pp. 53–78. Chicago: University of Chicago Press, 1973.

Dove, John R., and Gamble, Peter. "Our Darker Purpose: The Division Scene in *Lear*." *Neuphilologische Mitteilungen* 70 (1969):306–18.

Draper, John W. "The Old Age of King Lear." *Journal of English and Germanic Philology* 39 (1940):527–40.

Driscoll, James P. "The Vision of *King Lear*." *Shakespeare Studies* 10 (1977):159–89.

Dundes, Alan. "To Love My Father All: A Psychoanalytic Study of the Folktale Source of *King Lear*." *SFQ* 40 (1976):353–66.

Duthie, George Ian, ed. *Shakespeare's "Lear": A Critical Edition*. Oxford: Blackwell, 1949.

Dye, Harriet. "The Appearance-Reality Theme in *King Lear*." *CE* 25 (1964):514–17.

Eddy, Darlene. *The Worlds of "King Lear"*. Muncie, Ind.: Ball State University Press, 1970.

Egan, Robert. *Drama within Drama: Shakespeare's Sense of His Art*. New York: Columbia University Press, 1975.

————. "Kent and the Audience: The Character as Spectator." *SQ* 32 (1981):146–154.

Elliott, G. R. *Dramatic Providence in "Macbeth": A Study of Shakespeare's Tragic Theme of Humanity and Grace*. Princeton, N.J.: Princeton University Press, 1960.

Ellis, John. "The Gulling of Gloucester: Credibility in the Subplot of *King Lear*." *SEL* 12 (1972):275–89.

Ellis, Roger. "The Fool in Shakespeare: A Study in Alienation." *Critical Quarterly* 10 (1968):246–68.

Elton, William. *"King Lear" and the Gods*. San Marino, Calif.: Huntington Library, 1966.

Empson, William. "Fool in *Lear*." In *The Structure of Complex Words*. New York: New Directions, 1951.

Enright, D. J. *Shakespeare and the Students*. New York: Schocken Books, 1970.

Evans, G. Blakemore, ed. *The Riverside Shakespeare*. Boston: Houghton Mifflin, 1974.

Everett, Barbara. "The New *King Lear*." *Critical Quarterly* 2 (1960):325–39.

Farnham, Willard. *Shakespeare's Tragic Frontier: The World of His Final Tragedies*. Berkeley: University of California Press, 1963.

Felperin, Howard. *Shakespearean Representation; Mimesis and Modernity in Elizabethan Tragedy*. Princeton, N.J.: Princeton University Press, 1977.

Fiedler, Leslie. *The Stranger in Shakespeare*. New York: Stein and Day, 1972.

Fleissner, Robert F. "The 'Nothing' Element in *King Lear*." *SQ* 13 (1962):67–70.

Fly, Richard. *Shakespeare's Mediated World*. Amherst: University of Massachusetts Press, 1976.

Fortin, René E. "Hermeneutical Circularity and Christian Interpretations of *King Lear*." *Shakespeare Studies* 12 (1979):113–25.

Fraser, Duncan. "Much Virtue in 'Nothing': Cordelia's Part in the First Scene of *King Lear*." *Cambridge Quarterly* 8 (1978):1–10.

Fraser, Russell. *Shakespeare's Poetics in Relation to "King Lear"*. Nashville, Tenn.: Vanderbilt University Press, 1966.

French, A. L. *Shakespeare and the Critics*. London: Cambridge University Press, 1972.

French, Carolyn S. "Shakespeare's 'Folly': *King Lear*." *SQ* 10 (1959):523–29.

Frost, William. "Shakespeare's Rituals and the Opening of *King Lear*." In *Shakespeare: The Tragedies*, edited by Clifford Leech. Chicago: University of Chicago Press, 1965.

Frye, Dean. "The Context of Lear's Unbuttoning." *ELH* 32 (1965):17–31.

Frye, Northrop. *Fools of Time: Studies in Shakespearean Tragedy*. Toronto: University of Toronto Press, 1967.

Frye, Roland M. *Shakespeare and Christian Doctrine*. Princeton, N.J.: Princeton University Press, 1963.

Gardner, Helen, *King Lear*. The John Coffin Memorial Lecture. London: Athlone Press, 1967.

Goldberg, S. L. *An Essay on "King Lear"*. London: Cambridge University Press, 1974.

Goldman, Michael. *Shakespeare and the Energies of Drama*. Princeton, N.J.: Princeton University Press, 1972.

Goldman, Oscar, and Stetner, S. C. V. "Lear's Darker Purpose." *L & P* 18 (1968):82–90.

Gottschalk, Paul. "The Universe of Madness in *King Lear*." *Bucknell Review* 19 (1971):51–68.

Granville-Barker, Harley. *Prefaces to Shakespeare*. Vol. 2. Princeton, N.J.: Princeton University Press, 1946.

Greenfield, Thomas. "Excellent Things in Women: The Emergence of Cordelia." *South Atlantic Bulletin* 42 (1977):44–52.

Grinstein, Alexander. "King Lear's Impending Death." *AI* 30 (1973):121–41.

Harbage, Alfred, *Conceptions of Shakespeare*. Cambridge, Mass.: Harvard University Press, 1966.

———. Introduction, *The Penguin King Lear*. Baltimore: Penguin Books, 1970.

———, ed. *Shakespeare: The Tragedies*. Englewood Cliffs, N.J.: Prentice-Hall, 1964.

Hardison, O. B., ed. *Medieval and Renaissance Studies. 1965*. Chapel Hill: University of North Carolina Press, 1966.

———. "Myth and History in *King Lear*." *SQ* 26 (1975): 227–42.

Harris, Duncan S. "The End of *Lear* and a Shape for Shakespearean Tragedy." *Shakespeare Survey* 9 (1976): 253–68.

Harrison, George B., and McDonnell, Robert F., eds. *"King Lear": Text, Sources, Criticism*. New York: Harcourt, Brace and World, 1962.

Hathorn, Richmond Y. *Tragedy, Myth, and Mystery*. Bloomington: Indiana University Press, 1963.

Hawkes, Terence. *Shakespeare's Talking Animals: Language and Drama in Society*. Tatawa, N.J.: Rowman and Littlefield, 1973.

Heilman, Robert. *This Great Stage: Image and Structure in "King Lear"*. Baton Rouge: Louisiana State University Press, 1948.

Hennedy, Hugh L. "*King Lear*: Recognizing the Ending." *SP* 71 (1974): 371–84.

Hibbard, G. R. "'King Lear': A Retrospect, 1939–79." *Shakespeare Survey* 33 (1980): 1–12.

Hiramatsu, Hideo. "The Structure and Theme of *King Lear*." *Shakespeare Studies* 12 (1973–74): 31–45.

Hockey, Dorothy C. "The Trial Pattern of *King Lear*." *SQ* 10 (1959): 389–95.

Hole, Sandra. "The Background of Divine Action in *King Lear*." *SEL* 8 (1968): 217–33.

Holloway, John. *The Story of the Night*. Lincoln: University of Nebraska Press, 1961.

Horowitz, David. *Shakespeare: An Existential View*. New York: Hill and Wang, 1965.

Isenberg, Arnold. "Cordelia Absent." *SQ* 2 (1951): 185–94.

Jackson, Esther M. "*King Lear*: The Grammar of Tragedy." *SQ* 17 (1966): 25–40.

James, D. G. *The Dream of Learning*. London: Oxford University Press, 1951.

Jayne, Sears. "Charity in *King Lear*." *SQ* 15 (1964): 277–88.

Johansen, Jorgen. "The Structure of Conflicting Cosmologies in *King Lear.*" *Poetics* 6 (1972):84–127.

Jones, Emrys. *Scenic Form in Shakespeare.* London: Oxford University Press, 1971.

Jorgensen, Paul A. *Lear's Self-Discovery.* Berkeley: University of California Press, 1967.

Kanzer, Mark. "Imagery in *King Lear.*" *AI* 22 (1965):3–13.

Keast, M. R. "Imagery and Meaning in the Interpretation of *King Lear.*" *MP* 47 (1949):45–64.

Kermode, Frank. *Shakespeare, Spenser, Donne: Renaissance Essays.* New York: Viking, 1971.

Kernan, Alvin. "Formalism and Realism in Elizabethan Drama: The Miracles in *King Lear.*" *Renaissance Drama* 9 (1966):59–66.

Kernodle, George F. "The Symphonic Form of *King Lear.*" In *Elizabethan Studies in Honor of G. F. Reynolds.* Boulder: University of Colorado Press, 1945.

Kinney, Arthur. "Lear." *Massachusetts Review* 17 (1976):677–712.

Kirschbaum, Leo. *Character and Characterization in Shakespeare.* Detroit: Wayne State University Press, 1962.

Knight, G. Wilson. *The Wheel of Fire.* London: Methuen, 1949.

———. "Gloucester's Leap." *Essays in Criticism* 22 (1972):279–88.

Knights, L. C. *Further Explorations.* Palo Alto: Stanford University Press, 1965.

———. *Some Shakespearean Themes.* Palo Alto: Stanford University Press, 1960.

Kott, Jan. "*King Lear* as Endgame." In *Shakespeare Our Contemporary.* New York: Anchor Books, 1964.

Krieder, Paul V. *Repetition in Shakespeare's Plays.* Princeton, N.J.: Princeton University Press, 1941.

Lascelles, Mary. "*King Lear* and Doomsday." *Shakespeare Survey* 26 (1973):69–79.

Law, Robert A. "Holinshed's Leir Story and Shakespeare's." *SP* 47 (1950):42–50.

Leech, Clifford, ed. *Shakespeare: The Tragedies. A Collection of Critical Essays.* Chicago: University of Chicago Press, 1965.

Lerner, Lawrence. *The Uses of Nostalgia: Studies in Pastoral Poetry.* New York: Schocken Books, 1972.

Lesser, Simon O. "Act One, Scene One, of *Lear.*" *CE* 32 (1970–71):155–71.

London, Philip W. "The Stature of Lear." *University of Windsor Review* 1 (1965):173–86.

Lothian, John. *"King Lear": A Tragic Reading of Life.* Toronto: Clarke, Irwin, 1949.

Lucas, F. L. *Literature and Psychology.* Ann Arbor: University of Michigan Press, 1957.

Mack, Maynard. "The Jacobean Shakespeare: Some Observations on the Construction of the Tragedies." In *Essays in Shakespearean Criticism,* edited by James Calderwood and Harold Toliver. Englewood Cliffs, N.J.: Prentice-Hall, 1970.

———. *"King Lear" in Our Time.* Berkeley: University of California Press, 1965.

MacLean, Hugh. "Disquise in *Lear.*" *SQ* 11 (1960):49–54.

MacLean, Norman. "Episode, Speech, and Word: The Madness of Lear." In *Critics and Criticism,* edited by R. S. Crane. Chicago: University of Chicago Press, 1957.

Marks, Carol. " 'Speak What We Feel': The End of *King Lear.*" *ELN* 5 (1968):163–71.

Mason, H. A. "Can We Derive Wisdom about Old Age from *King Lear?*" *Cambridge Quarterly* 6 (1975):203–13.

———. *Shakespeare's Tragedies of Love.* New York: Barnes and Noble, 1970.

Matthews, Richard. "Edmund's Redemption in *King Lear.*" *SQ* 26 (1975):25–29.

Maxwell, J. C. "The Technique of Invocation in *King Lear.*" *MLR* 45 (1950):142–47.

McElroy, Bernard. *Shakespeare's Mature Tragedies.* Princeton, N.J.: Princeton University Press, 1973.

McFarland, Thomas. *Shakespeare's Pastoral Comedy.* Chapel Hill: University of North Carolina Press, 1972.

———. *Tragic Meanings in Shakespeare.* New York: Random House, 1966.

McGlaughlin, Ann. "The Journeys in *King Lear.*" *AI* 29 (1972):384–99.

McGlaughlin, John J. "The Dynamics of Power in *King Lear:* An Adlerian Interpretation." *SQ* 29 (1978):37–43.

McManaway, James G., ed. *Shakespeare 400: Essays by American Scholars on the Anniversary of the Poet's Birth.* New York: Holt, Rinehart, and Winston, 1964.

McNamara, Peter L. "*King Lear* and Comic Acceptance." *Erasmus Review* 2 (1971):95–105.

McNeir, Waldo F. "Cordelia's Return in *King Lear.*" *ELN* 6 (1969):172–76.

————. "The Role of Edmund in *King Lear*." *SEL* 8 (1968):187–216.

Mehl, Dieter. "King Lear and the 'Poor Naked Wretches.'" *Shakespeare Jahrbuch* (Heidelberg), (1975):154–62.

Miller, Robert F. "*King Lear* and the Comic Form." *Genre* 8 (1975):1–25.

Milward, Peter L. "The Religious Dimension of *King Lear*." *Shakespeare Studies* 8 (1969–70):48–74.

Morris, Ivor. "Cordelia and Lear." *SQ* 8 (1957):141–58.

————. *Shakespeare's God: The Role of Religion in the Tragedies*. New York: St. Martin's Press, 1972.

Mortensen, Peter. "The Role of Albany." *SQ* 16 (1965):217–25.

Myrick, Kenneth. "Christian Pessimism in *King Lear*." In *Shakespeare 1564–1964: A Collection of Modern Essays by Various Hands,* edited by Edward A. Bloom. Providence, R.I.: Brown University Press, 1964.

Nevo, Ruth. *Tragic Form in Shakespeare*. Princeton, N.J.: Princeton University Press, 1972.

Nojima, Hidekatsu. "Exit the Fool." In *English Criticism in Japan,* edited by Earl Miner. Tokyo: University of Tokyo Press, 1972.

Oates, Joyce Carol. "'Is This the Promised End?': The Tragedy of *King Lear*." *Journal of Aesthetics and Art Criticism* 33 (1974):19–32.

Olson, Elder. *Tragedy and the Theory of Drama*. Detroit: Wayne State University Press, 1961.

Ornstein, Robert. *The Moral Vision of Jacobean Tragedy*. Madison: University of Wisconsin Press, 1960.

Orwell, George. *Shooting an Elephant and Other Essays*. New York: Harcourt, Brace, 1945.

Partee, Morriss H. "The Divine Comedy of *King Lear*." *Genre* 4 (1971):60–75.

Pauncz, Arpad. "Psychopathology of Shakespeare's *King Lear*." *AI* 9 (1952):57–78.

Peat, Derek. "'And That's True Too': 'King Lear' and the Tension of Uncertainty." *Shakespeare Survey* 33 (1980):43–53.

Pechter, Edward. "On the Blinding of Gloucester." *ELH* 45 (1978):181–200.

Peck, Russell A. "Edgar's Pilgrimage: High Comedy in *King Lear*." *SEL* 7 (1967):219–37.

Perkinson, Richard H. "Shakespeare's Revision of the Lear Story and the Structure of *King Lear*." *PQ* 22 (1943):315–29.

Poggioli, Renato. *The Oaten Flute: Essays on Pastoral Poetry and the Pastoral Ideal*. Cambridge, Mass.: Harvard University Press, 1975.

Quinn, Edward G. *The Major Shakespearean Tragedies: A Critical Bibliography.* New York: Free Press, 1973.

Rabkin, Norman. *Shakespeare and the Common Understanding.* New York: Free Press, 1967.

Rackin, Phyllis. "Delusion as Resolution in *King Lear.*" *SQ* 21 (1970):29–34.

Reibetanz, John. *The Lear World: A Study of "King Lear" in Its Dramatic Context.* Toronto: University of Toronto Press, 1977.

Reid, Stephen. "In Defense of Goneril and Regan." *AI* 27 (1970):226–44.

Ribner, Irving. *Patterns in Shakespearean Tragedy.* London: Methuen, 1960.

Righter, Anne. *Shakespeare and the Idea of the Play.* New York: Barnes and Noble, 1963.

Rose, Mark. *Shakespearean Design.* Cambridge, Mass.: Harvard University Press, 1972.

Rosen, William. *Shakespeare and the Craft of Tragedy.* Cambridge, Mass.: Harvard University Press, 1960.

Rosenberg, John D. "King Lear and His Comforters." *Essays in Criticism* 16 (1966):135–46.

Rosenberg, Marvin. *The Masks of "King Lear".* Berkeley: University of California Press, 1972.

Rosier, James L. "The *Lex Aeterna* and *King Lear.*" *Journal of English and Germanic Philology* 53 (1954):574–80.

Rosinger, Lawrence. "Gloucester and Lear: Men Who Act Like Gods." *ELH* 35 (1968):491–504.

Rusche, Harry. "Edmund's Conception and Nativity in *King Lear.*" *SQ* 20 (1969):161–64.

Savvas, Minas. "*King Lear* as a Play of Divine Justice." *CE* 27 (1965–66):560–62.

Schneider, Carl D. *Shame, Exposure and Privacy.* Boston: Beacon Press, 1977.

Schoff, Francis G. "King Lear: Moral Example or Tragic Protagonist?" *SQ* 13 (1962):157–72.

Seiden, Melvin. "The Fool and Edmund: Kin and Kind." *SEL* 19 (1979):197–214.

Sewall, Richard B. *The Vision of Tragedy.* New Haven: Yale University Press, 1959.

Sewell, Arthur. *Character and Society in Shakespeare.* London: Oxford University Press, 1951.

Siegel, Paul. *Shakespearean Tragedy and the Elizabethan Compromise.* New York: New York University Press, 1957.

Sinfield, Alan. "Lear and Laing." *Essays in Criticism* 26 (1976): 1–16.

Sisson, C. J. *Shakespeare's Tragic Justice.* London: Methuen, 1963.

Skulsky, Harold. *Spirits Finely Touched: The Testing of Value and Integrity in Four Shakespearean Plays.* Athens: University of Georgia Press, 1976.

Smith, Donald M. "'And I'll Go to Bed at Noon': The Fool in *King Lear.*" *Essays in Arts and Sciences* 5 (1976): 37–45.

Snyder, Susan, "*King Lear* and the Prodigal Son." *SQ* 17 (1966): 361–69.

Soellner, Rolf. *Shakespeare's Patterns of Self-Knowledge.* Columbus: Ohio State University Press, 1972.

Speaight, Robert. *Nature in Shakespearean Tragedy.* New York: Collier, 1962.

Spencer, Theodore. *Shakespeare and the Nature of Man.* New York: Macmillan, 1942.

Stampfer, Judah. "The Catharsis of *King Lear.*" *Shakespeare Survey* 13 (1960): 1–10.

Stevenson, Warren. "Albany as Archetype in *King Lear.*" *MLQ* 26 (1965): 257–63.

Stockholder, Katherine. "The Multiple Genres of *King Lear:* Breaking the Archetypes." *Bucknell Review* 16 (1968): 40–63.

Stoll, E. E. *From Shakespeare to Joyce.* New York: Doubleday, 1944.

Summers, Claude. "'Stand Up for Bastards': Shakespeare's Edmund and Love's Failure." *College Literature* 4 (1977): 225–31.

Summers, Joseph H. "'Look There, Look There!': The Ending of *King Lear.*" In *English Renaissance Studies Presented to Dame Helen Gardner in Honour of Her Seventieth Birthday,* edited by John Carey. London: Oxford University Press, 1980.

Talbert, Ernest W. "Lear the King: A Preface to a Study of Shakespeare's Tragedy." In *Medieval and Renaissance Studies. Proceedings of the Southeastern Institute of Medieval and Renaissance Studies, Summer 1965,* edited by O. B. Hardison, Jr. Chapel Hill: University of North Carolina Press, 1966.

Taylor, E. M. M. "Lear's Philosopher." *SQ* 6 (1955): 364–65.

Taylor, Warren. "Lear and the Lost Self." *CE* 25 (1964): 509–13.

Toliver, Harold E. *Pastoral Forms and Attitudes.* Berkeley: University of California Press, 1971.

Traversi, Derek A. "Lear." *Scrutiny* 19 (1952–53): 43–64.

Van Domelen, John E. "Why Cordelia Must Die." *South Central Bulletin* 35 (1975): 132–35.

Van Doren, Mark. *Shakespeare*. New York: Doubleday, 1939.

Vickers, Brian. "*King Lear* and Renaissance Paradoxes." *MLR* 63 (1968): 305–14.

Vivas, Eliseo. "Tragedy and the Broader Consciousness." *Southern Review* 7 (1971): 846–65.

Watkins, W. B. C. *Shakespeare and Spenser*. Princeton, N.J.: Princeton University Press, 1950.

Webster, Margaret. *Shakespearean Tragedy*. London: J. M. Dent, 1957.

Weitz, Morris. "The Coinage of Man: 'King Lear' and Camus's 'L'Etranger.'" *MLR* 66 (1971): 31–39.

Welsford, Enid. *The Fool: His Social and Literary History*. London: Faber and Faber, 1935.

Welsh, James M. "To See It Feelingly: *King Lear* through Russian Eyes." *Literature/Film Quarterly* 4 (1976): 159–64.

West, Robert H. *Shakespeare and the Outer Mystery*. Lexington: University of Kentucky Press, 1968.

Whitaker, Virgil K. *The Mirror Up to Nature: The Technique of Shakespeare's Tragedies*. San Marino, Calif.: Huntington Library, 1965.

Wickham, Glynne. "From Tragedy to Tragi-Comedy: 'King Lear' as Prologue." *Shakespeare Survey* 26 (1973): 33–48.

Williams, George W. "The Poetry of the Storm in *King Lear*." *SQ* 2 (1951): 57–71.

Willson, Robert F., Jr. "Lear's Auction." *Costerus* 6 (1972): 163–77.

Wilson, Harold S. *On the Design of Shakespearean Tragedy*. Toronto: University of Toronto Press, 1957.

Wood, Glena D. "The Tragi-Comic Dimensions of Lear's Fool." *Costerus* 5 (1971): 197–226.

Young, Alan R. "The Written and Oral Sources of *King Lear* and the Problem of Justice in the Play." *SEL* 15 (1975): 309–19.

Young, David. *The Heart's Forest: A Study of Shakespeare's Pastoral Plays*. New Haven: Yale University Press, 1972.

Index

207